Dear Reader:

Some crime cases remain in our minds—and in our hearts—long after the jury has returned its verdict. With its shocking incidents of sex and violence, the case of serial killer Robert Lee Yates Jr. is one of the most compelling of all.

Respected family man, father of five, and Desert Storm veteran, Yates earned numerous medals for his nineteen-year military service. Yet, something compelled him to prey upon vulnerable women of high-risk lifestyles, shooting them in the head while they tried to satisfy his sexual desires. He left a trail of discarded bodies along well-traveled roads, but buried one victim right under his wife's bedroom window.

In this newly updated edition of *Body Count,* Edgar Award–winning author Burl Barer provides new information and insights on this case. From his cell on death row in Washington State Penitentiary, Robert Lee Yates Jr. seeks redemption through religion. But for the friends and families of his victims—and for the law enforcement professionals who put him behind bars—his legacy of evil is beyond forgiveness.

Already hailed by experts, reviewers, and readers, *Body Count* will enthrall and amaze you. Sit back and enjoy a fascinating story, told by one of American's finest investigative journalists.

If you would like to comment on *Body Count,* we'd love to hear from you at marketing@kensingtonbooks.com.

Don't miss Burl Barer's other real-life crime thrillers, available from Pinnacle!

With my best wishes,

Michaela Hamilton

Michaela Hamilton
Executive Editor, Pinnacle True Crime

BODY COUNT

BURL BARER

PINNACLE BOOKS
Kensington Publishing Corp.

http://www.kensingtonbooks.com

PINNACLE BOOKS are published by

Kensington Publishing Corp.
119 West 40th Street
New York, NY 10018

All Kensington Titles, Imprints, and Distributed Lines are available at special quantity discounts for bulk purchases for sales promotions, premiums, fund-raising, and educational or institutional use. Special book excerpts or customized printings can also be created to fit specific needs. For details, write or phone the office of the Kensington special sales manager: Kensington Publishing Corp., 119 West 40th Street, New York, NY 10018, attn: Special Sales Department. Phone: 1-800-221-2647.

Pinnacle and the P logo Reg. U.S. Pat. & TM Off.

ISBN-13: 978-0-7860-2927-3
ISBN-10: 0-7860-2927-7

First printing: September 2002
10   9   8   7   6   5   4

Printed in the United States of America

For Charlotte

O Lord, O Thou Whose mercy hath encompassed all, Whose forgiveness is transcendent, Whose bounty is sublime, Whose pardon and generosity are all-embracing, and the lights of Whose forgiveness are diffused throughout the world! O Lord of glory! I entreat Thee, fervently and tearfully, to cast upon Thy handmaiden who hath ascended unto Thee the glances of the eye of Thy mercy. Robe her in the mantle of Thy grace, bright with the ornaments of the celestial Paradise, and, sheltering her beneath the tree of Thy oneness, illumine her face with the lights of Thy mercy and compassion.

—Abdu'l-Baha, *Bahá'í Prayers for Women*

PROLOGUE

Patrick Oliver, twenty-one, and Susan Savage, twenty-two, grew up together in Walla Walla, Washington. Friends since childhood, the pair reunited in the summer of 1975 for a Sunday-afternoon picnic.

Patrick washed and polished his Mercury Cougar, then picked up Susan at her residence. On July 13, at exactly 2:15 P.M., the couple drove off to their undisclosed, and perhaps undecided, destination. "We'll be home in time for dinner" were the last words Patrick said as Susan and he got into the car.

The dinner hour came and went. At first, their parents were only mildly concerned—car trouble could explain the delay. The mood darkened as the sun set, and comforting optimism turned gradually to cold fear—fear of a serious or fatal car accident.

This possibility stirred tragic memories for the Olivers. Patrick's brother James was killed on the

Fourth of July, 1967, at the age of eighteen, when his car went out of control and hit a tree about eight miles west of Elgin, Oregon. James was killed, and younger brother Dan was hospitalized for some time at St. Joseph Hospital in La Grande.

Phone calls to area hospitals and the Washington State Patrol confirmed that there were no serious injury accidents that day. The distressed and desperate families contacted local law enforcement.

"We were asked to search for the missing couple, but the families had no idea exactly where to look," recounted Detective Mike Skeeters. "Oliver and Savage didn't say where they were going, only that they planned a picnic. All that could be done was to put out an alert for Oliver's car."

The following morning, the two families gathered at the Oliver home to brainstorm on Susan and Patrick's whereabouts. Oliver's aunt Nadine Gerkey offered an insightful hunch: if the picnic's purpose was to renew their fond childhood friendship, they would most likely go to a location filled with treasured memories.

A recreational area ten miles east of Walla Walla on Mill Creek, near the Wickersham Bridge, was a favorite outing spot for the Olivers, recalled Gerkey. Oliver and Savage enjoyed many fun-filled weekends relaxing on the grassy banks, shaded by large trees, and swimming in the softly flowing stream.

Dan Oliver and his uncle Frank Munns followed Gerkey's hunch. Driving the ten miles up Kooskooskie Road to Mill Creek, they soon discovered Patrick's Mercury Cougar parked on the roadside. Continuing their search along the creek bank, they spotted something unusual about a half mile west of Wickersham Bridge.

"I saw this sort of funny arrangement of debris down near the edge of the creek," recalled Frank Munns. "There was a lot of stuff piled up, and an old tarp thrown over it with a tire on top." Taking a closer look, the apprehensive searchers lifted the corner of what was actually an old army sleeping bag covering brush and debris. They saw a foot with a shoe on it sticking out from under the brush. "I am the one who discovered Pat and Susan on July 14, 1975," said Dan Oliver years later. "I saw their dead bodies on the west side of Mill Creek beneath a sleeping bag and a tire."

Exactly twenty-four hours after Patrick Oliver and Susan Savage pulled out of the driveway, Frank Munns and Dan Oliver walked into the Walla Walla County Sheriff's Office. Notified of the shocking discovery, Sheriff Art Klundt and Chief Criminal Deputy "Scotty" Ray immediately drove to the scene.

Beneath the implement tire, sleeping bag, and debris were the bodies exactly as Dan Oliver and Frank Munns reported: Savage, placed on top of Oliver, was naked from the waist down, and her green halter top was pulled up exposing her breasts. Oliver, clothed in his matching lightweight blue shirt and shorts, had a bullet wound directly through the heart; Savage's wound was directly behind her left ear.

An autopsy conducted on both victims by Dr. Abbas Sameh revealed that Oliver was actually shot three times—the first bullet went through his left forearm; the second passed through the right shoulder. This indicated that the killer was a marksman aiming for the heart and that Oliver put up his arms in a defensive reflex. The first two shots were only slightly off target; the third shot went directly through young Oliver's heart.

Dr. Sameh reported that Susan Savage also was shot more than once. Prior to the fatal shot behind her left ear, there was one to her left shoulder. "Doctor Sameh found no evidence of sexual assault," commented Sheriff Mike Humphries years later, "but there was a substance noticed on Ms. Savage that was never identified for the simple reason that her body was completely cleansed by the funeral home before the autopsy. Today, of course, we would recover every hair, fiber, or whatever and identify it. But this is the twenty-first century, and the murder was in the mid-1970s."

The sheriff's office requested, and received, assistance from the Spokane police in processing potential evidence retrieved from the debris piled upon the bodies. There were a small number of latent fingerprints, but they were insufficient for purposes of comparison to prints on file. "About as good as we can do," reported the lab technicians, "is to either say they were or were not left by any particular person in the event you locate a suspect."

Ray sent all the physical evidence, including bullets recovered from the bodies, to the FBI lab in Washington, DC. There was one thing, said Ray, which could crack the case. The FBI reported that the bullets came from a .357-caliber handgun. If there was a viable suspect who owned a .357, a ballistics test could determine with a high degree of probability whether or not the suspect's gun was the murder weapon.

Desperate for additional clues, Ray invoked help from the *Walla Walla Union-Bulletin*, the local newspaper where Oliver's aunt Nadine Gerkey was a respected reporter. Radio stations KTEL and KUJ joined in the media effort encouraging any and all individuals with information, ideas, or evidence to immediately contact Scotty Ray at the sheriff's office.

"Public response to our efforts to track down the killer has been very good," noted Ray, who acknowledged that the sheriff's office received an "enormous" number of calls from individuals offering information. Several people reported hearing gunshots at Mill Creek that Sunday afternoon, but the area was also a popular spot for target practice. Hearing gunfire wasn't unusual.

Diane Lackey, a teenager picnicking at Mill Creek with her boyfriend the same day as Oliver and Savage, was among those who contacted Investigator Ray. She had heard more than gunfire, and had seen more than the area's rural serenity. Lackey had heard a woman scream, and shortly thereafter, she had come upon a man crouching in the bushes.

To elicit more details, she agreed to being interviewed under the influence of sodium amytol by psychiatrist Frederick Montgomery. The interview's results were then shared with Walla Walla deputy prosecuting attorney Jerry Votendahl.

"Diane was, I think, extremely cooperative," reported Dr. Montgomery. "Following an altercation with her boyfriend, she walked to a small ravine and, while standing there, she noticed a young man between the ages of nineteen to twenty-four crouching in the brush with no shirt on. When they noticed each other, he stood up and they stared at each other for some time. She describes him as being weird-looking, with brown medium-length hair. He was of medium height, of a slender build, and wore jeans. They looked at each other for a period of time; then both became frightened and they both took off and ran. The boy running away from her, and the girl running back toward where her boyfriend was.

"Diane seems to recognize this individual," noted Montgomery, "and she states that she has seen him before some place in Walla Walla, but could not recollect when. I think she would recognize him again if she saw him."

Lackey added one more important piece of information—the man may have been driving a red compact car, similar to a Mustang. She noticed the car parked alongside the road when she arrived at Mill Creek. Several other people, including residents of the area, also mentioned a small red car parked near Oliver's vehicle.

The unidentified red compact car was among over two dozen vehicles that were either parked or cruising in the Mill Creek area at the time of the homicides. "The sheriff's office is doing what we can," said Ray, "to get these cars identified that people have seen up there. Deputies have interviewed about one hundred persons in the case, including individuals acquainted with the victims, and others who were in the area at the time of the shooting."

The entire town was emotionally invested in capturing the couple's killer. A citizens' group raised a $5,000 reward for information leading to the arrest and conviction of the guilty party. Walla Walla attorney Madison Jones, cochairman with fellow attorney Al Golden of the nine-member Concerned Citizens Reward Committee, was optimistic.

"The bigger the reward, the more likely someone is going to come forward with information," Jones said. "People in this town are upset about this thing. Susan Savage baby-sat for everybody in this town, including me." The day she died, Susan Savage had been wearing a cloisonné bracelet received as a thank-you gift from the parents of three neighborhood children for whom she baby-sat.

"Pat Oliver was from a well-known family in this town," stated Madison Jones. "I think that with a reward, we can continue to maintain the public interest. With a tragedy like this, it shouldn't go unnoticed after a few days. Look at the Lindbergh kidnapping. They didn't solve that for two or three years. They didn't find Patty Hearst for nineteen months."

Within two weeks of the murders, the sheriff's office confirmed that two officers working full-time devoted one thousand man-hours to the investigation. Hundreds of persons were contacted, and forty-three individuals provided taped interviews. Transcriptions ran to over two hundred pages, and the case files reached a thickness of more than two feet. Supplemental reports totaled over 150, and seventy-five items were collected as evidence. Despite the impressive numbers, authorities were no closer to catching the killer than they were on the day Savage's and Oliver's bodies were uncovered.

"Walla Walla was then and is now a very small community with very limited resources," commented Christopher Oliver, Patrick's younger brother, in retrospect. "The investigation started with several suspects. All these leads were a dead end. No real suspects, no true motives."

"Murders have three essential elements," explained Detective Skeeters. "They are as follows: motive, means, and opportunity. The 'means' in this crime was a handgun, the 'opportunity' was the seclusion of the couple's picnic site, but the motive was something that couldn't be ascertained."

"We are not prepared to offer any motive that we can back up," acknowledged Ray to the press at the month's end. Sheriff Klundt and he held strongly divergent opinions regarding motive: Klundt seriously considered the possibility that "it was just some kook who killed them for no reason." Ray disagreed, insisting that the killings were too deliberate to be the sudden act of some "kook."

"My hunch is that somebody followed them out there with the intention of killing them," said Ray. He also firmly suspected that the motive was jealousy. "It's got to be the motive. The girl was not raped, and there was no struggle," commented Ray, who also noted that the bodies were easily discovered. "There was no effort to hide the crime. Leaving Pat's car at the scene was like setting up a sign."

Ray and the other deputies then pursued a "process of elimination" by investigating everyone with whom the couple associated. Perhaps something in their recent past, lifestyles, or behavior contained the singular clue that would reveal the killer's motive and identity. It was time to take a deep look into the private lives of Patrick Oliver and Susan Savage.

"So who was Pat Oliver? He was born in Walla Walla. He was raised in Walla Walla. Unfortunately, murdered in Walla Walla," said his brother Christopher. "He was always adventurous. Pat was the third son of four boys. The Oliver boys were a unit. If anyone had a problem, we all got involved. If there was something new to experience, we all had to try it. Pat loved sports. He played baseball up to colt league. He played football; he was a halfback and linebacker. He played track. He was a very good skier. He liked the mountains and he hunted pheasants. Pat was a leader."

Patrick Oliver was a 1972 graduate of Walla Walla's DeSales High School. He was class president in his sophomore and senior years, team captain of his football squad, president of the letterman's club, and homecoming king during his senior year.

"After high school, Pat went to Washington State University," continued Christopher. "While some of his contemporaries partied, he studied inorganic chemistry, microbiology, and other premed courses. He was an honor student and had an opportunity to study in Paris his junior year." When Oliver returned from a year's study at the University of Paris and the Sorbonne in the summer of 1975, he decided to attend Walla Walla's Whitman College to study premed. He had only recently returned when Susan Savage and he went to Mill Creek.

"Susan was at a point in life that had the most promise," said David Savage, Susan's brother. She achieved an associate degree from Walla Walla Community College, received a bachelor of arts degree as an interior decorator from Washington State University, studied at the University of Guadalajara in Mexico, and was, at the time of her death, a respected employee at Viewbird Graphics and Corporate Design.

"I don't know why this happened," said her mother, Marybelle Savage, in 2001. "Why would anybody shoot your child? When you lose a child, you sometimes think you see her face in crowds," she said. "She would have owned her own business. She would have been married with a family."

Looking back, Christopher Oliver commented that "it would make sense to investigate who in the Walla Walla area had a license to both a small red car and a .357 handgun, but that wasn't the tack taken."

Assuming jealousy as the motive, investigators probed deeply into the couple's history and private lives. What they discovered was that Patrick Oliver and Susan Savage shared a relationship similar to that of a loving brother and sister—they were each other's most ardent supporter, but they never dated. The couple was not, and had never been, romantically involved.

"It was like that ever since they were kids, and all the way through school," said one longtime friend. "Susan was Pat's greatest booster. She thought he was tops; he thought she was the greatest. I guess they just knew each other too well to be anything more than good friends."

With the jealously motive abandoned, an alternate scenario was created. The new theory was international in scope and exceptionally expensive. "I can't really fault Ray or the sheriff," said Christopher Oliver years later, "but I think they wasted an enormous amount of time and resources with Interpol."

Because Patrick had only recently returned from Europe and Susan had spent some time in Mexico, Ray considered that perhaps something happened outside the USA that accounted for the killings. "We've drawn an absolute blank on any kind of motive from here," said Ray, "and I think we can eliminate Susan as being the target for the killer because she has been home from Mexico for quite some time. But Pat was only back for two weeks when he was killed."

Ray asked a resident FBI agent concerning the proper procedure for requesting assistance from Interpol. Complete information on Patrick Oliver's travels and activities were then sent to Interpol headquarters. It was learned that after Oliver left Paris, he went to Amsterdam for a short visit. The hotel in which he stayed was a suspected drug-distribution center and the scene of a large narcotics bust prior to his return to Walla Walla. The question evolved: was Patrick Oliver the informant who "blew the whistle" on the hotel's drug traffic? If so, perhaps an international drug syndicate hired a hit man to travel all the way to Walla Walla to kill Oliver in retribution or to silence him.

The investigation's focus for almost a year and a half was Ray's theory that a professional assassin, sent from Europe, killed the couple. "In my opin-

ion," said Sheriff Humpries in 2001, "they were
off on a wrong track. A hit man usually targets one
person, and they don't do placement of bodies.
Former sheriff Klundt's theory that perhaps it was
'some kook' was more on target and was supported
by psychologist John Berberich of the Seattle Police
Department who, as the case remained unsolved,
contacted Scotty Ray."

Berberich wrote that he had been thinking a lot
about the murders in Wall Walla. In his opinion,
the most likely explanation was that one or two
men had stumbled on the couple, observed them
for a while, and decided they wanted to have sex
with the woman. Her companion probably resisted
and was shot, and the female victim was shot to
cover up the crime.

Because the bodies were not mutilated, these
murders did not give Berberich the picture of having been done by a psychotic. He did, however,
note a "clear sexual component," in the female
victim's state of partial undress.

Berberich was three months into his employment
with the Seattle Police Department at the time he
advised Ray. "I had written one profile prior to
that which was of Bundy, and I did that in 1974
or '75," he stated in 2001. "The picture I tried to
present to Scotty Ray was that of a psychopath, a
personality type that tends to have the kind of
descriptors I included here."

"Berberich made some very interesting observa-
tions back then," commented Sheriff Mike Hum-
phrey. "As he mentioned, you can tell by the
placement of the bodies that this was a sexually
motivated homicide and not a murder for hire."

The Oliver and Savage families, emotionally devastated by the brutal murders, were further dismayed by the extended investigation's continual detours down dead-end roads. In time, the reward committee's optimism also faded as fanciful theories proved fruitless. The murders remained unsolved. "We were left with no resolution," said Chris Oliver. "But we never let go."

In 1975, while Scotty Ray pursued the nonexistent international hit man, a quiet and courteous corrections officer at the Washington State Penitentiary in Walla Walla resigned his job after only six months' employment. He moved away, taking with him his red Dodge Dart and his Ruger .357 handgun. His name was Robert Lee Yates Jr., and his primary passion was shooting.

"He shot all the time," said Linda Yates, his wife. According to her, his favorite place to shoot was about ten miles up Kooskooskie Road to Mill Creek, not too far from the Wickersham Bridge.

CHAPTER ONE

In his hometown of Oak Harbor, Washington, they don't call him Robert Lee Yates Jr. They call him "Bobby," differentiating him from his respected father, Robert Yates Sr.

In 1945, Bobby Yates's grandmother, wielding a double-edged ax, violently ended her husband's life. "I was there," recalled Yates Sr. "I heard the murder in the night." He found his father near death and his mother seated in a straight-backed chair in another room. "She had given birth to eleven children, been under the stress of having a husband working away from home, and she simply broke. She spent seven years in a state mental hospital," confirmed Yates Sr.

When speaking of Robert Yates Jr., family friend George Cantrell said, "This is a kid who was never in trouble. He was always practicing his upbringing—and it was a good one." Yates's upbringing was idyllic, healthy, moral, and exemplary.

Oak Harbor, situated on Whidbey Island, offers

stunning views of the majestic Olympic Mountains and the cerulean blue Pacific Ocean. Backpacking, hunting, dirt-bike riding, fishing, and other wholesome activities are the rule, not the exception, for life on Whidbey.

Robert Lee Yates Sr. was an elder in Oak Harbor's Seventh-day Adventist Church—a tiny congregation of less than one hundred people sharing common bonds of beliefs and values. Health, family, and the sacredness of Sabbath are well-known pillars of American Adventist culture. The elder and younger Yates were always close.

The boy and his loving father shared everything together. The only childhood secret kept by the younger Yates was sexual molestation by a neighbor boy five years his senior when he was only six years old. Father and son, however, shared all of life's joys. "They did a lot of activities together," said family friend Dorothy Cantrell. "Sports was their big thing."

His father coached Little League, and it was there that Robert Lee Yates Jr. learned the pitching skills later utilized while playing for the Oak Harbor Wildcats. "He could throw a fastball with precision," recalled former teammate Harry Ferrier. "Yates had a seven-one record his junior year in high school." According to former classmates, Yates was neither too outgoing nor exceptionally shy, neither a hedonistic animal nor a hermetic ascetic. He wasn't a wild ladies' man, but he dated with pleasant consistency. "He was kind of quiet," said Harry Ferrier, who now lives in Anacortes. "He was kind of like Joe Average."

For money, Yates mowed lawns, worked at gas

stations, and harvested peas with Gary Berner in the summer, making $1.80 an hour. "The worst thing I know about Bob is he wouldn't play football his senior year," says Berner.

His "steady" moved away from Oak Harbor during their senior year. With no date for the homecoming dance, Robert Lee Yates Jr. spent the evening playing canasta with his buddy Al Gatti at the Yates family home on East 300th Street.

"He was very much loved," said Gatti of his old pal Bobby Yates. "There was a lot of respect in that family. They were the type of people that you'd want as your neighbor. Mr. Yates—he'd give you the shirt off his back."

Yates and Gatti, two youths contemplating their futures, considered careers as biologists or game wardens. Gatti joined the army; Yates went to Skagit Valley College from 1970 through the spring of 1972, earning an associate art degree in general studies.

Respectful and courteous, Bobby Yates didn't yield to pop-culture trends or in-crowd behavior. When other youths grew their hair long, Yates kept his closely clipped.

"He didn't smoke and he didn't drink. Nothing or anything like that," said Yates's closest friend, Al Gatti. "We didn't give into peer pressure; that wasn't our thing. Our thing was hunting and fishing and hiking."

One popular hiking excursion for Yates and Gatti was a sixteen-hour round-trip backpacking outing in Washington's Cascade Mountains. The purpose: fishing an isolated lake famed for its twenty-inch trout. Yates remained an avid outdoorsman, boast-

ing to Gatti that his third daughter and he stalked
deer together—a cause for celebration because
none of his other daughters were attracted to the
sport. According to Gatti, Yates told him, "We had
a terrific time."

Yates was the twice-married father of five. At the
age of twenty, he married Shirley Nylander. The
newlyweds moved to College Place, where they
enrolled in Walla Walla College, a Seventh-day
Adventist school.

"I didn't get to know him that much," said Mary
Nylander, Shirley's mother. About eighteen
months after the marriage, Shirley moved out, went
home, and asked for a divorce. Yates didn't give
her an argument; he gave himself to Linda Brewer,
a pleasant young student at Walla Walla Community College.

"Yates's 1974 marriage to Linda was illegal, and
therefore annulled," commented Sheriff Humphries, "because his divorce from his first wife was
not final." Six months after the invalid ceremony,
Linda Brewer Yates, former high school classmate
of Susan Savage's sister, Nancy, gave birth to their
first child.

Robert Lee Yates Jr. always had a passion for
flight. Leaving Walla Walla, he enlisted in the
armed forces, becoming an accomplished pilot.
His wife, however, was more concerned about her
husband's other passions. Shortly after their marriage, Linda left him for thirty days when she
learned that he had drilled a hole in the attic wall
so he could watch the couple in the next apartment
have sex.

"I left him again in the mid-1980s," said Linda

Yates, "and moved back to Walla Walla with the children while he was on duty in Alabama. I loved the separation," she admitted, "but the girls were pleading to be with their dad. They didn't want to be poor and not have anything anymore."

While in the armed forces, Robert Lee Yates Jr. became a highly trained helicopter pilot. In his eighteen years of exemplary service, Yates received three meritorious service medals, three army commendation medals, three army achievement medals, and two armed forces expeditionary medals. He served in Germany and in Operation Desert Storm. Following the devastation of Hurricane Andrew, Yates participated in vital relief efforts, and he flew in a UN peacekeeping mission to Somalia. His fellow aviators praised his bravery and recalled him as "an excellent pilot, knowledgeable and very safety conscious."

In Somalia, Yates violated regulations by shooting a wild pig while flying a helicopter. Yates and his airborne buddies, after more than a month of army food, wanted a barbecue. "They tried to court-martial him because he didn't go through the proper channels," said a former military associate. "It all turned into a big joke after a while. It didn't hurt a damn thing. They were just trying to get some fresh meat."

In 1995, Yates was transferred from New York to Fort Rucker, Alabama—the "Home of U.S. Army Aviation." It was at Fort Rucker that Yates instructed helicopter pilots in the fine art of teaching other soldiers to fly OH-58 helicopters. He drilled seven hours a day and was one of only ten instructor pilots at that level. "We were in a pinch for instructors, and Bob filled the position nicely," said Rick Ponder, his boss.

"My husband's military colleagues always seemed surprised that he had a wife," recalled Linda Yates. "When we would go to parties together, he would drink heavily, moon other women, and tell them his name was James Bond, 007." Perhaps Robert Yates Jr. came to believe that he also had a license to kill.

With less than eighteen months left to finish a twenty-year career in the army, Chief Warrant Officer Robert Lee Yates Jr. abruptly requested voluntary separation from the army. This was undertaken with the same inexplicable suddenness as his resignation from Washington State Penitentiary.

Four months later, he received an incentive bonus for leaving early, and he moved from Fort Rucker to Spokane. "It was the tail end of another reduction in army forces," commented a former associate, "and I was under the impression that he accepted a special incentive that allowed him to keep getting about forty-five percent of his normal pay, probably about twenty thousand a year. Maybe he just got tired of the army. The helicopter he knew best was also becoming obsolete and being replaced by the Kiowa Warrior."

Maybe there was another, more imperative reason Yates retired from the armed services. On August 9, 1995, while Yates was stationed at Fort Rucker, prostitute Tarayon Corbitt was found murdered. Corbitt, a male fetchingly outfitted in female attire, was shot twice in the face with a .45-caliber handgun. Corbitt's corpse was dumped along the roadside between Ozark, the county seat, and Midland City, bordering Fort Rucker. It was only a matter of time before Dale County detectives turned their investigative gaze toward the Home of U.S. Army Aviation.

"Mr. Yates was very familiar with the area," said Dale County detectives. "He traveled to Fort Rucker several times during his career for flight school, warrant officer school, and advanced training."

Yates graduated from an instructor pilot course on August 18, 1995, just nine days after Corbitt was murdered. Nine days after that, Yates was awarded the Master Army Aviator Badge, a symbol of Yates's fifteen years of service as an army chopper pilot.

"It's just a theory at this point," explained investigators from Dale County, "but the theory is that as our search for Corbitt's killer closed in on Fort Rucker, Mr. Yates possibly panicked, resigned his commission, left Fort Rucker and his army career to avoid investigation."

"We have not determined if Yates owned a .45-caliber weapon," confirmed Sergeant Cal Walker of Spokane's homicide task force. "His first two victims, Patrick Oliver and Susan Savage, were killed with a .357-caliber handgun; the majority of his victims in the late 1990s were killed with small-caliber handguns."

Yates, who received a 407-year sentence for his confessed commission of twelve murders in Spokane, faced trial in Pierce County, Washington, in April 2002 for the murder of two Tacoma women. Melinda L. Mercer and Connie LaFontaine Ellis were both killed in the Tacoma area, their bodies dumped in remote locations. In both cases, they were killed during periods when Yates, coincidentally, was serving with the Washington Army National Guard at Camp Murray and Fort Lewis, near Tacoma.

"Even if Mr. Yates is convicted in Tacoma," said, Jerry Costello, Pierce County's chief criminal prosecutor, "interstate compacts are in place to allow him to be transferred to Alabama to face a jury if charges are ever filed against him there."

In 1996, leaving the armed forces behind, and possibly avoiding any connection with the deceased Corbitt, Yates moved his family to Spokane, Washington. With a population of 195,629 in the Spokane city limits, and another 417,939 in greater Spokane County, Spokane is located on the eastern side of Washington State, only eighteen miles west of the Idaho state line, and 110 miles south of the Canadian border. The Spokane area serves as the hub of the Inland Northwest, a thirty-six-county region encompassing eastern Washington, northern Idaho, western Montana, northeastern Oregon, and parts of Alberta and British Columbia, Canada. It is also only 140 miles from Robert Lee Yates's in-laws in Walla Walla.

"I had hoped that coming back home to Washington would help the marriage," Linda Yates said, "but it really didn't. The romance was gone, but I felt guilty about splitting up the family. The kids loved their dad, and I just kind of suffered through it. I didn't love him like a wife should. He killed that."

Unable to secure a pilot position, he worked for

Tony Givens, owner of Pantrol Inc. "Pantrol puts together electronic instruments for heavy machinery," explained Givens. "Yates worked for me assembling components until 1997. He was a good worker who mostly kept to himself. Nothing really stuck out about him," Givens said. "He was just an average Joe—pretty quiet. I didn't talk to him much. But he seemed friendly enough."

When orders dried up at Pantrol, Yates crossed the picket line at Kaiser Aluminum's Processing Plant in Mead, Washington, where his coworkers considered him "a very family guy" who took the leader, or "father figure," role in the group. "He got along with all of us," said Tim Buchanan, the man with whom Yates took his coffee breaks. Dan Russell, president of the striking Local 329, said, "Yates initially worked as a carbon setter, and that's intensive work that requires respirator-equipped laborers to toil around pots of molten ore that reach up to 1,700 degrees Fahrenheit. Sometime later," Russell said, "Yates's job changed to overhead crane operator in the pot room."

According to Susan Ashe, spokeswoman for Kaiser, "By all accounts, he was a good worker. He had a very good work record."

Robert Lee Yates Jr. joined the National Guard in April 1997. "He came to us very, very qualified. In the three years he was assigned to us, he was a good performer. He did an excellent job," said Lieutenant Colonel Rick Patterson, a National Guard spokesman. But pending medical evaluations, Robert Lee Yates Jr. was not allowed to fly. The dates of his grounding were from spring 1997 to spring 1998. The body count began.

During that one-year period, Robert Lee Yates Jr. killed Spokane women whose lost lives, one at a time, would not elicit outrage. "He learned as he went along," commented Sergeant Walker. "He learned that killing women with high-risk lifestyles did not garner the same community outrage as killing someone such as Susan Savage."

Yates's next self-acknowledged kill was the 1988 murder of Stacy Hawn, twenty-five, last seen alive in Seattle on July 7, 1988. Her skeletal remains were found five months later in Skagit County, Washington.

"Oh, he learned all right," said Cathy A., a former Spokane prostitute now living a respectable life in Renton, Washington. "He learned plenty just sitting with us in the Coach House coffee shop. All us hookers would sit around talking about who and what we did, and he would just be real quiet, pleasant, passive, and if one of us needed a ride somewhere, he would give us a lift. We didn't know him as Robert Lee Yates Jr., of course. Sometimes he was Dan; sometimes he was Bob. You never notice names; they change all the time."

"They said it was somebody we all knew and dated," said Leda, another Sprague Avenue prostitute. "Sure enough, it was." Yates was known as a reliable, safe regular.

"He paid me twenty dollars for an easy no-touch date," said Jennifer T. "I don't remember much about him other than he had big hands and a thick neck."

"Every time I dated him, which I did about nine or ten times," said Julie, "he had me get some crack cocaine for him and heroin for myself. He liked smoking it so much, I called him 'my little crack patient.' I shot him up with crank one time, too. I thought he was harmless." Today, looking over the list of murdered women, many whom she knew, she wishes she had killed him.

Yates first picked her up near Trudeau's Marina on East Sprague. "We went to Al's Spa Tub Motel, and twice we went to my apartment," she recalled. "He didn't seem to give a shit who saw him. Most married men are nervous.

"He only scared me once," she admitted, "and that's when I asked for more money. He looked angry as hell, and I mean real angry, but he drove to the cash machine and got the rest of the money.

"Our dates ended when I quit heroin for a while. Because I didn't need to support the habit, I stopped working as a prostitute," she said. "Bob was emotionless most of the time. Underneath that mild-mannered mask, there was nobody home. You looked in his eyes and they were dead.

"I hate to admit it," said Julie, "but I actually felt sorry for him when I saw on television that he had been arrested. If you'd have given me one hundred guys and said which is the least likely to do this, I thought he was a minus one. I wonder why he didn't kill me, too. Maybe it was because I didn't steal from him; maybe it was because I gave good head. I don't know. The fact that I'm alive is a God thing to me."

Julie wasn't the only woman stunned by the revelation of the serial killer's identity. "When I saw his face on TV after he was arrested, I about fell off my bar stool," said Aloha Ingram. "I thought, it couldn't be Bob. He was generous, soft-spoken,

and I had halfway fallen in love with him. He wasn't
kinky. He wasn't abusive. He wasn't real aggressive.
He was just normal. Very passionate and very concerned about my satisfaction. He'd kiss me from
head to toe. He was real intimate that way," she
said. "He always had his arm around me. It was
like a relationship, not a paying customer.

"I began to fall in love," admitted Aloha. "I even
told my family about him. He told me that he cared
about me. That's why I felt there was more there
than just a business contact." Of all the customers
in her years as a sexual professional, she had never
felt safer than when cuddled up to Robert Lee Yates
Jr., the compassionate romantic who murdered her
friends.

"I just thank God I never dated him," said Cathy
A. "I mean, either he liked you and let you live or
he blew your brains out. I got out of Spokane
because of the serial killer, and I got clean of drugs,
too. My God," she said with a perceptible shudder,
"I could have wound up decomposing in an empty
lot somewhere or rotting away in an alfalfa field."

CHAPTER TWO

August 26, 1997

It was a beautiful day for finding dead bodies. The warm summer sun shimmered down through high overcast clouds, and a soft breeze cooled 80-degree August heat. At 11:00 A.M., Vietnam veteran Larry Jones foraged for empty pop cans in an overgrown empty lot off Spokane's East Springfield Street. Searching for recyclable aluminum, he discovered a rotting corpse.

Concealed under a tree, and hidden in high grass behind some large metal tins, the half-naked body showed every indication of extensive exposure to the elements. Systematic analysis of the crime scene by Spokane police, headed by Detective John Miller, revealed over a gallon of dried blood in a nearby parking lot, leaving a dark brown trail up and over the curb. It was easily seen that the victim was murdered elsewhere, driven to the parking lot, dragged up the embankment, and dumped as refuse.

"The body is decomposed to the point that we're not even certain if it is male or female," said Lieutenant Jerry Oien, the commander of Spokane's Major Crimes Unit. "We're also not sure of the nationality." That is how the day began. From there, it only got worse.

Several hours later, on a Mount Spokane farm, Kevin and Cindy Kailin hurriedly bailed alfalfa in a heated rush against oncoming rain. Kevin Kailin sensed more than the breath of a storm. He smelled death.

"At about five-twenty P.M., my wife, Cindy, and I were in a field to look at a hay bailer," recalled Kailin, "and we smelled something. I followed the smell to the body—it was in tall grass about thirty feet east of a tree with a No Trespassing sign on it." The Kailins hauled off three hundred bales of alfalfa before calling the Spokane County sheriff. At 6:30 P.M., Detective Rick Grabenstein was dispatched to the crime scene, where Sergeant Martin O'Leary was the on-scene supervisor. Also waiting for Grabenstein was the homicide's lead investigator, Detective Fred Ruetsch.

The body was located on a brush-covered side road that descended about two hundred feet into an alfalfa field. "There was a lone large pine tree on the bank a short distance west of the body," reported Grabenstein. "Other than this tree, and the dense brush, the area was open and devoid of any vegetation that would provide shade.

"The body appeared to be that of a female, but was badly decomposed. The skin appeared leather-like," he noted, "and the body was infested with maggots. Although the race could not be initially determined, facial features suggested partial and/ or full African-American, Indian, or Asian descent."

The body was faceup, arms extended above the head and somewhat outward. The legs were nearly fully extended straight out from the body. "There was no indication of the body being posed," said Grabenstein. "The body was surrounded by the brush, which had been crushed by the weight of the body, and the surrounding brush restricted the view of the body to a distance of about fifteen feet and offered some degree of concealment. However, there was no apparent attempt to cover, or further conceal, the body."

The victim's clothing included a long-sleeved blouse or dress, unzipped and pulled up to the shoulder area, and a black brassiere. The bra had been pulled up over the victim's head, and the body was unclothed from the chest area on down.

"The area east of the body appeared as if it were a trail from the roadway to the field," Grabenstein said. "At the top of this trail, marks in the grass and brush, which had been bent over, indicated a probability that the victim's body was dragged up this trail into the brush where the body was subsequently located."

Clothing that remained on the body was drawn up around the shoulder area, consistent with the victim having been dragged by the ankles. The trail into the brush, however, indicated that the victim was dragged headfirst.

Identification Officers Carrie Johnson and Julie Combs arrived on scene at 7:50 P.M., and the entire area was photographed. Due to impending darkness, detectives suspended further investigation until the following morning at nine o'clock. The scene was left intact, and patrol officers kept it secure throughout the night. Everyone except security deputies cleared the area at approximately 9:30 P.M.

The body, true to professional crime-investigation protocol, was not removed. "All professional law-enforcement personnel know that you don't move the body until you absolutely have to," commented Sergeant Walker. "You only get one chance to study the victim's body in the context of the crime scene, and once the body is moved, that opportunity is lost forever. You secure the scene, you guard the scene, and you process the entire crime scene, including the body, in the clear light of day."

Key to the investigation of a violent sex crime for which there is no known perpetrator is the science and art of profiling both the crime scene and the offender from the physical and psychological evidence. The methodology is based on Locard's Principle of Exchange: "Anyone who enters the scene both takes something of the scene with them and leaves something behind." The crime scene is a living document, and preservation of the scene's purity is critical. After securing and preservation comes processing; this includes documenting the physical evidence, being attentive to detail. Even the smallest item, such as a red fiber from a car rug taken off the victim's body, can provide valuable insight.

Each law enforcement agency has its own crime scene protocol. An essential factor is consistency of protocol. Planned consistency is simply good investigative practice. Detectives always consider whether a scene is primary or secondary. If the body is in an isolated location, a spiral search pattern using the body as a starting point will often be utilized.

According to forensic scientist Brent Turvey, profiling the crime scene may give investigators a more narrowed pool of suspects, insight into motive, and linkages of a given crime to other similar crimes. "The opportunity to profile an unsolved crime," insists Turvey, "is not to be ignored or wasted."

The crime scene investigation on Forker Road resumed in earnest the following morning, August 28. Additional evidence was located along the south side of the dirt access road just to the south of where the body was located. These articles included a yellow condom, one pair of size-seven black high-heeled shoes, a pair of black underwear, and one broken auto radio antenna.

After the location of the body was recorded, investigators approached the north side of the body through the brush. The bushes were initially checked for any trace evidence; then they were cut away as the search continued toward the body.

"The only evidence located on any of the brush north of the body were possible bloodstains," reported Grabenstein. A sample of the apparent bloodstains was collected, as were samples of the brush and vegetation. As the brush was cut away from the north side of the body, articles near the victim's left arm became visible: a pair of zippered-front black pants (size small) and a bloodstained towel.

"The body was now noted to have long dark hair believed to be black or auburn," said the detective. "The hair was so matted with body fluids and foreign material that making a precise color distinction was somewhat difficult. The body appeared to be that of a person of small build, although decomposition made estimating a weight difficult."

The victim wore pierced earrings and two finger rings. On the left middle finger was a thin plain gold band. On the right ring finger, a gold ring with a setting including a single white pearl in the center with a small green stone on either side. "The body was noted to have purple nail polish on both the finger- and toenails," Grabenstein recalled, "and the toes had what appeared to be fine particles of silver or white 'glitter' on the polish."

Degradation of the body made it near impossible to immediately identify any trauma wounds. Large areas of flesh were missing, destroyed or damaged. However, there was a defect noted in the left shoulder area of the blouse, as well as a round perforation in the back of the left shoulder with a smooth edge, indicative of a bullet wound.

Detectives could not know, prior to autopsy, that this was indeed a gunshot wound. Even with an autopsy, they would have no way of knowing that this body's wounds were almost identical to those inflicted over twenty years earlier on Susan Savage of Walla Walla, Washington.

Within twenty-four hours, the two homicides were high-profile cases dominating newspaper headlines and television news. Spokane's city and county detectives were under more pressure than astronauts.

Dr. George Lindholm and PA Randy Shaber performed autopsies on both bodies in the Holy Family Hospital morgue. Detectives Ruetsch and Grabenstein, plus Identification Officer Julie Combs, attended the 10:22 A.M. autopsy of the body found in the Kailins' alfalfa field.

"Doctor Lindholm noticed that the blouse worn by the victim still had a mother-of-pearl right-wrist cuff button present," said Ruetsch, "but the left-wrist cuff button was missing." Also missing was one of the victim's false eyelashes. The victim, shot in the chest and the left shoulder, died from a gunshot wound directly behind the left ear. The murder weapon was a .22-caliber handgun.

The body found in the unused lot on East Springfield also died from gunshot wounds to the head, but from a .25-caliber handgun. Fingerprints identified the victim as twenty-year-old Heather Hernandez, supposedly of Phoenix, Arizona. Hernandez was an enigmatic drifter who lived on the streets. At the time of her death, no one in Spokane knew complete details of her life, exactly where she came from, her family history, likes, loves, or aspirations.

As for the body found in the alfalfa field, she was identified as nineteen-year-old "Jennifer Kim," one of the city's youngest and prettiest prostitutes. Kim and Hernandez knew each other, but they were not directly associated. Kim was not the young

woman's real name. Her true name was Jennifer
A. Joseph.

At 6:00 P.M., on August 29, 1997, Detective Rick
Grabenstein telephoned Chaplain McKinney of
Pierce County at the Spanaway, Washington, home
of the victim's father, John Joseph. McKinney
broke the news of Jennifer's death, but it was left
to Grabenstein to provide the unpleasant details.

"I spoke with him briefly," confirmed the detective. "He was advised that his daughter had been
shot to death, of the general condition of her body,
and the date that it had been discovered, and that
he could contact the coroner's office to make
arrangements to obtain her remains. Further
details of her murder were not discussed."

It was then that Mr. John Joseph revealed his
daughter's true age. "She was born October 6,
1980," he said. Jennifer Joseph was only sixteen
years old.

Chaplain McKinney asked Grabenstein for assistance in contacting Jennifer's mother in Hawaii.
With the aid of Communications Officer Victor, a
fax was sent to the Wailuku Police Department.
Within four hours, Mi Hae Joseph learned of her
daughter's tragic death. At the request of detectives, both parents provided investigators with samples of their blood in the event that it ever became
necessary to establish a biological link between
themselves and their beloved daughter.

Jennifer Joseph was an army brat who followed
her father around the world, growing up in such
places as Denmark, South Korea, and on both
coasts of the United States. Between the ages of
nine and thirteen, she took piano lessons. "Jenni-

fer had a beautiful voice, singing in a church choir and the school choir as she grew up," recalled her father.

Emotional, impressionable, and irrepressible, Jennifer Joseph had a mind of her own, a strong will, and an aggravating allergy to pets. Denied the companionship of live animals, Jennifer opted for a room full of plush pups and other stuffed substitutes. "She'd been popular, did well in elementary and junior high school," her father said. "But when she started going through adolescence, things changed. She started hanging out with the wrong crowd, her grades slipped, and she eventually dropped out of school." She did, however, promise to return to school in the fall if she could continue her travels during the remaining summer.

Just prior to her disappearance, she told her father not to worry about her, as she could take care of herself. John Joseph, who heard from his daughter regularly, was unaware of her foray into prostitution. "He knew that she was in Spokane with her new boyfriend, who was also from Tacoma," said Detective Grabenstein. "He believed that the boy, with some help from him, was covering expenses. The boyfriend recently returned to Tacoma and was anticipating that Ms. Joseph would soon join him."

Detectives Ruetsch and Grabenstein made plans to get hold of Joseph's boyfriend in Tacoma. First, however, they delivered several items to the forensics division for laboratory examination. Among the thirty items, each sealed in a plastic bag, were Joseph's clothes, shoes, hair samples, a towel, the broken car radio antenna, and a test tube containing two swabs with iridescent material.

"The items were examined for the presence of trace evidence," recalled forensic scientist Kevin C. Jenkins. The results were more than favorable. "The following items," Jenkins reported, "may be evidentially significant: shoes and towel (Items two, three, and seven). A total of seven blue carpet fibers of two different shades were found, one from each of the shoes and five from the towel. In addition to the carpet fibers, green cotton fibers are common as well as brown acrylic fibers commonly used in sweaters and stocking hats, and [they] may be found in upholstered items." Jenkins also found several hairs not belonging to the victim. The trace evidence was preserved for future examination and comparisons.

The best way to know when somebody died is to find out when was the last time somebody saw him or her alive. All the pathologist can do is provide time parameters based upon physical characteristics.

While Jenkins was doing microscopic investigations, Detectives Ruetsch and Grabenstein were handling the macroscopic. As a general rule, one of the standard procedures in a homicide case is conducting a neighborhood canvass. As the two women were not murdered in their homes, were transported after death, and were far more mercurial in their social interactions, the sphere of search and inquiry was far vaster than if they had been victims of a "traditional homicide."

"When you're dealing with the murder of a woman with a high-risk lifestyle, "commented Ser-

geant Walker, "it's difficult to get cooperation
from their friends and coworkers. The last thing
prostitutes and drug dealers ever want to do is talk
to a cop. After all, most of our interaction with them
is not to their liking—law enforcement personnel
tend to arrest them. This doesn't exactly build great
bonds of affection and camaraderie. Face it, even
the most law-abiding citizens often refrain from
getting involved with the police—you can imagine
how difficult it is to get prostitutes, drug addicts,
pimps, or drug dealers to confide in us."

Victimology, the study of the victim's life and
lifestyle, is one of the most critical parts of an investigation. Detectives Grabenstein and Ruetsch
wanted to find out as much about Jennifer Joseph,
her habits and associates, as was humanly possible.

"The crime Analysis Fl computer was used to
attempt to determine any associates or addresses
that Jennifer Joseph may have had in the Spokane
area," explained Ruetsch. "The results indicated
a strong possibility that Joseph was well acquainted
with D.D., a local gentleman associated with an
escort service who had also recently been arrested
for possession of a controlled substance. His address on Montgomery Street was the same address
Jennifer Joseph supplied to law enforcement officers on a number of police contacts. The only
difference," said the detective, "was the apartment
number."

The apartment's resident manager told Ruetsch
and Grabenstein that the man they knew as D.D.
called himself "Roberts," and he moved in on
March 7, 1997. "I've probably seen more than
thirty girls going in and out of his apartment since

he moved in," she said. "All the girls are very pretty and well dressed. They would all load up together in a car and leave until about three or four A.M. Right now, he's behind in his rent, and if he doesn't (pay) he'll be getting a letter from the company."

Grabenstein showed her photos of Jennifer Joseph and Heather Hernandez. "I have seen a small, petite Oriental girl in and out of the apartment in the past, roughly in the last part of July," she said, "and that photo looks a lot like the girl I saw, but I can't be positive. Anyway, the guy who rents the apartment used to drive a white Cadillac exactly like the brown one he has now, but I haven't seen it in a while. He leaves several days at a time," she told detectives, "and he says that he's a roofer and that his working crew is doing a job in Gresham, Oregon." The last time she saw "Roberts" was Wednesday, August 27, the day after Jennifer Joseph's body was discovered.

"We need to speak with him," Ruetsch told her. "When he comes back to the complex, please notify us immediately." His hasty departure following the body's discovery could be coincidence, or it could be flight to avoid capture. At this point, all was speculation.

Systematically seeking out everyone who could have seen Jennifer Joseph the night she vanished, Grabenstein and Ruetsch treaded the same Sprague Avenue path as Spokane police detective Miller, who was investigating the Hernandez homicide. "Police and sheriff's detectives are working together," said Undersheriff Mike Aubrey, "to find a possible link between the deaths of Heather Hernandez and Jennifer Joseph."

On August 27, the day after Joseph's body was found, and the same day Roberts left Spokane, a pimp on East Sprague was seen brandishing a broken piece of car radio antenna. "By the time this was brought to my attention," said Detective Fred Ruetsch, "the pimp, who had an outstanding warrant for his arrest, had left the Spokane area. I did, however, contact the prostitute who worked under him."

Speaking to her on the phone, Ruetsch asked her if she remembered that night and, more specifically, the car antenna. "Sure I remember. The reason he had the antenna," she explained, "was because he was gonna make it into a crack pipe." After gaining new insights into the multitudinous uses of automotive accessories, Ruetsch inquired if she had any idea who killed Joseph and/or Hernandez. "No. I'm clueless," she said. "I can't imagine anyone doing shit like that. Pardon my language."

Off-color remarks and street-level obscenities were the detectives' least concerns. Prostitution and drug possession—often termed "victimless crimes"—are insignificant compared to homicide. Interviewing several prostitutes in rapid succession gave Grabenstein and Ruetsch additional insights into Joseph's and Hernandez's lifestyles.

"I knew both Jennifer and Heather 'cause I worked the same corners as them," said one Sprague Avenue regular. "I came to Spokane from Tacoma in February 1996 because over here the cops aren't so rough on you as over there. In Tacoma, they throw you into jail every chance they get. Here, they give you a citation and a talking-to.''

The most important talking-to in recent memory was not from Spokane law enforcement, but from Heather Hernandez. "She got hold of me and asked if she could, you know, 'associate' with me and my man because she had a falling-out with hers,'' the woman explained. Her man was the same man whom the apartment manager knew as Roberts, and it was he who represented Jennifer Joseph as an escort. "Heather's man was doin' some other lady, and Heather was hurt over it. Anyway, Heather and I both left the Bel-Air Motel at six o'clock to work East Sprague. We walked to the area of the Honey Baked Ham Restaurant, and I was almost immediately picked up by a date. I got back about twenty minutes later, and Heather was not around. I wasn't too concerned. I just figured that she was with a customer. All this occurred on a Friday night. It was the day before Jennifer disappeared, and that was a Saturday.''

Detective Miller suspected Hernandez's man, commenting, "These girls had been playing games with their pimps, and they can get disciplined for that.'' Sergeant Walker confirmed this initial suspicion. "The idea of pimp wars did occur to investigators. You have to take all things into consideration, and that was a possibility.''

The woman acknowledged that Hernandez's former man might be angry at Heather for working "under different auspices,'' but she thoroughly discounted any possibility that the women's deaths were due to any kind of "pimp war.''

"They don't do that sort of stuff around here,''

she told detectives. "Maybe in the movies they do, but not on East Sprague. We try to watch each other's backs most of the time. Sure, there are some psycho nutcases working out here, but you gotta worry more about the customers than the other girls or their so-called pimps.

"I saw Jennifer the next night," she continued. "She was wearing black pants, a long-sleeved silver button-front shirt, and some type of dress shoes. Oh, and she had the same purse that she always had, which was a small plastic zip-lock pouch about four inches long, two inches wide, and one inch thick. It was clear except for all the glitter. Inside the pouch was change, condoms, and a canister of mace. I told her to take the mace out of the pouch and put it in her right pocket where she could get to it, and would keep it away from the guy in the driver's seat if she were a passenger." A thoughtful pause postponed her recollections' final punctuation. "I guess it didn't do her much good, did it?"

Jennifer Joseph took a taxi from the motel to East Sprague, sharing the cab with Tiesha, another prostitute whom she first met in Portland, Oregon, earlier that summer.

"The cab would come and pick us both up at the motel," said Tiesha, "and take us wherever we wanted to go. Most times, we would call for this same cab to pick us up when we were finished."

This one particular cabdriver was often requested by a number of the prostitutes, explained Tiesha, "because he was respectful toward women and wasn't judgmental even though he knew we were prostitutes. He didn't even trade sex for taxi fares. He wasn't like some other cabdrivers," she said, naming one or two whom she found particularly repellent.

According to Tiesha, it was "against policy" for Jennifer and her to engage in chitchat, walk together on the street, or spend too much time with customers. "We did get to talk once in a while," said Tiesha. "Jennifer talked a lot about her father. She said that he was mad at her because she left home, and she told me that she didn't think her dad would even let her come home if she wanted to. She even said that her dad had rented out her room, but I didn't believe that, and I don't think she really did, either. I think it was just something she was saying, you know, just to say it."

Asked if she knew why an essentially drug-free sixteen-year-old girl would choose prostitution as her summer employment, Tiesha gave detectives a simple, direct, and inarguable answer: "She liked the lifestyle."

Not all other prostitutes, however, liked Jennifer. "When I first met her, I didn't like her because she was Korean," admitted one streetwalker questioned by Detective Grabenstein. "Korean girls make a lot of money 'cause for some reason, all the guys want 'em. So Jennifer was always very busy, being picked up by customers one right after another. I mean it was 'wham-bam-door slam' and on to the next one. She would get in the car, drive away, come back, get out, and get in another one. Meanwhile, I'm still pacing back and forth on the corner waiting for my next date."

The graveyard-shift employees at the Chevron station close to Jennifer Joseph's favorite corner remembered her well. "She used to come in here quite a bit," recalled one counter person. "She was always pleasant, friendly, and courteous. I knew she was a prostitute by, well, some of the things she said and by the fact that she bought quite a few condoms—mostly LifeStyle brand, the ribbed kind. The other girls told me that she made up to seven hundred dollars a night."

A security guard working in the parking lots on 3900–4000 East Sprague frequently observed prostitutes doing business and made entries in her journal regarding activities that affected her clients. "I recognized the media photographs of Jennifer Joseph," she told detectives. "I had contact with her a few times and observed her on other occasions without contacting her. She would be picked up at least four times in twenty minutes," recalled the security guard. "I told the young woman to make her contacts somewhere else other than the Pepsi parking lot. She agreed and was very nice about it. The other thing I noticed was how often she was picked up, driven around the block, and then dropped back off. I think maybe her price was higher than some men were willing to pay."

Joseph was also seen fending off one man's unwanted physical advances. "At first, I thought they were embracing, but then I realized that she was trying to push him away. I recall that he drove a white car, a two-door, but I don't know the make, model, or license number. I did write it down on a scrap of paper, but I can't find it."

Grabenstein and Ruetsch compiled an extensive list of suspect vehicles. They also inquired regarding known violent and dangerous tricks; they didn't rule out regular customers with benign reputations.

"We didn't have the individuals' names, but we had physical descriptions of both the men and their vehicles." Familiar cars and trucks cruising the high-prostitution-activity area included a white 1990 Chrysler New Yorker, a dark Chevrolet Camaro, a white Chevrolet Camaro, a maroon Buick, a Ford Thunderbird, an older Ford LTD, a dark Oldsmobile Cutlass, a light-blue Chevy Blazer, a large white Chevy Suburban with a company logo on it, an older dark-blue or black van, a brown 1970s-era van, a pickup truck with a camper on the back, a four-door Nissan, a white Porsche, and numerous pickup trucks with big wheels.

September 2, 1997

Yolanda Cary, the prostitute who interacted with Jennifer Joseph's boyfriend when she failed to return home for dinner, recounted to detectives about the last time she saw Jennifer Joseph and the vehicle in which she was riding.

"We were all staying at the same motel, but Jennifer and I weren't in the same room," said Cary. "I last saw her on Saturday night, August sixteenth, at about ten-thirty P.M. I'm sure of the time because I looked at my watch at the same time that I saw her. I was working on a corner just about a block east, near Sprague and Thor," she explained. "We'd been talking a bit earlier, and she told me that she was going to quit working and leave for home about midnight. Anyway, the last time I saw Jennifer, she was in the passenger seat of a white sports car heading east on Sprague. I didn't get a good look at the driver, but I'd say that he was a white male about thirty to forty years old. I think the car was a Porsche.''

Grabenstein and Ruetsch transported her to the East Sprague area; she identified the intersection of Sprague and Ralph as the one where Jennifer Joseph was working. Because she earlier told Jennifer's boyfriend that she had seen her get into a Porsche, the detectives drove her to a used-car lot.

"In that lot was a white Porsche nine twenty-eight," Grabenstein recalled, "and we pointed it out to her. She then said that this was not the type of vehicle that she had observed. Parked along the curb nearby was a white 1975 Chevrolet Corvette coupe, with a fabric cover over the grill and headlights on the front. She pointed out the vehicle and said that this was the exact model and color as the vehicle the victim had been in, except that it would have had no black bra on the front.''

The identification of a white Corvette as the car in which Jennifer Joseph was last seen by a coworker was only potentially significant. Investigators wanted a description of every car and every customer that Jennifer's street-savvy contemporaries considered suspect. The names of vehicles were better known than the names of customers. Most men use an alias or nickname when doing business with street prostitutes; the women do likewise.

"Just because Jennifer rode off in a particular car doesn't mean that was her last date,'' explained one seasoned Sprague Avenue veteran. "If it was a quick 'car date,' it could have been all over by the time they drove through a couple intersections.

You get in the car, he gives you the cash, and you go down on him. Maybe you pull into a parking lot or an alley, and then there are some guys who're perfectly happy to have you do it while they're driving. Well, it's all over real fast, he's happy, you've got more money, and in less than ten minutes, you're either back on the same corner you were before, or he drops you off somewhere else."

On a busy night, quick car dates are the "fast food" of prostitution. "Some girls charge forty dollars for head; others will do it for twenty," she explained. Some nights, even the ones who charge $40 will drop their price if things are slow, the night cold, and their financial situation desperate. "Jennifer Kim—that's what she called herself—was the 'high-priced spread,' " commented a sardonic older streetwalker. "Young like that? Shit. She could charge more, and here's the important part: she could get picked up faster and more often. In other words, she could have been out of a Chevy and into a Ford in less than ten minutes. Get it? God only knows who had her last."

Whoever had her last had a small-caliber gun to her head, and he pulled the trigger. The same scenario fit the death of Heather Hernandez. As her homicide was inside the city limits, Spokane police detectives worked the case, while the sheriff's office worked the Joseph case.

Continual dead-end detours down convoluted cul-de-sacs of suspicion would dampen the spirits of lesser souls, but dogged dedication is a hallmark of professional detectives. The more suspects they can eliminate from suspicion, the better, and Spokane County detectives were still awaiting the return of "Roberts"—the man who shared the same address as the late Jennifer Joseph.

At two minutes after noon on September 3, 1997, Detective Ruetsch received a telephone call from the apatment complex's resident manager advising him that the brown Cadillac belonging to Roberts was back.

"I was unavailable to respond immediately," recalled Ruetsch, "so I had a district car swing by the apartments to check on the Cadillac. Primarily, I wanted to know whether or not the antenna was intact." This was an important question because a broken car antenna was found near the body. "A half hour later, I received a call from Deputy Jack Rosenthal, who advised that the antenna was there and did not appear to be broken or recently replaced."

Outgoing and gregarious, Roberts openly acknowledged his chosen career path in the escort-service industry. "My responsibility is to find girls for the customers and to keep people from harassing them," he willingly elaborated. "I have associates that go and talk to people who are harassing the girls. The customers contact the girls via their pagers when they want to do business."

"He readily admitted," recalled Grabenstein, "that he rented the apartment under a false name because he knew he could not obtain credit under his real name." Roberts was "borrowed" from a man in Post Falls, Idaho.

"I had surgery on my shoulder and was not working," said the real Mr. Roberts. "Well, he loaned me some money. In return, I was asked to cosign on his cellular phone application." The first cell phone bill was for over $1,000. "That bill was paid, and I didn't get any more. But now," he lamented, "it turns out that there is a thirty-five-hundred-dollar outstanding bill on the phone, and collection agencies are after me for it."

His name was also the one used to obtain the apartment on Montgomery. "I only found out about that because another collection agency is after me for back rent on the place," he explained. "I didn't give anyone permission to use my name to get that apartment, and I suspect that the information I provided when I cosigned for the cell phone was also used on the apartment application."

Detectives were more concerned with aggravated homicide than unpaid cellular-phone bills and overdue rent. D.D. was honestly distraught over news of Joseph's death, and he had no objection to a complete examination of his car for any trace of evidence, nor did he resist the request for a sample of his blood. He also willingly offered to take a polygraph test. One more suspect was thus eliminated from an ever-widening spectrum of possible perpetrators.

CHAPTER THREE

September 5, 1997

At 8:40 A.M., Detective Rick Grabenstein received a telephone call relaying a message from a local prostitute. "The information was concerning a full-sized Chevrolet van, believed to be a late-1970s model which was dark brown in color with a center panel on the side that was beige in color with a dark brown flame pattern in the lighter center section. The vehicle also had an eagle painted on the back door or spare-tire carrier. It was driven by a white male, middle-aged, and probably with brown hair."

"My parents don't know I'm a prostitute," the woman told Grabenstein when he interviewed her in person, "so if you ever have any reason to contact them, please don't tell them." Asked why she suspected the van's driver, she offered an intuitive explanation. "I saw the van earlier this summer, and it didn't have tinted windows, but now it does.

Anyway, the guy in the van drove by where I was working about eight times. He finally pulled over to the curb," she said, "and I guess he was expecting me to come over, but I didn't because I just had this bad feeling about him. He drove away, and that was that. I just followed my intuition—I got bad vibes, you know. I did talk to another girl who said that she dated him and that he was harmless, but I don't know. I go with my gut, and my gut said, 'Don't get in the van.' I guess Heather Hernandez either didn't have the same gut reaction, or if she did, she ignored it."

"Why do you say that?" asked Detective Grabenstein.

"Well," she replied, "because I saw her get into that van a couple days before they found her dead body."

"That's not the only uncleared homicide possibly linked to Yates's van," commented Detective Grabenstein several years later. "In the summer of 1996, I investigated the murder of Shannon Zelinski. Her body was found near a school bus stop. She died as a result of a gunshot wound to the head."

It was at the same time of the year, according to Linda Yates, that Robert Yates Jr. took his daughter Sasha to work at Certified Security Systems at 11:00 P.M. At 2:30 A.M., Robert Yates still hadn't returned home, so she locked up their Fifty-ninth Avenue residence. At 6:30 A.M., she heard her husband banging on the front door. "When I opened the door for him," recalled Linda Yates, "he came in and immediately gathered up all sorts of cleaning supplies. There was lots of blood in the back of the van, and the cushions of the fold-down bed were soaked with blood, too. He told me that a man on Ray Street was walking his dog on a leash and that the dog jumped in front of the van, and he hit the dog. He said that he couldn't avoid hitting it and that he put the poor thing in the back of the van and took the dog and owner to a veterinarian. He claimed the dog bled all over the cushion in the back of the van. He removed the foam rubber in the cushion and destroyed it, and then bought new foam rubber to replace it," explained Linda Yates.

Grabenstein, of course, knew nothing of Robert Lee Yates Jr. or his ownership of a 1988 Chevrolet van. The detective made note of the prostitute's uneasy feelings about the van's driver, but there were also similar hunches about the drivers of big rigs, compact two-seaters, luxury cars, and grungy trailers. If you're a detective, you make note of them all and track down as many as you can. First on the detectives' agenda was a trip to Tacoma to track down Jennifer Joseph's boyfriend, Marlin, who, according to Yolanda Cary, searched Spokane's streets before returning brokenhearted to Tacoma.

"I'm not her pimp, if that's what you're thinking," Marlin told detectives when they contacted him in Tacoma, Washington. "I met her at a party in Tacoma about two to four months ago. I've been to her house, and I've met her dad and her brother. Her father told me that she needed to get someone to take care of her, and he jokingly told me that she would drive him crazy.

"Once we got to Spokane from Tacoma," he

said, "we checked into the Red Top Motel, where we paid one hundred ninety per week. Anyway, she would leave the motel at about three in the afternoon to work for some escort service. I don't know exactly where she went, or what she did, and I never took her there. I don't really know my way around Spokane at all."

Joseph's boyfriend last saw her on Saturday afternoon, August 16, 1997, at about 3:00 P.M. "As usual, she left the motel in a cab," he said. "She was wearing long black pants, a gray silk blouse with long sleeves and a zipper or buttons in front, and black velvet dress shoes. No, I don't know what kind of underwear she had on. Her hair was curled and just below the shoulder in length. I think her hair was worn down and not pulled back."

"The only jewelry he recalled that she would have been wearing," reported Grabenstein, "was a cross necklace. He didn't recall her wearing any rings. Later that night, the victim called him at the motel."

"It was about nine P.M.," recalled her boyfriend. "She called me and told me that she would be home at about midnight. Other than asking me what I was going to cook for dinner, there was nothing else discussed."

Marlin did discuss loaning money to a fellow named Swan, but that discussion didn't involve Jennifer. Mr. Swan needed a loan and requested money from Jennifer's boyfriend. Marlin didn't have the cash on him, but he assured Swan that once Jennifer got home around midnight, there would be money available. When Jennifer failed to come home, the loan became irrelevant; Marlin became increasingly concerned.

"I started asking other girls if anyone had seen her," he told detectives. "One girl said she saw Jennifer getting into what she thought was a white Porsche, and that was about ten-thirty P.M. She said that the guy driving was white and in his midthirties or early forties. I guess he'd been driving around the area for a while—you know, kinda cruisin', waving at the girls, and that sort of thing. I don't know her name, but I can describe her—a white female, twenty-four or twenty-five years old, with blond hair, and she's a little heavyset. I think she was staying at the same motel and she seemed to go down the steps in the northwest corner of the complex to an area in back of the west side of the motel. Whatever her name is, she was the only one who seemed to know anything at all.

"I remained in Spokane for seventy-two hours after she disappeared and made several attempts to locate her. I called her father's house twice in the following days to find out if she had gone home."

Disconsolately he returned to Tacoma, assuming that she may have taken up with someone else or would possibly return home at a later time. "It had crossed my mind," he admitted, "that she might be dead. The reason I didn't make a missing persons report was because this wasn't the first time that she had disappeared for up to two days at a time since I'd known her."

Joseph was neither a drug addict nor a recreational user, but the only time she had ever vanished for two days at a time was when she had experimented with crack. "I know she hadn't had any drugs for at least thirty days because I was with her during that time and she was drug free.

"I brought her belongings home with me," he tearfully told detectives, "hoping that Jennifer would show up and everything would be fine. When I heard that she had been found dead, I could not even look at them, so I gave them to a friend of mine to keep safe. I knew someone would come looking for them sooner or later."

His first indication that Joseph was dead came via telephone from Spokane on August 27, the day following her body's discovery in the alfalfa field. "I heard that a dead girl had been found in a place with a lot of rubbers and that the cops were asking if anyone knew any features that might help them identify the victim." He had the caller relay to authorities the description of Jennifer's distinctive tattoo of two roses. His fears were confirmed when he read the subsequent article in the Sunday *Tacoma News Tribune* that identified the victim, along with funeral arrangements.

"He turned over four containers of personal belongings that belonged to the victim," reported Grabenstein. "These articles were noted to contain at least two purses, several pairs of shoes, a CD folder, and numerous clothes. The articles were transported back to Spokane for further examination."

Marlin directed the detectives to his car, and he had no objection to his vehicle being thoroughly searched for evidence. He also willingly provided blood samples. "He was most cooperative," recalled Detective Grabenstein, "and was honestly devastated by the victim's death."

"He was initially reluctant to take a polygraph test," recalled Detective Fred Ruetsch, "because his parents told him it wasn't a good idea due to his nervous personality. After a short discussion with both Detective Grabenstein and me concerning the workings of a polygraph, he agreed to accompany us to the Tacoma Police Station, where we turned him over to Detective Larry Miller." Miller administered a polygraph examination and concluded that the young man was being truthful when he said he was not involved in the death of Jennifer Joseph.

"What never made sense to us," later commented Sergeant Walker, "was that Joseph's 'escort representative' and her boyfriend didn't seem to know each other. Here was Joseph living with one fellow, yet obviously associated with D.D.'s escort enterprise, and the two men claimed to not have any interaction at all."

That conundrum was the least of law enforcement's worries. It was almost sixty days since the discovery of Joseph and Hernandez. Police prayed for a breakthrough, and on September 15, they had their first ray of hope.

September 15, 1997

A potential breakthrough offered instant encouragement—Spokane police temporarily detained a man held for an unrelated violation and impounded his car. Not only did his vehicle match one of those on "the list," but in his possession were two handguns: a Raven Arms .25 and a Jennings .22 automatic. "The calibers of these weapons," said Detective Ruetsch, "were perfectly consistent with those used in the homicides of Jennifer Joseph and Heather Hernandez."

Ruetsch, accompanied by Detective John Miller, drove to Garland Towing, where the suspect's car was impounded. "It was an older Chevrolet Camaro that had been recently spray-painted black," recalled Ruetsch. "The chrome had not been taped over very carefully, and the rust and the vinyl top were also spray-painted to include lots of overspray on the taillights and brake lights." Most important, there was no antenna visible on the car. "There was also what appeared to be a bloodstained bedspread wadded up on the backseat."

Later that afternoon, Ruetsch and Grabenstein interviewed the passenger riding in the car at the time of the driver's arrest. "She stated that both firearms belonged to her, and she willingly gave permission to have the weapons test fired to assist our homicide investigation."

Fred Ruetsch sent the weapons and the ammunition to the Washington State Patrol Crime Laboratory System. He requested a comparison of the Raven Arms .25 semiautomatic ballistics to the bullet recovered from the Heather Hernandez homicide. He also requested a comparison of the .25-50 grain ammunition. Awaiting results, Detectives Ruetsch and Grabenstein returned to Spokane's streets.

Lynn Everson, a counselor at the public HIV clinic in downtown Spokane, knows the status of AIDS in Spokane County, and she also knows the names and faces of almost every prostitute on East Sprague. "The AIDS rate in Spokane County is very low," said Everson. "Part of the reason for that certainly is that we try to work with the women to keep them as safe as possible and because condoms are free and available to them at two different locations, and that helps women to be safer."

As for Heather Hernandez and Jennifer Joseph, she remembers them both. "I had only one encounter with Joseph. She asked for the list of 'bad tricks.' "

The "Bad Tricks List" is a compilation of one hundred descriptions of customers known to be violent, deviant, and/or dangerous. "Women are advised to not get into these cars," Everson explained, and offered some examples from the Tricks list.

"Red cab semi truck, white male tried to drag worker outside the truck. White van, older, looks spray-painted, white male, rapist tried to gut worker. Ninety-five percent of the people on the list," Everson said, "are white males with trucks." The hot August night Jennifer Joseph chatted briefly with Everson, she helped herself to several free LifeStyle condoms.

"As for Heather Hernandez," continued Everson, "she struck me as very levelheaded, with a good sense of humor. I never saw her drink or use drugs, and she never appeared to be under the influence of either."

"I don't think she ever used any kind of drugs," said "Young B.," the man—*her* man—who knew her best of all. "If she did, I wasn't aware of it." Immediately following his initial interview concerning the Hernandez homicide, and before follow-up questioning could take place, he disappeared from Spokane. This sudden departure did not elevate him to "prime suspect" status. Such mobility is not uncommon for gentlemen of his lifestyle. It was, however, indicative of the reluctance for police interaction that plagued the investigation from day one.

September 22, 1997

At approximately 11:00 A.M., Detective Ruetsch observed the previously mentioned white Chevy Suburban parked partially in a garage entryway door on Augusta Street. "On October 1, 1997, Detective Grabenstein and I drove to the company headquarters of the firm to whom the Suburban was registered, and [we] contacted the secretary, asking to speak with the president of the company."

The company's president, warmly cooperative, asked how he could be of assistance. "We told him that we were investigating the death of a prostitute here in Spokane," said Detective Fred Ruetsch, "and that during our investigation, a witness told us that they had observed the Chevy Suburban owned by his company possibly attempting to contact prostitutes on East Sprague."

The company's president told Ruetsch and Grabenstein that this particular Suburban was driven by one of any number of employees and that "he would look into it for us and get back to us as soon as possible."

That same afternoon, Ruetsch received the

call—the president was unable to determine which of his many employees might have been driving the vehicle on East Sprague. He offered to provide detectives with a list of his employees' names, if that would be of any value. Detectives accepted his offer, but the names, for the most part, were as common as John Smith, and none of the names were flagged by Spokane police as having drug-related lifestyles, nor were any of the employees known for blatant and repetitive frequenting of Sprague Avenue prostitutes. The president, going the extra mile, provided investigators with a series of photographs taken at the company's Christmas party. Hopefully, the individual whom they sought could be spotted in the pictures. "We had no such luck with that. We also heard back about the ballistics tests on the guns from the Camaro."

"The Raven pistol, item thirteen, was submitted with a broken firing pin," reported Edward L. Robinson, firearms examiner for the Washington State Patrol. "The pin was replaced with an exemplar, and test firing was completed without malfunctions. This pistol has a trigger pull weight of six pounds, which is within average parameters. Test-fired bullets from the Raven pistol were compared to an open-file bullet. . . . These items all share similar general characteristics; however, the microscopic comparison of individual characteristics was inconclusive."

The Jennings pistol was also test-fired by Robinson, and it, too, functioned normally. "This pistol has a trigger pull weight of eight pounds, which is within average parameters. Test-fired bullets and cartridge cases from the Jennings pistol were com-

pared with open file bullets and cartridge cases.
. . . both with negative results.''

September 24, 1997

Robert Lee Yates, Jr. saw the flashing lights of
Officer Corey Turman's patrol car in his rearview
mirror. Yates dutifully pulled his white Corvette
over to the curb just blocks away from where Jennifer Joseph was last seen. Officer Turman, who regularly patrolled the "prostitution zone" on East
Sprague, was asked by homicide detectives to keep
on the lookout for a white Corvette. "I hoped the
driver would make a mistake so I would have an
excuse to stop him," Turman later recalled.

There were two mistakes that night involving
Turman and Yates. First, Yates neglected to signal
a lane change when swerving around a city bus.
The second mistake was more serious. Turman's
report accurately recorded the time, date, and the
driver's name and description. He even wrote that
the 1977 sports car was in excellent condition.
Under "model," however, he wrote "Cam" instead
of "Corvette"—he misidentified the vehicle as a
Chevrolet Camaro rather than a Chevrolet Corvette.

"Slip of the hand," remarked Turman years
later. "You're thinking apple and you write
orange." At the end of his shift, he delivered his
report to crime analyst Jack Pearson. From there,
it would be brought to the attention of the Spokane
police major crimes unit. "It should have," said
Pearson in retrospect, but it wasn't. A field report
noting that the driver of a white Camaro failed to

signal a lane change did not attract the immediate attention of homicide detectives.

"We decided against asking the public to help find the Corvette," said Detective Fred Ruetsch. "We worried that the killer, if he indeed drove a Corvette, would quickly ditch it. He might destroy other evidence, too."

"We suspected that the same person killed Hernandez and Joseph," Detective John Miller acknowledged later, "but we weren't completely convinced that a Corvette was involved. We had suspects who drove other cars . . . In addition, I could just imagine the complaints from innocent Corvette owners if we went public. If I owned a Corvette, it would irritate me."

The first ray of hope was an illusory flicker, and the first solid connection to Yates and his white Corvette lay dormant due to a simple penmanship error. This was not going to be a quick solve; not quick at all. Three more women, regular prostitutes on East Sprague, Lynn Everson told detectives, had not been seen in some time: Their names were Laurie Wason, Shawn Johnson, and Darla Scott.

A check with the missing persons crew revealed that Darla Scott's conspicuous absence had already prompted her distraught twin sister, Marla, to file a report. Shawn Johnson's counselor had also contacted missing persons agents, explaining that Johnson was awaiting admittance into a local methadone program but never returned. "She was dressed," said the counselor, "as though she were going to work on East Sprague as a prostitute."

Shawn Johnson's mother, describing her daughter as "a known drug user who had been living with her ex-husband's brother in the Deer Park area,'' also contacted police when the usual contacts between mother and daughter suddenly ceased. Johnson, of Native American descent, had received land claims payments, and had used Indian Health Care for her medical and dental. Her previous employment included the Wandermere Chevron Station, Taco John's, Maid-o-Clover, and John Doempier Oil Company in Spokane. She had children, an occasional boyfriend, and the requisite number of angry associates outraged at unpaid debts, shoplifting incidents, and vanishing drug money. Her lifestyle and behavior were not dissimilar to that of Darla Sue Scott's.

"I never date guys who've been smoking crack," said Darla Scott on April 12, 1996. Interviewed over a fast-food lunch of fish and chips from Zip's in downtown Spokane, Scott enthusiastically discussed the perils and possible pitfalls of her chosen career as "sex service professional."

"If men smoke too much crack, they can't get an erection," Scott insisted. "If they get mad about it, they might take it out on me. I don't want to get beat up because some guy can't get it up. I refuse to put myself at risk like that." Seventeen months after granting this previously unpublished interview, Darla Sue Scott was murdered by a man who couldn't get it up, at least not while she was alive. When she was dead, however, he had no trouble at all.

"The last glimpse I had of Darla was from my front porch," said her former boyfriend, Arthur. "I'd been doggin' her a bit, and I sat up there and watched her walk back and forth waiting for this date to pick her up. She told me that this guy had been violent with her on a previous date. She not only dated him again, she got drugs for him—you know, that's what they do."

"They" refers to prostitutes who introduce dates to drugs. "First of all," explained one well versed in the art of deception, "you now have the trick more or less dependent on you because, as a new user, he doesn't know how else to get the drugs. And because he doesn't know the real players, prices, and amounts—he wouldn't know a 'teener from an eighth—you can cheat him blind. Plus, you can always just outright rip him off by telling him you were robbed or cheated when you really just used the drugs yourself. Of course, sooner or later he wises up. By then, he's in the game and has become a player. I don't mean he lies, cheats, and robs people, too; I just mean he's 'smart to the business.' He never trusts you like he did at the beginning, unless you wise up and stop thinking about ripping him off. If you see him as an associate, you can do deals together, and both of you either pretend that you never did rip him off in the 'old days,' or you both know that you both know, but he just lets it go. After all, you both may need each other someday. Until he gets wise, however, you got yourself an easy score."

The other, or reverse, aspect of the scenario is the male view of this hustle. "These women think we're all stupid as shit," remarked one street-savvy trick. "What many of them don't know, or maybe they do know, is that we *allow* them to cheat us, or rob us, or lie to us, just to see if they *will*—it's both a test and entertainment."

"Hell, yes," agreed another man with a hearty laugh. "I'll allocate forty dollars for theft or reward, and this is how it goes: I'll tell the girl I want to buy forty dollars' worth of stuff and that I'll share it with her, plus if it is good, I'll buy us a lot more. What they don't know is that I'm telling them the truth. If they come back with some sob story of how they were robbed, I know they are liars and thieves, but I pretend that I believe them. If they come back with good stuff and we share it, then I keep my word, plus I give them a forty-dollar bonus. Most of these girls steal the first forty dollars and are too damn short-sighted to go for the free stuff and the bonus. But I've already figured that into my budget under 'entertainment.' "

Of course, some men simply have no patience for lies and thievery. The fastest way for a prostitute to get killed is to disrespect her client, attempt to defraud him, or rip him off. The second fastest way is for the client, whom she has now made an addict, to find out that she's an "informant"—a crack snitch. For a "respectable man" acting out perverse, violent, psychopathic behavior one or two nights a month, killing a prostitute-snitch could be easily justified as prudence personified. How he would know that the prostitute was a snitch to the cops is simple: another coke snitch would tell him.

"The number one topic of conversation with these women is each other—gossip and backbiting," explained one formerly amongst them. "They'll use together, steal together, and talk about each other behind each other's backs constantly. A coke snitch-whore will be the first to snitch on a snitch."

Bob Dylan's famous words "To live outside the

law, you must be honest" find their tragic fulfillment in the murder of those whose back stabbing
possibly contributed to their own demise. "Darla
came over to the house, was really high, and very
upset," recalled a female friend. "She said she was
going to go meet this guy who had beaten her up
before, and she was afraid that he was going to do
it again."

"You can see why I couldn't stand that scene,
and Darla's immersion in it," said Arthur. "And
you might wonder why Darla would see a man that
had been violent with her in the past, or why she
violated her rule against dating guys who were dick-
numb from dope. Simple—she wanted the money.
Once Darla decided to do something, you couldn't
stop her. When I last saw her, she was wearing my
Mickey Mouse shirt. You know, the one they found
covered in blood out on Hangman Valley Road."

CHAPTER FOUR

November 5, 1997, 9:46 A.M.

On the morning of November 5, Harold Lebsock's dog found a dead body near Hangman Valley Road. "Every day, Mr. Lebsock walked his dog through this particular area," reported Deputy Jack Rosenthal, "and for the previous five days, the dog had been noticeably attracted to a certain section of landscape outside Lebsock's view. Finally, curiosity compelled Lebsock's personal investigation. His dog has been sniffing in the area where the body was located. He didn't look in the area himself until this morning."

Deputy Rosenthal entered the area alone, and only once, taking pictures as he went in. The body was approximately sixty feet off the roadway, next to a small creek running parallel to Hangman Valley Road. "A depression under the corpse gave the appearance that it had been buried at one time," said the deputy. Moving in closer, Rosenthal observed that "the head, one leg, and one arm was showing. The rest of the body was buried. On the arm that was visible was a long sleeve from a shirt. It was blue in color, and there was material, possibly the same as the shirtsleeve, laying on the ground next to the body location."

Rosenthal spent a total of five minutes in the body's immediate area. At exactly 10:21 A.M., he notified headquarters of his findings. Within minutes, Detectives Grabenstein, Francis, Madsen, and Ruetsch, accompanied by Sergeant York, responded from the Public Safety Building.

Armed with appropriate information and directions, Detective Grabenstein retraced Rosenthal's steps into the wooded area. "Just prior to reaching the actual grave site, an area of previous excavation was observed," reported Grabenstein. "It appeared that the perpetrator may have attempted to dig the grave in this area but changed location for some unknown reason, possibly for easier digging or better concealment of the activity."

The body, partially covered with dirt, was lying with the head to the north and the feet to the south. It was on its back, with the right side of the head, upper chest area, and upper arms exposed. "Also exposed was what I believed to be the right leg," said Grabenstein. "It was doubled up and lying across the midsection of the body with the knee pointing to the east. The left leg was exposed from the midcalf region to foot area."

Significant degradation to most exposed portions of the body was noted, primarily animal-caused, along with some degree of putrefaction. "The right side of the head was devoid of flesh and scalp and was nearly skeletonized," stated Grabenstein. "Marks apparently inflicted by the teeth of predators were visible on the right side of the skull, and there was also a rounded defect present in the right rear portion of the skull that appeared consistent with a bullet wound."

Predators also fed upon the left shoulder. Red-colored flesh was visible in open wounds, the remaining portion of the left arm from above the elbow was missing, as were the right ankle and foot. The left leg was visible from approximately the knee to the foot, with the lower portion of the calf and foot cradled in dirt.

"The flesh appears mummified but intact," the detective reported. "The chest and lower portions of the torso are covered with a small amount of dirt. One piece of clothing is visible on the upper portion of the body that is a light blue, long-sleeved shirt. It appears that the material was damaged at the same time as the damage was inflicted on the body. On the right side of the body, a portion of the shirt shows the character Mickey Mouse in the normal black and red colors, leaning on a red capital letter *M*."

Detectives from the Washington State Patrol soon arrived to set up their "Total Station" and began diagramming the scene as other investigation procedures progressed. Slowly and carefully, the detectives began a strategic excavation, much like that of an archeologist.

"Excavation continued from a distance of approximately twelve inches to approximately thirty-six inches from the body's left foot. This was again excavated to a depth of approximately six feet with the soil removed and sifted," explained Sergeant Walker. "It was then excavated approximately an additional six inches to facilitate removal of the body at a later time."

"The sifting of soil and the gathering of evidence didn't stop there," said Grabenstein, emphasizing the procedure's detailed thoroughness. "After initial excavation of the area east of the body, further material was removed nearer to the body and sifted. As items of possible evidentiary value were located, they were recorded as to the area from where the soil bearing the article had been removed. As the articles were located, they were photographed with their designated item number, and then the number was again photographed in the area of excavation where that portion of soil had been."

During the excavation, circumstances of significant interest came to the detective's attention. The victim's head and left shoulder were resting on grass and vegetation. This indicated that it had been lying on the original surface of the ground at the time of burial.

"In other words, the area where the head was resting had not been dug out to form the grave," he said. "Soil was mounded near the head, on top of the vegetation, indicating that soil had been dug up and placed on the original ground surface."

By 4:00 P.M., excavation was completed on the east and south side of the body to a point where the body could be removed. Coroner Amend was summoned to the scene, as well as Ray Corkrum of the Cremation Society.

A piece of black plastic sheeting was placed in the bottom of the excavated area east of the body, and further minimal excavation was done along the west side of the body to allow it to be moved more easily. "The body was then rolled from its resting-place onto the plastic," recalled the detective. "Some of the dirt adjacent to, and adhering to the body, dislodged, and the larger portions were collected."

The body and remaining material were placed in a white body bag and delivered to the Forensic Institute by Corkrum. Due to darkness and a threat of rain, the area was covered with nylon. The following day, excavation continued while Detectives Madsen and Francis went to the Forensic Institute for the autopsy conducted by Dr. Lindholm. The victim was determined to be a white female, estimated live weight approximately 120 to 140 pounds, height 67½ inches, and her age range was twenties to thirties.

Dr. Lindholm's preliminary examination of the body determined that the victim suffered two gunshot wounds. One bullet entered the left temporal region, approximately one inch above the auditory canal; the second passed through the upper helix area of the ear. "The direction of the gunshot wounds," explained Francis, "was from left to right, exiting the victim from the right upper side of the skull. The victim, it was determined, was female, and the cause of her death was two gunshot wounds passing through the brain. The size of the perforations in the head suggested a .25 caliber or smaller. Other evidence collected at autopsy included oral, anal, and vaginal swabs."

On November 12, at 10:30 A.M., forensic odontologist Dr. Frank Morgan, using dental records, was able to identify the remains as those of Darla Sue Scott, born as a twin on September 18, 1968. "Detective (Dave) Bentley and I attempted contacting Darla's sister at her residence, but she wasn't home," reported Francis. "We then telephoned the Tacoma and Yakima Police Departments to have their chaplains notify Darla Scott's parents."

"Weighing in at just over three pounds at birth, Darla could have fit in a shoe box," recalled her mother. "She struggled for life for two months. On her child's fifth birthday, we said farewell to our Darla. Once again, fitting in a shoe box."

"Getting pregnant and having a baby was Darla's idea," said the child's father. "She believed that somehow that would keep her from going back to the street life, but it didn't." Scott got off drugs during her pregnancy "for the baby's sake," but her rehabilitation was short-lived.

"Darla went through at least five drug-treatment programs," he recounted to detectives, "but she would only last in there for maybe two weeks, or as little as three days, before she would be back on the street selling herself for drugs."

"No amount of love," confirmed Darla's mother, "could keep her feet from traveling a dark path. If left to choice, Darla would not have totally abandoned her parents, her twin sister, and her father, and the father of her child."

Prior to her disappearance, Darla would call her daughter's father at least every two or three weeks. "Sometimes she would be out of town with a truck driver," he said. "When she called, I could tell that she was clean and sober."

The last personal contact between Darla Scott and her child's father was in early October, not long before her disappearance. "She was on East Sprague by Kmart," he recalled. "She was waiting for a drug deal. I tried to convince her to come home with me, but she wouldn't do it."

The truck driver he mentioned enjoyed Darla Scott's companionship, convivial conversation, and sexual virtuosity—but he insisted that Darla remain drug free. "Darla liked traveling with him," said one of Darla's longtime acquaintances, "because it took her out of the scene and kept her clean." Ironically, Darla Scott logged more time drug free with the truck driver than she ever did in a rehab program.

The six-foot-tall, 185-pound truck driver frequently hauled frozen foods for his employer. He rented a room when in Spokane, and the woman who was his landlady spoke openly to Detective Grabenstein about her tenant and his relationship with Scott.

"The last time I saw Darla, she had just returned from a trip in his truck, and it was the day before her birthday," she said. "Apparently, he had plans to take her out to dinner for her birthday, but she left to meet one of her friends and never came back. This upset him quite a bit. You see, when Darla was with him, she wasn't using. So when Darla went back to her other friends to resume her normal lifestyle of drug use, he was very aggravated."

"I love Darla," he reportedly confessed to his landlady, "but I can't stand what she's doing any longer. I'll only be rid of her and all her problems when she's dead."

Another longtime beau was good-hearted and good-humored Arthur, who spoke of her with lingering, bittersweet affection. "I was her boyfriend until Christmas of 1996, but I couldn't tolerate her working the streets. It just got to me. I wasn't jealous; that wasn't it. It was just the whole scene was unhealthy and dangerous, and I was just getting either too old or too mature to put up with it. She couldn't give it up, or wouldn't give it up, I don't know which, but I just wouldn't stay in a relationship with her under those conditions. We were going to get together on her birthday, and she said she would call me that day, but I never heard from her."

When Darla Scott's twin sister first reported her as a missing person, many of Darla's friends were not concerned. "I figured she was on the road with that truck driver," confirmed one prostitute. "She'd mentioned that he'd asked her to take off with him, and that meant that she could be out of town for quite a while."

There were rumors that associates of murdered heroin dealer Vito Tombari pegged Darla Scott for murder. "The rumor was that Darla turned in Vito on a drug charge, and some folks were out to get her," explained a Spokane street person formerly in Darla's circle. "I dunno—Vito is, I heard, the father of her sister's kid, so it gets too weird. They say that five pounds of heroin disappeared when Vito was killed. I'll tell ya one thing, Darla was heavy into drugs—mostly crack, but toward the end, she was doing heroin. Darla's life was mostly about buying dope, selling dope, stealing dope, and get this—she was a fuckin' snitch for the cops.''

"Darla was one of our number one informants," confirmed Sergeant Walker. "When her drug-world associates asked her what she was doing in a police vehicle, she would tell them that she was dating that particular officer, which was complete nonsense. She wasn't dating law enforcement; she was informing law enforcement."

Despite her flaws, or perhaps to balance them, Scott manifested a pretzel-logic sense of loyalty to old friends. Whenever she set them up to be arrested by the police, she underplayed their acts of illegality. Incarcerated associates were, for the most part, willing to cut her slack.

"I don't blame Darla," said one former resident of the Spokane County Jail. "The cops had her under their thumb—the only way she could keep on the street, and feed her drug habit, was to do what they wanted, and what they wanted was for her to roll over and give people up. Well, she gave them me, but we remained friends. In fact, she visited me every week while I was in jail."

There was always the possibility, of course, that someone against whom she provided a deposition—usually on videotape, as she was too drugged out to show up in person and appear credible—killed her in retribution. One of the first questions seriously considered by homicide detectives was if her murder was motivated by revenge.

"If every person she cheated, stole from, ripped off, or ratted out were a suspect in her murder," said one of Scott's acquaintances, "the suspect list would make Schindler's list look like a fuckin' Post-it Note for shoppin' at the Circle K."

Everyone agreed that "Darla, bless her heart, was a thief. She would rob anyone if she had half a chance," recalled a male acquaintance. "In fact, she once bragged to me about stealing five hundred dollars from a perfectly polite traveling salesman who offered her that much money for spending the night with him. She took the money, said she was stepping out to buy a pack of smokes, and never came back."

"Darla and I have been friends since the sixth grade," said one young woman sadly. "From what I understood, the twins were adopted at birth. They were well cared for, and I don't think either of the girls was ever abused. Both the parents sort of had disabilities, and could be a bit overbearing, but they didn't have any sort of awful home life."

Darla confided in her friend about her prostitution activities, telling her that oral sex was the activity that Darla engaged in most of the time. "From what I could tell, Darla would do anything for money, and she never indicated that there was any type of sexual activity or behavior that she avoided. Even though Darla talked about using condoms, she was just as likely to reuse them or not use them at all."

"I wasn't surprised that someone finally killed Darla" said one ex-prostitute to Detective John Miller. "She would rip off everyone, and she would rob her johns. Darla told me that she carried a small pistol in her waistband, and she would brag that she used it to rob her customers."

"That's absolute bullshit," insists Arthur, Darla's

longtime, long-suffering boyfriend. "Darla was scared to death of guns, scared of just about everything, and she was a crybaby. Darla's first response in any unpleasant or threatening situation was to run and cry. I mean, that was Darla. She might make up bullshit stories to tell other women on the street, but Darla didn't ever have a gun, wouldn't want a gun, and if she saw one, she would run and cry."

Despite her thievery, Darla easily infatuated her regulars, and more than one became dangerously obsessive. Whenever a customer fell head over wallet in love, Darla would discard him for a newer, less clinging sugar daddy. One man with whom she had a long-term financially based relationship was a married pawnshop proprietor. "Some folks thought that she was blackmailing him, threatening to tell his wife if he didn't give her money," said Arthur. "But his wife knew what was going on the whole time."

The pawnbroker's long-term loans were offset by his short-fused temper. "One day, he broke into my father's house by smashing in the back window," recalled Arthur. "We were letting Darla stay there, and he goes inside and tries to force her to leave with him. His friend Sergeant Moore of the Spokane police, I believe, conveniently detained me on the way home. This would, I guess, give him time to get in and get Darla. Well, the timing was off. I get to my dad's house and there is that pawnbroker guy struggling with Darla, and she's stark naked. Well, not only does she refuse to go with him, she gives him hell—telling him to get his ass out of that house, and then she added, 'While you're at it, leave fifty dollars on the table when you go!' You know what? He actually dug fifty bucks out of his wallet and put it right there on the table on his way out.''

''Immediately prior to her disappearance,'' related another lifestyle associate of Scott's, ''he—the pawnbroker—became furious with Darla because she left him sitting around like a dog while she was up in my apartment. He stormed out and then called and left her a message on the answering machine: 'Darla, you bitch! You fucking whore! I should have come up there, kicked the door down, and dragged you out of there.' Well, it was a day or two after this message and their confrontation that Darla went out to run some errands and never came back.'' Detectives spoke extensively with the former pawnbroker and his aggravated spouse. Both were eliminated as suspects.

''Darla stayed all over the place, her and other girls,'' said one of Darla's former associates. ''She stayed with a security guard for a while, way back she used to be at Arthur's, and then at Arthur's father's house. Then, for a while, she stayed over at Mr. Wilson's, who lived at his mother's place. Darla and some other working girls used to hang out there quite a bit. Maybe you should talk to him.''

''My mother passed away in September of 1996,'' Wilson explained. ''Prior to her death, I took care of her for three to four years. After she died, I was lonely.'' Detective Fred Ruetsch showed Wilson photographs of Darla Scott and 1996 homicide victim Shannon Zelinski, both of whom he recognized. ''Yes, I remember them. They, and some of the other girls, often stayed here at the house, but I never used their services—I just needed their company. There were several of those women in and out of my house, and I did not really know all their names. Oftentimes they stole money or property from me. I guess I was an easy touch."

Detective Ruetsch asked Wilson if he owned any handguns. "I used to own a .38 five-shot revolver that I bought from my daughter," he replied. "I sold it to Gun Emporium here in Spokane. I also own a rifle that my son's had for the last eight or nine years."

"When I asked him had he any other guns," recalled Ruetsch, "he stated that he used to have a gun that was stolen from him in approximately 1996, which he described as a .32 automatic. He advised that whoever stole it left behind a clip and a box of ammunition, as well as the bill of sale for the gun, which he said that he bought for seventy-five dollars about a year before it was stolen."

Wilson had a fairly good idea of who stole the weapon, or at least a likely suspect, but he had never made a police report regarding the weapon's theft. "When the interview was over, I asked him to go through his personal belongings and attempt to locate the bill of sale, the clip, and the ammunition that he had for the stolen gun."

"I found the sack that had the ammunition in it," Wilson told Ruetsch by telephone later that day. "I found it down in the basement, but there was nothing inside it. I don't know what happened to it. It's possible that my grandson took them, although I don't know that for a fact. But I am fairly confident," he told the detective, "that I no longer have the gun, the ammunition, the clip, or the bill of sale.''

As detectives retraced Darla Scott's meandering path and temporary residences, they saw repetitive patterns of taking advantage and violating trusts— not always by Darla herself, but often by those who followed her into homes and apartments offered to the distraught and homeless by the lonely and depressed.

"Darla was the only single woman my mother ever let stay at the house," remembered Arthur. "Mom wouldn't let single girls or troublemakers stay in our home. Darla was the one girl that Momma made an exception for, and Darla knew it. So Darla never disrespected my mother or the family, never stole from her, nothing like that. No, when it came to my family, Darla behaved herself. Of course, when she went elsewhere, all bets were off.''

While authorities characterized Scott's lifestyle as "on society's fringe," it was beyond the fringe, and one step beyond anything her contemporaries in "mainstream society" could imagine, much less endure on a daily basis. Life is always a crisis when you're addicted or habituated to an illegal substance.

"Darla and I would go to the same drug houses," explained one woman to detectives, "so we knew the same dealers, including one woman who would get real pissed and threatening if she found out that you bought from somebody else." Scott also told her and several other people that she had ripped off more than one "drug cop"—or at least patrons claiming to be police officers. One heroin dealer strongly warned Scott not to rob her clients, especially police clients, as that could get her killed.

"Darla worked for two escort services some time back," the woman elaborated to Detective Grabenstein. "One was run by a white couple who lived on Pines behind a Seven-Eleven. This service was, I think, sold to this black guy, you know who I mean." Detectives knew. "The second escort service was run by, oh, whatshisname who lived in the area behind Yokes on North Foothills Drive.

"And," she stated emphatically, "I know that she *did* have sex with cops—off duty, of course. She told me that when she was working for one of the services, she showed up at the motel to meet her client and it was a police officer. She didn't know his name, but she recognized him. Of course, neither of them mentioned his employment. She said she had that happen twice, two different cops, two different motels."

"What we're interested in," said Detective Grabenstein, refocusing the conversation, "are any patrons who assaulted or threatened you." She mentioned one individual who did not assault, but who did scare her. "He was wearing a dress shirt, slacks, and looked like he'd been wearing a tie. He was driving an older Buick four-door that was yellow or tan in color. He had a pick, shovel, and camouflage clothing in the backseat of the car. He wanted me to spend the night with him and that he would pay me four hundred dollars that he had in a safe at the house."

The money was acceptable, but she didn't trust him. "After I agreed to go with him, his eyes began darting back and forth rapidly, and he had a nervous laugh—you know, he laughed like an idiot after everything he said. Well, I figured he was a fucking wacko and that the pick and shovel might be for burying me, so I jumped out of the car the next time he stopped at a streetlight.''

She also told detectives about a white male, "stocky like a bodybuilder," who attempted to rape her. "He was physically choking me, and I thought I was a goner. I got away, and I later heard that he stabbed a prostitute and threw her out of his car.''

Another contact, a black male approximately fifty years old, who associated at the Coach House, picked her up, took her to Airway Heights, and accused her of coming to his apartment in the Otis Hotel and stealing his wallet. "She was able to talk her way out of this situation," recalled Grabenstein, "but she feared that he would kill her.''

"About three weeks before Jennifer Joseph was killed," remarked another prostitute, who called detectives on November 14, 1997, "I was picked up by a man in an older brown Chevy van. After we moved, he told me that he was a police officer and that he was going to arrest me if I didn't give him sex for free. Then he pulled a shotgun on me. Well, shit. I jumped out of that damn van so fast and ran like hell. I made note of his license plate number and gave it to the man I was living with at the time—I can't remember his name. This guy in the van followed me for about a week after that, and it scared the crap out of me.''

Not all prostitute customers are rude, violent, dangerous, or disrespectful. A "good date" can be both a professional and personal pleasure, and working girls discuss who is a "good date" and who is a must to avoid. Ironically, men who frequent prostitutes and call girls do likewise. There are entire Internet Web sites dedicated to "Prostitute Reviews." Much as critics review movies or plays, customers review the women's performances, prices, attitudes, and behavior. "Bad dates"—women who rip off their clients—are flagged with detailed warnings.

For many, Darla was a "bad date." Her reputation spread wide, but there were always more men in more cars. "I know for a fact," insisted a former coworker of Scott's, "that neither Darla Scott nor her friend Linda Maybin would ever get into anyone's car unless they felt safe with them. After all, Darla was so scared of getting hurt or killed out there that she stopped working the streets altogether. She just took dates through the escort service, or men introduced to her as good dates by other working girls. If she drove off with a guy, it was someone she felt wasn't too damn dangerous, or at least someone who she believed was not going to hurt her. Who was it? Damned if I know. She saw a lot of guys, and a lot of guys saw Darla."

"The last time I saw Darla was in October," said Darold Johnson, operator of First Step Services, a Spokane homeless shelter. "She came in, as she usually did twice a week, and made quiet small talk with the folks at the shelter—the place was a refuge from the daily drudgery of her street life. She wasn't proud of what she did for a living. She didn't know how to do anything else. She knew that. She didn't deserve to die for it."

Neither did Melinda Mercer, good-natured Seattle waitress and part-time prostitute, whose naked body was found December 7, 1997, in Tacoma—a town on the opposite side of Washington State.

Edward Jamison discovered Mercer's nude body at 3800 South Fiftieth, Tacoma, Pierce County, Washington. A crime scene investigation was done by Detective Dave Devault, Detective D. L. Correll, and Detective M. Margeson, plus J. Kristoffersen and T. Taylor, forensic specialists.

"Located at the scene was an expended .25-caliber CCI brand casing," reported Devault. "No purse, wallet, or money was recovered. A vehicle was used to transport the victim to the body-recovery site." On the same day, December 8, that the autopsy was conducted in Pierce County by Medical Examiner John Howard, two more "suspect vehicles" were eliminated from the Spokane list: the light blue Chevy Blazer and the black Oldsmobile Cutlass. Both vehicles belonged to a couple familiar with Darla Scott, her sister, and others of Scott's cronies.

"Both vehicles have probably been seen on East Sprague on numerous occasions," reported Detective Madsen, "because her husband and she would pick up Darla Scott and some of the other people down there and give them rides."

As for the autopsy results on the body found in Pierece County, "Recovered from [around] the victim's head were four plastic bags," noted Dr. Howard. "Cause of death was determined to be three gunshot wounds to the head, with two projectiles recovered. Oral, anal, and vaginal swabs were also taken." The victim was identified as Melinda

Mercer, daughter of Karyl Greenwood of Centralia, Washington.

"She was running in a fast world up in Seattle," said her mother, "but she was the most loving girl, the most innocent victim ever. She never deserved this. Nobody deserves to be shot in the head three times."

"Melinda Mercer had no ties to Tacoma," Tacoma police spokesman Jim Mattheis told reporters. "She had been living in Seattle, working part-time as a waitress in the Wallingford District, and working the streets some as a prostitute."

Mattheis didn't overlook the similarities to the Spokane deaths of Joseph, Hernandez, and Scott—the rural or sparsely populated areas where the bodies were found, plus the fact that all died of similar gunshot wounds. Mercer was shot in the head at some other location, and her body dumped in the field near South Fiftieth Street and Burlington Way. On that same weekend, Robert Lee Yates Jr. served on active duty with the National Guard at Fort Lewis, near Tacoma.

Following his aerial maneuvers, Yates returned home for the festive Yuletide season of comfort and joy. There was no solace for the family of Shawn Johnson, though. One week before Christmas 1997, Michael Connors, one of several maintenance workers at a sewage-treatment plant, found Johnson's corpse on Hangman Valley Road, not far from where Harold Lebsock had discovered the remains of Darla Sue Scott.

"The killer made no attempt to bury her, not even in the most shallow of graves," said Sergeant Walker. "Instead, her body was concealed under leaves and brush. Detectives Grabenstein, Henderson, Francis, and Madsen, as well as Ident Officers Julie Combs and Deb Rowles, did the crime scene investigation. As with the other victims,'' stated Walker, "no purse, wallet, or money was recovered, and the body was transported to the recovery site by vehicle."

On December 12, 1997, Dr. George Lindholm and PA Randy Shaber performed the autopsy. The victim was identified as Shawn L. Johnson. Two plastic bags covered her head; two gunshot wounds entered her head. "Oral, anal, and vaginal swabs were also obtained," states the official report. "Investigation revealed that Johnson was involved in prostitution and illicit drugs."

"I knew Shawn was dead before police found her," admitted Shawn Johnson's heroin connection. "I was in custody in Adams County at the time they found her body, and an investigator from the drug task force told me that my number was found in her stuff. That makes sense, because I did a lot of business with her, and she owed me about one thousand dollars for heroin that I'd sold her. I wasn't too worried about getting paid," he said, "because at the time she got in debt to me she had a real job working at the Chevron station on North Division. But she got fired and then began to work the streets as a prostitute. Well, this caused me some concern because now I didn't know how I was going to get paid. She and I stayed in regular contact, and, of course, I was trying to gradually get her bill paid off. We got along fine; there was no friction—we both knew she owed me the money, and she was usually pretty good about paying her drug debts.''

When suddenly he could no longer locate her, he feared the worst. ''I knew she would never run away because she had a son and a car. The car was a small white station wagon that she used to let me borrow on occasion. Then Shawn vanished. I figured that the serial killer had gotten to her.''

''This drug dealer,'' later commented Detective John Miller, ''was easily eliminated as a suspect in her homicide as he was in jail from November 13, 1997, until January 7, 1998.''

There was far more to Shawn Johnson's life than procuring drugs and soliciting sex—both temporarily relevant illegalities. ''All I ever wanted,'' wrote Shawn Johnson in her personal journal, ''was a family, a home, children, and, of course, someone who cares about all of the above and me.''

For the family of Shawn Johnson, her tragic demise was more painful than her oft-lost battle with addiction. ''When we were kids, Shawn and I would put on plays for our parents and neighbors,'' recalled Debbie Fine, her sister. ''We'd dress up in costumes and the whole bit. We used the living room or the front yard as a stage, and we'd have a narrator, set chairs out, and invite all the neighbors over.''

''The last time we saw her,'' recalled her tearful daughter-in-law, Shannon Johnson, ''was my wedding day, October eleventh.''

Shawn's son Eric married Shannon, who lamented that ''she will never be able to see her grandchildren. She will never be able to see her youngest son grow up to be an adult.''

"My daughter was trying to get help when the serial killer took her choices away," said Johnson's mother, Margaret Dettman. "To find out, with a knock at your door, that your daughter was murdered and you can never see her again is to feel so much agony you can't even speak."

Grieving with Dettman over the loss of her daughter was longtime family friend Pennie Yates, cousin of Robert Lee Yates Jr. "Knowing her personally, and knowing her daughter was a victim, is very difficult," said Pennie Yates. "We all know Margaret. I mean, you don't know what to say."

"I pray that God is giving her the peace that we hoped she'd find while she was alive," said a family friend. "That opportunity was taken from her. It's tragic. It's heartbreaking, but that's what's real, and we'll have to deal with it the rest of our lives."

CHAPTER FIVE

Spokane was compelled to face an unsettling reality—a serial killer acting out deranged fantasies of dominance and death in the beautiful "Lilac City" of Spokane, Washington. Having a serial killer on the loose is not a source of civic pride, and law enforcement personnel never delight in unsolved homicides, a rising body count, and an exponentially increasing number of bereaved, heartbroken families.

On December 22, 1997, the special Serial Killer Homicide Task Force was formed; it was comprised of detectives from both the Spokane Police Deparment, under Chief Terry Mangnan, and the Spokane County Sheriff's Office, under Sheriff John Goldman. Among the first detectives assigned to the task force were Spokane police detectives John Miller and Minde Connelly and Spokane County Sheriff's detectives Grabenstein and Ruetsch. The task force was dedicated to catching Spokane's serial killer.

In Los Angeles or San Francisco, a dozen or more detectives would have been assigned to the team, but Spokane had neither the man power nor the budget for a task force of that magnitude. What the Spokane task force lacked in numbers was compensated for by the degree of unwavering dedication and consummate professionalism. Upon formation, the Spokane task force consulted with King County's Green River task force for tips on running a large investigation, and they sought guidance from the FBI. Again, stressing the importance of victimology, they compiled and compared lists of friends of each of the victims, seeking similarities or patterns.

"The lives of the victims, and other women reported missing at that time," said Sergeant Walker, "overlapped considerably. They knew each other, although sometimes not very well; they frequented the same places, worked the same streets, and shared many of the same customers. Hence, the investigation of each homicide overlapped with the investigation of the others."

For homicide detectives, each investigation is a matter of life and death. Every victim, regardless of past indiscretions or prior convictions, is regarded with honest and unfailing reverence. "We are very protective of our victims' dignity," insists Walker. His use of "*our* victims," in this context, rather than "*the* victims," demonstrates a sense of personal relationship and commitment.

"No killer, no matter how degrading the acts perpetrated upon those he kills, can ever usurp the inherent dignity of human life," said Walker thoughtfully. "Protection and preservation of the murdered individual's dignity becomes a subtle, seldom-expressed subtext to homicide investigations."

Detectives must be empathetic to the sensitivities of the victims' families, resilient to often-unreasonable expectations, and thick-skinned when opportunistic pundits second-guess and insult them on radio and television. Detectives repeatedly requested that media outlets not term the homicides "prostitute murders."

Media professionals in Spokane certainly understood the request's importance, but there were those who either didn't understand or didn't care. "What investigators were up against was public apathy, plain and simple," explained Walker. "When a prostitute is murdered, there is not a united public outrage. It's sad, but for some reason these victims, who were wives, mothers, and/or children to someone, are not regarded by some people as being of the same value as everyone else."

This apathy finds reflection in the story of Kristen Stiles, a twenty-eight-year-old stripper who, according to colorful prose in the *Seattle Times,* "wears a red dress, drinks strawberry milk shakes, and holds a cigarette ringed with pink lipstick." Ms. Stiles was a high school friend of Darla Scott's who was devastated by the discovery of her former chum's decomposing corpse.

Stiles turned to her mother for emotional comfort. Her mother, however, heard the gruesome details with complete emotional detachment. "So what," said the mother, "she was a prostitute."

The fundamental principle animating the apathy toward the suffering of prostitutes is that these women—by nature of their career, lifestyle, or abilities—are deemed less than human. Respectable women look down on them, and disrespectful men regard them more as appliances than people.

"These women are not seen as human beings," insists Lynn Everson of the Spokane County Health Department. "They're seen as objects without feelings or thoughts or values. And they aren't valuable except as objects to satisfy someone's urges. And because they've often come from places that are so violent—sexually, physically, and emotionally— the chaos and the violence out on the street seem normal."

Everson's portrayal of prostitutes is consistent with the standard clinical and support agencies' representation of prostitutes as young, single, addicted, undereducated, and from backgrounds replete with poverty and abuse. "The average age of entry into prostitution is fourteen," says Everson, "Studies say that between seventy-five percent and ninety percent of those women were sexually abused as children."

These prostitute stereotypes—young, abused, and addicted—are partially challenged by recent field studies conducted in the United Sates and Canada by sociologist Frances M. Shaver of Concordia University. "The majority [of prostitutes] began their careers between the ages of sixteen and twenty," reported Shaver. "Although young, this is far above the thirteen- and fourteen-year-olds emphasized in the popular media."

Speaking at the 1996 International Conference on Prostitution, Shaver cited research demonstrating that the level of sexual abuse among prostitutes is no more, and in some geographic areas, significantly less, than among the population at large. Thirty-three percent of female prostitutes in Vancouver, Canada, for example, suffered childhood sexual abuse compared to 54 percent of the respondent female population of Canada. "These findings should challenge us to reevaluate our thinking about prostitutes and prostitution," said Shaver. "More research must be done before concluding that the level of sexual and physical abuse of working prostitutes when they were children is higher than the level of abuse in the general population."

Frances Shaver, a Concordia University sociology professor, concluded that stereotypes about prostitutes are just that: stereotypes. "Prostitutes practice safe sex and do not present an undue risk of AIDS or HIV. Prostitutes are not desperate women. In addition, we found that only seven percent of prostitutes use drugs, contrary to popular belief."

"I believe," said Shaver, "that sex work should be decriminalized so that prostitutes will be treated with more respect, so they can be treated fairly under the law when they are harassed, instead of getting harassed by the law."

"Harassment comes with the trade, partly because it is persecuted by the police," said one of Shaver's researchers. "It's not an easy life. You see the effects. They get burned out. There's a lot of harassment."

"Because of the marginalization of those who work on the street, compounded by the criminalization of prostitution, it is difficult for prostitutes to seek recourse for crimes committed against them," said Carol Leigh, coordinator of a San Francisco outreach project through the Coalition on Prostitution.

"Prostitutes are unable to make complaints against officers in cases of illegal arrest, misconduct, and abuse, as they are highly dependent on the good graces of the police, who 'oversee' street activities. Prostitutes are also unlikely to go to the police, because of her or his criminal status, in cases of domestic violence, or if they are raped or robbed."

Everson, Shaver, Leigh, and others may disagree on statistics and solutions, but they agree completely that no woman, be she prostitute or stock broker, sets herself up for violence. "You hear people say, 'If the women weren't out working the streets, this would not happen to them. They would not have been killed or hurt.' That is a clear case of blaming the victim," insists Everson.

"Prostitutes do not set themselves up for violence," agrees activist Jenette Marlowe. "Nobody asks to be assaulted. Prostitutes have never had the right to work free of prejudice, hatred, violence, or fear."

"I hope that anyone reading this will understand my desire to have those in prostitution understood as victims," said Lynn Everson, and most recovery programs and women's groups tend to portray prostitutes as victims. Many prostitutes, however, find this characterization objectionable.

"If she sees all of us as already being victimized—and our customers as furthering that victimization—then she is denying the reality that most of us are capable and competent to make a conscious decision to work in this business," says Holly, a street prostitute with twenty years experience.

"Some recovery programs and women's groups like to regard prostitutes as victims," Jenette Marlowe commented politely, "despite the fact that many current and former prostitutes believe themselves to be nothing of the kind. This victim mentality is a convenient way of absolving oneself of blame for making ill-conceived or unwise choices. Typically applied to female rather than male prostitutes, it reinforces the archaic notion that women don't know what's good for them and are incapable not only of making their own decisions, but also of taking responsibility for those decisions."

"I'd ask anyone to close their eyes and imagine a pimp," said Everson. "My guess is that most of you imagined a black man with a big hat and a Cadillac. The reality is very often a mother or father selling a child, profiting from the child's earnings selling sex to adults, all the while abusing that child regularly. Pimps range in age from sixteen to seventy, and they are every color and every race. Our stereotypes about who these people are almost always wrong."

The actual percentage of prostitutes represented by pimps of the "big hat and Cadillac" breed is remarkably low. Even in San Francisco, Shaver's research shows that stereotypical pimps represent less than 4 percent of the city's sex workers. As for anecdotal evidence of victimization, Everson has powerful stories.

"I worked with a woman whose mother sold her for the first time at age twelve," said Everson, "and a man whose father sold his ten-year-old son to a chicken ranch, a place where adults have sex with children when he was only ten. None of these children made a free choice to be where they are. Very few people in prostitution can stand to have sex with strangers unless they are numbed by drugs and alcohol."

"I was being given beer and hard liquor when I was seven or eight years old," confirmed one prostitute who, true to Everson's example, started at an early age. "My folks thought it was funny to get me drunk. By the time I was ten, or maybe eleven, I was smoking pot; by twelve or thirteen, I was snorting coke and smokin' crack. Do you really think that I wanted pot and crack instead of Barbie and Ken? My family life wasn't like any family I saw on TV. I got the hell out when I was fourteen. You know what I found out? You can't rent an apartment. You can't get a job. Oh, you do have choice, of sorts: you can choose to sell drugs, or choose to sell yourself. Selling drugs doesn't take much skill, and the only real talent I'd developed by the time I was fifteen was giving a really spectacular blow job. I realized early on," she said with an elaborate stage sigh, "that no matter how good I was at it, or how many hours of practice I put in, I'd never perform at Carnegie Hall." She laughed at her self-deprecating joke. "However," she added with bittersweet self-awareness, "I could perform in the alley *behind* Carnegie Hall."

"It's no joke, the way some people feel about us," remarked another working girl. "So-called respectable women look down on us, like they're not prostitutes themselves, which they are just as much as us, probably. As long as their husbands bring home the bacon, they gladly eat pork. But if their man has money troubles, or he don't get a promotion or a raise, and can't or don't buy 'em the shit that they want, the bitch cuts him off. Of course, she can't cut him off completely, because she doesn't know where he's getting it, which is, hopefully, from me.

"Even then, a lot of guys treat us like shit, too, even the ones that pay us. It's like they don't think of us as real live people, like we're androids or whatever you call 'em, you know, robots that look real, but don't feel nothin'. Well, I got news for ya. I happen to be an honest-to-God human being. Yes, I'm a prostitute. I charge money for sex. So what else is new? Look at it this way: for less money than taking a date out to dinner and a movie, I'll give you what it is you just hope to get otherwise. The problem, of course, is that I could wind up getting killed by this goddamned serial killer."

"Saying that all the serial killer's victims are prostitutes is like saying all his trout are fish," said Cathy A., who's spent most of her adult life working the track. "I bet this guy has dated almost every working girl on Sprague Avenue, and most of them are still alive. Whatever his victims have in common, it isn't simply what they do for a living."

Sergeant Walker addressed speculation of the killer's motive with measured, blunt professionalism. "Those of us in law enforcement have years of experience dealing with this issue, and the truth is that the only person who could tell you why he did it, would be the killer himself. He's got tons to tell us," said Walker, "and he is the only person who knows the answers to the many things we have to assume.''

"Those women, regardless of their stature in life, deserved the same quality of investigation as anybody on the face of this earth," said Detective Ruetsch, "and that's what we attempted to do."

"Women on the streets were terrified," recalled Lynn Everson. "Some women believed that they would know the killer when they looked into his eyes, or that they would sense the evil. Others said that if he picked them up and tried to hurt them, they would leave their mark on him. It turns out that the women he killed never had any idea that it was him, that he was the serial killer."

"We figure it's someone we all know," offered one nervous young lady, picking at a cuticle as she discussed possible suspects. "Either a cop— my vote is Sergeant Moore because he treats us like shit—or one of our regular customers that we feel safe with."

There was one other possibility that seemed to disturb her the most. "Or the killer is another one of us—or maybe one of us and somebody else working together. God, I hate to think that," she said, glancing around the Coach House coffee shop as if fearful that the killer was overhearing the conversation. "I mean, what if the killer is sitting right here, right now, or is someone I see every day, or use with or date. It gives me the fuckin' creeps."

"There's this one guy," offered another woman, "who drove a white Corvette, about the only white Corvette I've ever seen out here. He made several passes by me. Most johns, after a couple of times driving by, will pick you up, but this guy just kept cruising.

"When he stopped, something triggered my inner warning device. I got bad vibes—that sixth sense I use for my survival told me, 'Don't ever get into the car with this man.' Whenever I meet someone, I go by how I feel. Oh, he was pleasant enough and friendly, but I go by my instincts. You know, he was asking me kinda 'What's a nice girl like you doing on a street like this?' sorta thing. He asked me if I was on drugs, had a pimp, and stuff like that. And I told him no, I was working to survive. I never dated him because he gave me the willies. He'd run and fetch smokes and coffee for me, and not charge me nothin', but I wouldn't ever consider going with him. I saw him quite a few times in the summer of 1997. He'd stand out there on the street right in front of God and the cops and everybody just talkin to me, suckin' up my time."

There was something other than bad vibes that gave her the creeps. "The real creepiest thing is that when I just happened to mention being scared about the serial killer, he told me that I didn't have anything to worry about because I was a good girl. It didn't occur to me until later that—I mean— how the hell would he know if I had anything to worry about? I didn't like the look in his eyes, anyway. The eyes are the windows to the soul, so they say. Well, the windows were open, but there wasn't a soul home."

One might imagine that these Sprague Avenue women would want to "get off the streets," but this is not always the case. While many prostitutes would probably move off the street if they could find an alternative way of making a living, many would not.

The street offers certain advantages to the sex trade professional. Among these advantages are the ability to see clients beforehand, the relative safety of working in numbers, the social aspect of working among colleagues, the absence of over-head costs, the freedom to choose one's working hours, and the comparatively fast turnover of customers.

There are also disadvantages to street work, not the least of these being the possibility of arrest. "Giving prostitutes police records not only reduces their chances of finding a job," insists activist Marlowe, "but encumbering them with stiff fines, when they have no other sources of income, means that they will have to immediately go back on the street in order to pay the fine."

Street prostitutes pay more than fines. They also pay for rent, food, clothing—all the basics of life—not only for themselves but for their families. "Almost thirty percent of all street prostitutes are the only income provider for their family," states researcher Shaver, "and are at least responsible for one other person in addition to themselves."

"Look at the extra hours these women, including me, put in the week before Christmas," said one Spokane hooker. "You know they've got children, folks, families, and they want their Christmas Day to be as normal and happy as everyone else's."

The day before Christmas, another woman associated with addiction and prostitution, Sunny Gale Oster, was added to the list of those missing, a

list including Shawn A. McClenahan, Linda Marie
Maybin, and Laurel Wason. This made four women
of known prostitution backgrounds to suddenly,
and inexplicably, leave the scene.

"Little is known about McClenahan, except that
she is from the Spokane area and has previous
convictions on drug charges," Captain Doug Silver
of the Spokane County Sheriff's Office said.
"Wason, the married mother of a twelve-year-old
son, left her Kennewick home on October thirtieth
and has been missing since then."

The public's help was also requested in locating
Linda M. Maybin, thirty-seven. "She was last seen
on November twenty-second," said Spokane
police, "and was reported missing by friends."

Oster, a close friend of Linda A. Maybin's, was
last seen by street friends in November 1997 at the
now-defunct First Step Services. First Step offered
women a place to go when they needed help, and
local prostitutes came to rely on First Step's "open
door and protective hand" on the corner of East
First and Napa.

Situated in an unimpressive physical landscape,
the emotional terrain was noted for compassion,
care, and sensitivity. First Step served as a communications center, lunchroom, safe house, and meeting place for both Spokane's homeless and its
prostitutes.

By the first month of 1998, First Step was already
out of step with the harsh realities of local zoning.
City-code-enforcement officers served a notice of
violation pointing out that First Step Services was
not zoned or licensed to operate as a mission or
detox center. "If this stands, I'm done," said First

Step owner Darold Johnson. He was all too familiar with what happens to the homeless and disenfranchised when people look the other way—he knew almost every woman killed, missing, or feared killed, including Sunny Oster.

"The last time I saw my sister, Sunny," said Audrey Oster, "was the summer of 1997 when she visited us in Auburn. We played like kids, went to church, and swam in Lake Tapps. When we were kids, she could jump and dive even before I was ready to let go of the side of the pool and get my head wet. She took my fear of water. Today I love it."

"It was ten forty-five, August 7, 1956," recalled Sunny's mother, "that I gave birth to a little girl. It was a really proud day. Her father was excited. She was perfect in every way. She was teeny and petite, giggled all the time. Troublemaker too. Spirited. I remember one time when she was little, she was out on the porch giggling and I went to investigate. And she had her little hands cuffed up, and inside was a garter snake and it was tickling her."

Sunny's essentially happy childhood included an exemplary relationship with her sister, Audrey. "They were both drum majorettes," said her mother. "They enjoyed that so much. It was something for the two of them to do together." Something happened to Sunny Oster that didn't happen to Audrey—something unpleasant and traumatic. All human beings seek pleasure and avoid pain. Sunny muffled her pain and distracted her mind with drugs. "The family knows what started it," confirmed her mother, "but we kind of just whisper about it."

Unexpectedly pregnant, Oster dropped out of Auburn High School when she was seventeen. Her struggle with drug addiction soon followed. At the age of forty-one, the mother of two sons, Brandon and Derek, longed for a life of normalcy. "She wanted what I had," said her sister. "She wanted a family, a house, to cook dinner. To do the same things I do. She wanted a relationship with her kids. She missed them and loved them."

Drug addiction, despite suppositions to the contrary, does not destroy altruism, selfless dedication, or caring self-sacrifice. "When I came out of the hospital with cancer, Sunny took care of me," recalled her stepmother, Cecelia Oster. "This was just ninety days before she went missing. She helped me to the bathroom, cleaned, and added liquid food for my feeding tube. She had to set an alarm to feed me through that tube in the middle of the night, just as if I was a baby. She did that all for me, out of love."

Love was not Sunny's only qualification—she was an experienced nurse's aide. "She took such good care of me," recalled her stepmother, "I treasured every day we shared—we talked; we laughed; we lived."

In her early forties, with adult children of her own, Sunny Oster took another shot of courage, and one more run at addiction-free sobriety. She had her heart set on a Spokane drug-treatment facility, but her family pleaded with her to attend one closer to home.

"Dad didn't want Sunny to go to Spokane," said

her sister. "He wanted her to go to drug treatment near home so we could visit her. He felt something inside that told him it was not right for her to go."

Oster, at a friend's encouragement, checked herself into the American Behavioral Health System, a Salvation Army facility in Spokane, for treatment of her cocaine addiction. She arrived on September 16, 1997. An inventory of her belongings included one bracelet, one crucifix, five pairs of earrings, and one Bible. She was officially discharged from the facility on October 2, 1997.

On September 28, prior to her official discharge date, Oster placed a collect call home to her father from somewhere other than the treatment center. At 5:47 P.M., October 1, 1997, she called her sister's home collect from that same number.

"Sunny Oster called her sister's house one more time on October fifth," reported Detective Grabenstein. "Her sister was out of town in California, and Sunny spoke to her brother-in-law. She was quite drunk and wanted him to drive over to Spokane to pick her up. Due to her condition, he politely declined."

Instead of returning to Auburn, Oster turned to the Maple Tree Motel on East Sprague. She checked into room 20, stayed through October 11, and returned October 18 for one night in room 22.

The Maple Tree's manager, disconcerted by Oster's behavior, advised Detective Grabenstein on October 31 that Oster "may be a prostitute." Oster's name didn't come to his attention again until December 24, Christmas Eve Day, when Sunny Oster's family reported her missing.

The day after Christmas, December 26, Laurel

Wason and Shawn McClenahan were found dead. McClenahan, and the still-unaccounted-for Linda Maybin, like Darla Scott, were known as "informants," or "crack snitches."

A crack snitch, in the opinion of most addicts and users, is despicable. "In my view of things, what it amounts to is this," explained one irritated former addict. "The cops essentially encouraged them to continue their lifestyle of addiction and prostitution. In return for not getting arrested, they tell the cops which of their friends and associates to arrest instead. Being a snitch is the fastest way to get marked for life. And the second fastest way to get killed—the fastest, of course, is to rip off your customers."

In some cities, the first time someone is uncovered as a snitch, they are marked for life with a diagonal razor slash across the face—an indelible mark advising one and all that the person is never trustworthy. The second time that person is revealed to have snitched, they are marked for death. Maybin, Scott, and McClenahan never received the first mark, but Spokane subculture differs in some respects from other cities.

Linda Maybin, Darla Scott, and Shawn McClenahan all had professional representation through Christine's Escort. McClenahan, not only worked for Christine's, she also was working as a police informant buying crack cocaine from her employer, J. R. Koesterman. Court documents confirm that Shawn McClenahan's work as an informant helped convict Koesterman of five felonies, including possessing crack cocaine and forgery, a felony conviction shared by employee Linda Maybin.

Darla Scott, an acknowledged police informant, lived at Koesterman's house in the summer of 1995. When arrested and convicted, Koesterman fled the state; his female partner went to prison. Christine's Escort, as a business enterprise, was taken over by Wendell L. Bonton. Linda Maybin gave Bonton's address to the State Department of Corrections as her own address one month before she was reported missing.

"There are a number of similar-type associations among these women," acknowledged Captain Doug Silver. "They traveled in the same circles." He declined, at that time, any further comment on the interrelationship of the escort service, the women, and their role as "informants."

Taking a close look at the within-the-scene behavior of Scott, McClenahan, and Maybin, some patterns and possibilities began to emerge. They ran in the same "crack crew," and all would die at the hands of the serial killer, almost one upon another.

"You tellin' me that is just a coincidence," asked Arthur, Darla's former boyfriend, rhetorically, "that three women who knew each other well, ran together, ripped off johns together, and snitched either on each other or together, would all be killed by the same guy, almost right in a row? Nah, someone had to bring them all together, plus identify them all as good dates for the killer, and the killer as a good date for them. I'm not saying the killer had a willing accomplice, but there has to be a common link."

"I would ask the question," offered Cathy A., former Spokane hooker, "was there a Spokane prostitute who dated the serial killer, who turned him on to each one of those women?

"Sure, there was," she continued, answering her own question. "What about Aloha Ingram? She knew all of them, maybe she was dating the killer and passing him on to them. After all, how many coke whore-snitches are there in Spokane who set up dates for other coke whore-snitches if the client asks them to suggest other girls?"

Sharon G. didn't bother using a calculator. "Uh, I'd say too many to count. Most of them, of course, would usually recommend someone they believed wasn't as good as them sexually, or as pleasant personally—you never turn a client on to someone he might like better than you. That would be suicide. Or, in this case, murder."

"I dated Shawn McClenahan on two occasions, back when I was still drinking and separated from my wife," recalled a retired truck driver who met her by chance, not arrangement.

"I drove a route between Spokane, Seattle, and Portland with occasional side trips to Denver and Salt Lake City. The first time I dated Shawn, she gave me a blow job for twenty dollars, and the second time, we had intercourse. Both times we did it in my car, used a condom, and she never took off all her clothes."

The trucker, now a recovering alcoholic, owned the previously mentioned maroon Buick. Investigators, following up on all tips, considered him a possible suspect. All suspects, without exception, were questioned; all possible suspects, without question, provided answers and blood samples. "Over one thousand individuals, possible suspects, submitted blood samples to the homicide task force for laboratory analysis," acknowledged Sergeant Walker, "including the driver of the maroon Buick."

"I used that car, the Buick, for both dates with Shawn," recalled the trucker, "and they would have been on Friday or Saturday nights because I never used prostitutes on work nights." On both occasions, he found her in the Kmart parking lot on East Sprague. The final encounter with his Kmart "Red Light Special" was within a few weeks of Christmas 1997. "She was very mellow, and didn't seem high or loaded to me. In fact, we exchanged phone numbers. I called her once, left a message, but I didn't hear back."

When sobriety returned to him his wife and his life, the recovering alcoholic jettisoned Shawn's phone number. "I liked Shawn, and I felt sorry for her," he told Detective Ruetsch. "I stashed away a hundred-dollar bill for Shawn and drove by Kmart to give it to her as a Christmas present, but I couldn't find her."

Shawn McClenahan was found crying in the parking lot of Rainbow Foods at 5:45 P.M., on Christmas Eve, by an elderly male acquaintance, unaware of her addiction or her profession. "I had been in Spokane shopping that day," he recalled. "I drove my little red Mazda pickup into town and stopped by Rainbow Foods. Shawn noticed me and came over to talk. She was crying and very upset."

Amidst the aural ambience of Christmas carols, idling automobile engines, and the happy hubbub of last-minute holiday shoppers, McClenahan confessed her anguish. "I'm a drug addict," she said, as if saying it aloud would make it go away. "I'm addicted to heroin, but . . ." She paused, wiped her runny nose on the back of her hand, and blurted out, "But I'm going into a methadone program, and I'm getting off drugs, and I'll be okay and, and maybe . . . maybe"—Shawn pulled up her famed reserve of positive good humor—"next Christmas I'll be so presentable I'll be gift wrapped under the tree instead of unraveling out here on the street."

"This was the first time I ever knew that she had a drug problem," he said. "She was upset with herself about it, but she told me that she was going into a methadone program where she could get off drugs. She then told me that she was meeting a girlfriend, but that she would call me later in the evening. That was the last time we spoke." He assumed Shawn would see her sister and other relatives on Christmas Day—she previously mentioned such intentions.

"It was the conflict between her love of family and her addiction to heroin that caused her so much personal pain," said longtime acquaintance Arthur. "I trust Shawn has found peace, or that peace has found Shawn."

Attorney Rick Dullanty found Shawn the day after Christmas 1997 while taking an afternoon stroll with his twenty-year-old son. Shawn wasn't in the parking lot of Rainbow Foods or Kmart. She was head-to-head with the dead body of Laurel Wason. On Friday afternoon, 2:00 P.M., December 26, Dullanty and son noticed two legs clad in blue jeans protruding oddly from soggy leaves in a wooded Spokane County gully.

"At three o'clock in the afternoon, I was in the

office working on another matter when Sergeant VanLeuven told me that patrol officers had located a body at East Fourteenth," recalled Detective Ruetsch. "When I arrived on the scene with Ident Officer Carrie Johnson, Deputy Spivey showed us the location of the body, which was in a ditch apparently dug out to prevent erosion and aid runoff.

"I could see the legs of one body pointed to the west, and I realized that I could also observe another leg pointed toward the east," he said. Upon investigation, it was discovered that the legs, one missing a foot, were not connected to the same body. "There were too many body parts for just one victim," recalled Ruetsch.

Covered with leaves, twigs, and branches, both bodies appeared to have been there for some time. There was approximately one-half to one inch of snow on the ground, and the weather forecast called for more snow that night. With less than a half hour of daylight remaining, Johnson took numerous photographs of the crime scene while Ruetsch removed a new twenty-five-foot by ten-foot roll of Visquine, a heavy-duty plastic, from the trunk of his car.

"Because the bodies and the drainage ditch were much lower than the surrounding elevation," reported Ruetsch, "I was able to cover the area without the Visquine touching the bodies. Guards were posted at both Fourteenth and Carnahan, as well as Twelfth and Havana, and a command post was established on Fourteenth, approximately fifty yards from the bodies."

Arrangements were made for investigators and support personnel to meet at nine o'clock the following morning. Three of the four task force detectives—Fred Ruetsch, Minde Connelly, and John Miller—plus identification experts Bev Naccarato and Carrie Johnson processed the crime scene. One most unusual aspect of this particular "dump site" was the incongruity of the vegetation covering the bodies—it obviously came from somewhere else.

"There was so much trash," said Sergeant Walker, "that detectives couldn't tell what was evidence and what was just garbage, but the debris on top of the bodies was something else again." The various bits of decorative bark, twigs, leaves, and concrete found concealing the dead women's remains impressed Detective Minde Connelly as exceptionally significant.

"I made this aspect of the investigation my mission," said Connelly. "I'm an avid gardener, and it seemed to me that perhaps the killer was a landscaper, gardener, or worked in a nursery." Hoping that detectives could match this odd combination of plants to someone's business, backyard, or flower bed, Connelly set about the task of creating little portable reference books for her fellow detectives.

Detectives would not publicly speculate if these two newly found bodies were related to the other killings in the area. Ident Officer Carrie Johnson, however, privately contemplated the distinct possibility that these bodies were linked to the serial killer. "I thought to myself, 'This guy has absolutely gone berserk,'" Johnson recalled. "'This is not going to stop. It's only going to get worse.'"

Both victims were shot twice with .25-caliber

Magtech slugs, and both women were apparently dumped at the same time and covered with the same bizarre hodgepodge of yard debris.

Two other murders had transpired that same week—the shooting deaths of twenty-year-old Jeremy Moore and thirty-eight-year-old Peter Peterson, whose body was dumped on Upriver Drive. He died from a single gunshot to the chest. Investigators could not say with any degree of assurance whether or not the deaths of Moore and Peterson were connected to the obviously related homicides of Scott, McClenahan, Johnson, and Wason.

"There sure as hell might be a connection, at least with Peterson's murder, but I can't exactly unravel what it is," admitted a baffled Sprague Street regular. "Consider this: Linda Maybin used to hang out at this drug house in North Spokane. The guy who Linda bought drugs from at that house was murdered a few weeks before Christmas. Next, Peterson is murdered Christmas week. Now, get this," she continued, "Peterson's brother, Barney, was murdered in 1991, and a suspect in that killing stayed at that exact same house. Plus," she said dramatically, "when a customer called Christine's Escort, where Darla and McClenahan worked, the person who answered the phone was Linda Maybin. Go figure."

In subcultures fueled by paranoia-inducing intoxicants, conspiracy theories and complex plots are as common as "methbugs"—imaginary insects crawling under the skin. Theories are one thing; hard facts are another. Detectives want facts, data, dates, and details.

"I was Shawn McClenahan's best friend for three

to four years," the woman known as Barb tearfully told detectives. "On Wednesday night, December seventeenth, Shawn and 'Q' came over to my trailer, and then [they] came back on Thursday the eighteenth. They were together, the two of them, and Shawn was crying because he was belittling her.

"It was between six and eight o'clock when they showed up," said Barb, "and Shawn was dope-sick. She went into the back bedroom and did a shot to get well." The three were together only a half hour when McClenahan stated that she had to go out onto the street and work.

"Q was supposed to watch Shawn's back while she was working, but I know that he didn't do it worth shit. All he ever really did was slap Shawn around."

"He did worse than that," commented one witness who knew Shawn and Q quite well. "Shawn lived with me and my family since early November. Q is a speed freak, and he would physically hit Shawn. One week prior to December seventeenth, the two of them were in a fight such that Q assaulted the hell out of her. He then took all his belongings and left the residence. However, he called her on a daily basis between eight and nine times a day to talk to her." The last time this family man saw Shawn McClenahan was two days after Shawn visited her father, a stroke victim in rehabilitation at St. Luke's, on Wednesday, December 17, at about 7:30 P.M. She and two others left his residence in an older van of unknown color and model.

"Shawn only worked until about ten o'clock," recalled Barb, "then called it quits. She mostly gave blow jobs, used condoms, and she only liked to date more mature customers because mature men are, well, more mature, respectful, and a lot more safe than some hopped-up punk with a hard-on."

Be he teenage punk or spunky senior citizen, Shawn McClenahan's final date put two bullets in her head and then covered it with three plastic bags.

"She was a beautiful, loving, wonderful, compassionate girl, ready to help everyone that came in contact with her," recalled Shawn McClenahan's mother. "She was born on May thirtieth, the old Memorial Day, 1958. When she was born, my doctor said to me, 'Well, you'll never forget her birthday.' He didn't know how prophetic those words were."

"My sister attended schools in Spokane, Washington. She attended Spokane Community College and worked very hard to get her degree," said Shawn's sibling Kathy Lloyd. "She then went on to work in area hospitals. She did well until she was diagnosed with carpal tunnel and could no longer work." Depression over the loss of her career, coupled with an increased dependence upon pain pills, took a hard toll on Shawn McClenahan. "Eventually, the pain and the drugs took over her life," commented her sister, "and she fell into prostitution to get the money for heroin."

Family members reported that McClenahan used heroin on a gram-per-day basis, and had been using it for four or five years. They also were aware that she worked as a prostitute. Married, she had separated from her husband over Thanksgiving. She was, as far as her family understood, living with a brother of her previous ex-husband.

Shawn and Kathy, despite their widely divergent lifestyles, shared a bond unbroken. "Shawn was a people person who had a high interest in young children, and she would frequently volunteer at the school where I work. She also enjoyed being around the elderly, and was always so caring and loving. She was wonderful with our father, who had had a stroke. She had my sense of humor, which we both thought was wonderful and unique. She had many, many friends. I became known in Spokane, not as Kathy, but as 'Shawn's sister.' I am still amazed at how many people, from all walks of life, knew her and spoke so highly of her. Her very large baby picture hangs over my fireplace—when this picture was done, it was so remarkable that it was displayed in the window of the photography studio.

"Shawn was about five foot seven, slim, had brown medium-length hair and the most beautiful eyes I have ever seen. Shawn also had a love of antiques, and we would spend the summers together going to garage sales. We both collected toys. We had talked many times of opening our own shop when I retired from teaching. We were much more than sisters; we were best friends. And with her death, a large part of myself also died."

Immediately prior to her death, McClenahan was accepted into a methadone program. She had been living with a family near Fourth and Altamont, and was baby-sitting their children. Her immediate family last saw Shawn on December 5. Three days later, Kathy Lloyd received a birthday card from her sister. "I wish I could live with you," wrote Shawn, "but I understand no one wants me around."

One man who enjoyed having McClenahan around was a seventy-five-year-old gentleman residing at Lake Coeur d'Alene, Idaho. "I was quite fond of her and thought she was a very nice person," said the saddened senior citizen. "I'd known Shawn for several months, and we had become good friends. Our relationship was nonsexual," he told Detective Miller, "and I never had any idea that she was a drug addict or a prostitute." He did know that she was an occasional baby-sitter for her friends' children, and he had often driven Shawn and her young charges to play at the park.

"I've had two hip replacements and need another hip surgery because I have a very difficult time walking and taking care of myself," he said. "Shawn had agreed to come stay with me later this year so I could have that surgery. The last time I saw her, she didn't say where she was going, only that she was meeting with a girlfriend and that she would call me later, which she never did."

"She wanted desperately to get out of the life that she hated so much," said her mother. "I would have loved to see her succeed." During May and June of 1997, Shawn McClenahan, then known as Shawn Beck, attended the Alcohol/Drug Network recovery program in Spokane and S.P.A.R.C. Outpatient Services.

"Shawn had two sisters and two brothers, three of whom live in, or around, the Spokane area. Her other sister currently lives back East. Shawn had one son, Joel. Her first grandchild was born in early January 1998. She was so looking forward to this event," said her sister Kathy.

"We didn't get to see her very often," her mother said, "and when we did get to see her, sometimes she was in the hospital undergoing treatment. Shawn told Kathy that she was looking forward to going into a methadone program in two weeks."

Dr. Vincent Dole and Dr. Marie Nyswander of Rockefeller University first used methadone, a long-acting synthetic narcotic analgesic, in the maintenance treatment of drug addiction in the mid-1960s. Methadone is administered daily in a constant dose after patients are stabilized. There are now more than 115,000 methadone-maintenance patients in the United States.

"She was a strong person in many, many, many ways. She could, perhaps, have kicked that habit," McClenahan's mother said. "I don't know. But we miss her and we will never, ever get over losing her."

The family of Laurel Wason was equally bereaved. "My sister, Laurel Wason, was a very active person," commented Darcy Acevedo, "but drugs took over the last few months of her life." The two sisters often discussed the pain and peril of addiction. Wason, loving mother and nationally recognized fancier of purebred rottweilers, enjoyed six healthy years of remission. Then, two summers prior to her tragic death, she relapsed.

Six drug-free years for a heroin addict was, at that time, against all odds. "Wason is proof of two things," commented a fellow recovering narcotics addict. "One, an addict can stay clean at least six

years, and two, that the addiction never leaves—
it waits for you, patiently.''

Numerous highly controlled studies of addicts
who were compelled by the courts to endure three
years of ''treatment,''—non-methadone—followed by rigidly monitored ''parole,'' revealed that
only 3 percent remained drug free for more than
twenty-four months.

Wason's family firmly believed that Laurel would
again break the bonds of addiction. ''She was very
determined that she would kick the habit,'' said
Acevedo. ''My sister was only thirty-one years of
age at the time of her death,'' she said. Had Wason
been allocated eighty-five years of life on earth, she
was still far from middle age on the day they buried
her. ''When I was missing her,'' said her sister, ''I
would drive down around Sprague and look for
her. The last time we saw each other was Halloween
night—she was walking down East Sprague in a
black trench coat.''

''Laurie Wason was my daughter,'' said Clara
Page. ''The impact [her murder] has had on my
family and me has been an unbearable pain. I've
had nightmares, sleepless nights, crying. . . . I
haven't been the same person, and I never will be.
I miss my daughter so much.''

No one could miss the three plastic bags over
her daughter's head, and the equal number on
Shawn McClenahan. The plastic bags covering
McClenahan's head were carefully removed during
her autopsy on December 29, 1997.

The outer bag was from Safeway, the middle bag
was unmarked by advertising, and the inner bag
was from Kmart, featuring colorful Sesame Street

characters and logo. On Wason, the outer bag was from Shopko, and inside was a folded paper towel. The second bag was from Albertsons, as was the third.

"Two gunshot wounds were clearly visible on the left side of the head in the jaw/ear area," Ruetsch's notes state from the autopsy. "Both appeared to be contact wounds. Two bullets were later removed from McClenahan's skull. On Wason, there were in fact determined to also be two gunshot wounds to the left side of the head near the ear area, and both appeared to be contact wounds, very similar in nature to McClenahan's wounds, and two bullets were also removed from Wason's skull.

"Identification officers used their forensic light-source machine in an effort to look for fibers and/or hairs on the clothing and body of McClenahan," reported Detective Ruetsch. "A total of eleven manila envelopes containing hairs and fibers from various parts of the clothing and body, observed at various wave lengths, and through various colored glasses, were recovered, including hairs from inside her bra, and a longer hair from both the hip and pubic area were retrieved. This was deemed significant," Ruetsch noted, "as her pubic area was shaven." Laboratory analysis of the hairs from inside the bra revealed that they were cat hairs.

Located within the front left-side pocket of McClenahan's jeans was a scrap of paper. Written in Shawn McClenahan's own hand was a man's name and telephone number. Detectives copied down the details for future follow-up.

"Of special note," said Detective Ruetsch, "was that although both bodies were recovered at the same time and location, and supposedly exposed to the same conditions, such as weather and temperature, the body of Wason was significantly more decomposed than that of McClenahan."

"As they will not give me the autopsy report, nor tell me when she died," posted Kathy Lloyd to the Web page at missingpersons.com that she maintained in memory of her sister, "I have to believe that she was not murdered the same day that she was found. Shawn was a very family person and I know she would have been at my house on Christmas Day." According to all sources close to Shawn McClenahan, her sister is correct.

"You've got to wonder," commented Sergeant Walker in retrospect, "what the killer was doing with the bodies, where he was keeping them. Where was Wason's body prior to being dumped with McClenahan's? And what about . . ." Walker stopped midsentence, glanced down at the full-color crime scene photograph of Wason and McClenahan's half-buried bodies, and shook his head. "Look at that. Just look at that. What the hell was this guy thinking, anyway?"

CHAPTER SIX

"We simply do not think the same way that a serial sex killer thinks," said Detective John Miller. "You can't use logic to tell you what these people are thinking." Acts that strike us as bizarre, illogical, and inexplicable are well within reason for the violent serial sex offender.

"A rapist, for example," said Dr. Steve Rubin, one of America's leading experts on sex offender behavior, "is violently hostile and sexually aroused at the same time. That combination is implausible, and probably impossible, for the nonrapist."

If detectives apply their own values when viewing the scene of a violent sex crime, they're going to be at a complete loss for an explanation, or a reason, for the behavior. "When a sex crime 'makes no sense,'" explained forensic scientist Brent Turvey, "it's easy to rely on easy explanations, like 'Some kook did it for no reason,' which is exactly what Walla Walla sheriff Klundt said at the time of the Oliver and Savage homicides."

These "kooks" have reasons. Violent serial sex offenders do not commit their crimes by accident. A distinct purpose, or goal, motivates the behavior. For investigators who are at a loss to explain motive in such cases, and who find attempts to analyze behavior frustrating, Turvey suggests that investigators describe the offenders by their behavior, and then ask "What desires do those behaviors satisfy?"

The accepted method in solving crimes is basing behavior on motive. In violent serial crimes, the motive is unknown—it is not about jealousy, money, or revenge. By approaching the problem from the opposite direction, the unknown motive is explained in terms of known behavior.

The violent behavior of these "kooks" and "sickos" makes perfect sense to them, agree the experts. They have fantasized about this act thousands of times without actually doing it. "It is not hard to understand why they continue these acts," says Dr. Rubin. "They continue for the same reason anyone repeats pleasurable behavior. If you try out a new restaurant, and you enjoy the food, you're going to return again and again. It's much the same with the serial sex offender. The question isn't 'Why do they keep doing it?', but rather, 'Why did they do it the first time?' "

For most people, fantasy is entertainment. It is temporary, mildly amusing, and understood as purely imaginary. If the fantasy involves aberrant or abhorrent behavior, there is no real harm done. "The reason most of us never seriously consider acting out dangerous, illegal, or immoral fantasies," explained Dr. Rubin, "is because we can also imagine the consequences—danger to others, ourselves, et cetera. The sex offender often is unable to consider consequences—they don't cross his mind. He only thinks of the pleasure involved in doing that particular act again.''

According to J. A. Fox and Jack Levin, authors of *Mass Murder: America's Growing Menace,* domination unmitigated by guilt is a crucial element in serial crimes with a sexual theme. The authors further explain that sadistic sex—whether both parties are willing or not—expresses the power of one person over another, but in serial homicides, the killers experiences the ultimate feeling control over his victims.''

As long as what transpires remains true to the fantasy, the control is unquestioned and satisfying. The serial sex offender brings his fantasy script out of his imagination and gives it life in the real world. Much as a writer or director casts the roles in a film or play, the sex offender creates the plot, envisions the direction, and then casts the role of the victim. In truth, he casts the leading-lady role again and again, each individual play calls for an encore, and each encore is curtains for his costar. Later, when the props and body parts are packed away, the artistic director either awaits or ignores the reviews on the evening news.

''A cunning serial killer who does not make tactical mistakes is virtually uncatchable, no matter how many police or FBI agents might be desperately searching for him,'' wrote a regular contributor to the Internet discussion group alt.true.crime. In this view, serial killers only got caught if they made mistakes in choosing their victims, disposing of the bodies, or interacting with the media. ''The bottom line," he insisted, "is that serial killers get caught because they trip themselves up."

City Manager Bill Pupo of Spokane acknowledged citizens' impatience for the killer to "trip himself up" or get apprehended as the result of the intensive investigation. "The task force is just in its nurturing stages right now," said Pupo. "The expectation of the community is based largely on what they watch on prime-time television where a case is solved in an hour. That's not the way it is in real life. Just because you can't see something happening, doesn't mean nothing is happening."

In truth, plenty was happening. The homicide task force was pursuing every lead, tip, and hunch with as much efficiency and professionalism as possible. "Tips came in constantly," said Sergeant Walker, "and the public would be amazed to find out how many completely innocent people were considered real suspects by their neighbors, landlords, ex-wives, former lovers . . . you name it. We can't exactly ignore someone when they say, 'I have information on your serial killer . . . ,' even if that information is nothing more than illusion, supposition, suspicion, or the outcome of some previous argument or disagreement."

Detectives, for example, invested significant effort in tracking down the driver of a white 1990 Chrysler New Yorker often seen on East Sprague. This vehicle was mentioned as one that seemed to follow Jennifer Joseph. The driver's apartment manager's son also advised detectives that the man was trouble.

"We showed him pictures of Joseph and Hernandez," recalled Detective Grabenstein, "and he

denied knowing them or ever having contact with
them. When we told him that he had been seen
in the area of Sprague near his residence in an
apparent attempt to make contacts with prostitutes
working in the area, he denied that as well."

"You must have got this from the manager's
son," he told Grabenstein. "I've had problems with
that guy." Asked if he owned any firearms, he easily
acknowledged possession of a .25-caliber Raven pistol and a pump 12-gauge shotgun. The Raven pistol, blued, was stored in its original box in a small
metal cash box kept in the bedroom closet. He
also had ammunition in the same container. The
box of fifty UMC brand full-metal-jacket bullets,
head-stamped "RIP," was full.

"We asked him if we could take the gun for a
test fire, and he had no objections at all," reported
Grabenstein. "As for the 1990 white Chrysler New
Yorker, it actually belonged to someone else, but
he had been attempting to buy it and had been
driving it for some time with the owner's permission. We asked to search the vehicle, and again he
had no problem with that, either. The reason his
car was seen so frequently is simply because he
lived in the neighborhood, and any time he left
his apartment, or returned home, he drove by that
part of Sprague."

Detectives were not only tracking down vehicles,
motel records, and rent-a-car receipts, they were
investigating the exact store locations from which
the killer procured his plastic bags and paper towels. "We're putting some parts of it together," Captain Silver said of the case on January 5. "We are
linking some of them. Evidence shows connections

between four of the seven most recent victims
whose bodies have been discovered during the last
six months."

As for where the killer was acquiring his victims,
the theater of audition was Sprague Avenue. Each
strolling prostitute was a potential one-show-only
leading lady of the evening. The next victim was
ascending the starlight stairway from Sprague
Street's back alleys to the *Spokesman-Review*'s front
page, following in the final footsteps of Shawn
McClenahan, Laurel Wason, Shawn Johnson, Jennifer Joseph, Heather Hernandez, and Darla Sue
Scott.

January 6, 1998

Spokane police were also trying to link up with
four more missing women. "Denise Raye Holmes,
also known as Dena Clifford, has four outstanding
warrants for her arrest," said a police spokesman.
"The thirty-eight-year-old woman is five feet four
inches tall, one hundred forty pounds, with blond
hair and blue eyes. Also reported missing is Sheila
Marie Burnette, who disappeared last summer. She
is twenty-nine, five feet six inches tall, one hundred
forty-five pounds, with blond hair and blue eyes."
Also reported missing were Brandy Mitchell,
twenty-three, and Jessica Ann Fitzgerald, twenty-
three. "We do not believe at this time," said police,
"that these disappearances are related to the
recent murders." Law enforcement had no direct
evidence supporting any relationship between the
missing women and the serial killer. They did, however, certainly consider the deadly potentialities.

Linda Maybin, thirty-four, had told her friend Brian that she was afraid of the serial killer. The last time he saw Maybin, they had talked about the murders, and she told him, "Don't go nowhere, 'cause I'm coming back." Brian also knew Darla Sue Scott.

"I first met Darla Scott approximately two and a half to three years ago. In fact," he told Detective Madsen on January 6, "I left my wife to be with Darla, and I wanted to marry her, but it did not work out. I have not associated with Darla in the past year and a half or so, but I've seen her on occasion. The last time that I saw her was early-to-mid September when I was on the bus, and I saw her working the street down on Sprague Avenue."

He told Madsen of another occasion when he was at a drug house on East Jackson. "I was there when Darla came out of the back bedroom. We just said hi to each other as she left. Anyway, after I quit hanging around with Darla, I started hanging around with Linda Maybin. That lasted up until approximately one year ago."

The last time he saw the missing Linda Maybin was a day or two before Thanksgiving. "She called me up and indicated that she wanted to meet with me to have dinner, that she had an idea who was killing the prostitutes, and wanted to discuss this with me. Also, Linda said that she was afraid that she may be the next to be killed. We made arrangements to meet that evening, but she didn't show up."

When Maybin failed to keep their dinner date, he drove to an apartment complex where he knew a lot of the prostitutes often found shelter. "I knew that Linda had been hanging out there recently. The guy who lives there is this nice guy. So I go there and I find Linda had overslept. Just as we're getting ready to go out to dinner, a tall white male showed up. He started talking to Linda, and she said that she had to leave with this man and would be back in approximately twenty minutes.

"She told me to wait, but she never came back—the guy came back and said that she went to work the street. I never saw or heard from her again."

Following the dissolution of his romantic bond with Maybin, he linked with another woman of similar talents, proclivities, and lifestyle. "She lived with me on North Ash Street in the first part of 1997, but I had to kick her out in May of 1997 because she forged and cashed about seventy of my personal checks."

"I didn't forge any of his damn checks," countered the insulted woman to Detective Madsen. "He was the one writing his own bad checks, and he's just trying to blame it on me. The one who wrote bad checks, and forged business checks for big bucks, was Linda Maybin. Just ask around. There are people who hate Maybin for pulling that shit. Hell, if someone was after her for stunts like that, no wonder she's missing."

January 8, 1998

"Brandy Mitchell, earlier reported missing, is alive and well," said police spokesman Dick Cottam, "and Jessica Fitzgerald was seen in Spokane this week. "Task force members are following up

on those tips," Cottam said. Both women had previously been reported missing.

"You get to the point," said Spokane educator
David Simmons, "that as soon as they tell you someone is missing, you start saying prayers for the
departed."

January 9, 1998, 9:00 A.M.

"I'm a thug, not a killer," stated the suspect
flatly, "and I'll take a lie detector test to prove it."
Detective Connelly stepped out of the room at the
Spokane County Jail to see if a polygraph was available; Detective Fred Ruetsch continued the questioning.

"I ain't never killed anybody, no females anyway,
and besides that," the suspect said emphatically,
"if I find out who killed these women, I'll kill him
myself. I knew Laurie Wason and Darla Scott from
the streets, and I knew Shawn McClenahan from
rehab."

"He was brought down from the jail and taken
to the polygraph office at one-thirty P.M.," recalled
Ruetsch. By day's end, one more suspect was
cleared of suspicion.

January 19, 1998

Two hundred Spokane residents raised their
voices in prayer and song in honor of "Our Friends,
Our Sisters," the eighteen women murdered on
the streets of Spokane since 1984. The service
began at 6:30 P.M. and was followed by a candlelight
vigil on East Sprague. "The gathering is a peaceful

memorial for those who wish to acknowledge the value of human life," said a church spokesperson.

"These women, because of their lifestyles, were often so despised, used, and misused," commented an attendee. "But they were also just plain folks who went to school, raised their kids, had fun, cried real tears, and were often loving human beings despite their troubles and addictions."

This event, one of the first conceived in a heart-felt desire to honor the hapless fallen, demonstrated a degree of civic solidarity, and it promoted cooperation in the search for the deadly, deviant killer. It also offered Spokane police an opportunity for utilization of high-tech covert-surveillance video gear.

"I accompanied Corporal Tom Sahlberg and Detective John Willard to work in a covert capacity doing surveillance at the Central Methodist Church," reported Officer John McGregor of the Spokane Police Department. This operation was fully prepared and under way by six o'clock on the evening of the memorial.

"The church service was open to the public," recalled McGregor. The event, much publicized, was scheduled for 6:30 P.M. "This officer [McGregor] set up and operated night-vision video equipment located to the east of the church, while Detective Willard used standard-vision video equipment in the black-and-white mode for better light gathering. This was set up to the west of the church.

"Inside the church, Corporal Sahlberg wore a hidden camera to capture on videotape those persons inside the church as he attended the service. At the conclusion of the service, the attendees gathered at another church at Pacific and Magnolia where a candlelight vigil was held. The group then walked northbound to Sprague, then westbound to Pittsburgh, then southbound to Pacific, and ended at the church. This procession was videotaped, and the faces of those attending captured on tape."

During the procession, Officer McGregor observed a red compact car driven by a white male, approximately thirty years of age. "This person did not appear to be a part of the group, but appeared to be interested in what was occurring. The car was followed out of the area by Detective Willard, and the videotapes were given to Detective John Miller of the SPD Major Crimes Unit."

This exercise in cinema verité was held one day before FBI agents arrived in Spokane to aid and assist the homicide task force. Spokane law enforcement contacted the FBI because of the agency's obvious experience and expertise. Just as medical specialists may be experts in a particular disease and know far more than the best local general practitioner, the FBI has the advantage of a national or even international perspective on certain types of crimes. The reference points of the FBI are broader and more inclusive. One aspect of FBI assistance is the use of their profiling process.

Profiling often relies on typologies—descriptions of various types of offenders. The investigator draws up a series of questions for a crime scene and the offender's behavior, then picks answers from a psychologically based typology.

"The major failure of most typologies of violent serial offenders is perspective," says Brent Turvey.

"The offender is described in terms that express the investigator's understanding of the motivation behind offender's behavior. This can be very subjective and may be misleading to an investigative effort to understand an offender and link him to another crime." Turvey made it clear that profiling does not mean coming up with a theory and then inserting an offender as best he fits. "Profiling means letting the physical evidence tell an investigator what behaviors occurred."

Working on the principle that behavior reflects personality, FBI agents evaluate five specific items prior to offering suggestions for investigation:

1. The criminal act itself
2. The crime scene's specifics
3. The victim—victimology
4. Preliminary police reports
5. The medical examiner's autopsy protocol

"Profiling," explained FBI Agent Judson Ray, "is a collection of all the disciplines and an understanding and a good depth of knowledge about forensic psychology, forensic pathology, cultural anthropology, social psychology, motivational psychology." According to Ray, the profile process works when "all of the [elements] are properly aligned and understood with a sense of investigative technique behind you, [and] you have all these things kind of synchronized."

The FBI's Spokane homicide task force created a "serial killer profile," but the task force was unimpressed. "The FBI profile of the killer is of little help and contains little detail," commented Doug

Silver. "The first thing they told us after they gave us the profile is not to use it. You hope it gives you direction. It just doesn't."

The actual profile simply said that the killer was probably a white man, between twenty and forty years old, who might be a loner. "That's a fairly generic description of most serial killers, and also describes thousands of perfectly innocent men in or around Spokane who have never killed anyone."

Detectives also consulted psychological profiles prepared outside the FBI. Each profile attempted defining the perpetrator's characteristics, traits, location, and/or motive. "He's a street person," said Vernon Geberth, author of *Practical Homicide Investigation,* and former homicide commander of the New York Police Department.

"The killer knows these women and runs in their circles. A street person with a criminal record is the likely killer," he said. "The ones who operate among prostitutes come from the area. He's part of the terrain. He's part of the environment. The killer is intimately familiar with these women," advised Geberth, "either as a pimp, john, or junkie."

Former FBI profiler Patricia Kirby was convinced that the killer did not look the least bit suspicious. "He's an average workaday Joe—seemingly harmless, but calculated and ritualistic in playing out homicidal fantasies. The street-smart victims let down their guard because the killer looks so ordinary.

"The killings follow a carefully planned script," opined Kirby, "from who he abducts and how long he keeps them alive to where and when he dumps the bodies. He's obviously taking them off the streets. Taking women who are prostitutes indicates some type of symbolism or some type of fulfillment of his fantasy.''

Understanding fantasy may be valuable, but it doesn't provide names, addresses, or physical descriptions. In truth, it is far easier to profile accurately and apprehend the perpetrator of a single homicide or a single-incident multiple homicide than it is to profile and apprehend a serial killer.

"That's an absolute fact," stated Tacoma homicide detective Robert Yerbury. "A serial killer is usually someone no one suspects. What are you going to do, ask people 'Who *don't* you suspect?' In a traditional homicide, you can work from possible motive. With serial killers, you don't have that so-called luxury.''

"We consulted [the profiles], but we didn't rely upon them. It's one of many tools, but not the total answer," Captain Silver said, noting that Seattle's Green River serial-killings investigation "had three or four profiles.''

"Three or four profiles for the Green River killings makes sense," commented Tacoma journalist Travis Weston, "because, by all indications, there were three or four different killers all dumping bodies near the same Green River area.''

The killings of seven Spokane women since the summer of 1997 certainly resurrected the specter of Seattle's Green River killer, and the homicide task force evaluated possible links with eleven other murders dating back to 1984—the year the Green River killings halted at a body count of forty-nine women.

"With a serial murder, investigators have to do more than what they are used to doing," stated Bob Keppel, an investigator with the Washington State Attorney General's Office, in Seattle, who helped investigate the Green River slayings. "There is the need to go outside your own jurisdiction to look for suspect information."

Following the FBI's consultation with the task force, authorities issued a press release stating that "we're very confident in saying that our individual, or individuals, is in no way connected to the Green River killer." This expression of confidence in the uniqueness of Spokane's serial killer did nothing to assuage civic anxiety or proffer protection for females with high-risk lifestyles.

Spokane detectives, to their credit and everlasting honor, quickly realized that the adversarial relationship between the law and the ladies of the evening, many of whom also sold and consumed illegal drugs, made the women easy prey.

While Spokane police were making important inroads of communication with working sex professionals on East Sprague, their law enforcement counterparts in Tacoma lagged seriously behind. "Our vice unit keeps up regular contacts in the city's underworld," said Tacoma police spokesman Jim Mattheis, "but I'm unaware of any departmental outreach program."

"It's a very common and predictable conundrum," commented broadcast journalist Chet Rogers. "The cops are the law, and the prostitutes are lawbreakers. It's hard for prostitutes to turn to the cops for protection when the cops' duties often include arresting them."

Pierce County homeless advocates acknowledged that Tacoma police were perceived as "out
to get" street people. "There's clearly animosity,"
said Erica Estabrook, working at a homeless shelter
in downtown Tacoma. "Law enforcement tradi-
tionally in Tacoma harasses people on the street.
It seems like they're trying to make it illegal in this
city for people to be homeless."

There are actually laws in Pierce County forbid-
ding certain women previously convicted of prostitution or drug charges to be seen on the streets of
downtown Tacoma. When an attempted outreach
program decided to start distributing flyers to
Tacoma prostitutes so they could keep tabs on dangerous customers, many women said they'd only
be involved if police were not.

"In Spokane, two detectives working with the
serial killer task force have been spending time on
the street, talking to women," said Lynn Everson
in 1998. "They've developed a trust relationship
with the women, and some women even carry the
officers' phone numbers with them. In fact, when
one ex–drug user left Spokane and moved to California, she telephoned me and reminded me to
let the police know she was safe. She knew if they
didn't see her, they'd be concerned that she was
okay."

"If Spokane's killer is lurking in Pierce County,"
acknowledged Tacoma police spokesman Jim Mattheis, "our department will certainly devote more
attention to building better relations with homeless
women. We're going to have to," he said.

"Tacoma is worse than Spokane, that's a fact,"
commented a sex worker familiar with several

cities. "Seattle is worse, too, and San Francisco is terrible. Down there, the cops can just go ahead and kick the shit out of you all they want—and they do."

"The real problem," says Kimberly, a prostitute from British Columbia, "is that prostitutes are not used to getting police support. Now, there is nothing better than a good cop, and some cops are very dedicated to protecting all women, no matter what we do for a living. But even then, there is a lack of respect for me as a witness because of the nature of my work—the justice system treats me as if I should expect to get hassled. Let me give you an example I'm personally familiar with—it didn't happen in Spokane, but it's pretty typical: A street prostitute was beaten, choked with a rope and left unconscious in an alley. She had severe bruising on her neck and face. The next day when she approached two female police officers to report the incident, they asked her what did she expect in her line of work and refused to take a report."

Detective Robert Yerbury of Tacoma works all his cases with zeal and dedication, be the victim's social position prostitute or missionary. "Some people think that just because a woman is a prostitute, that we don't take their murder seriously, or that we don't work the case with the same diligence as we would otherwise," said Yerbury. "That is simply not true at all. We don't give up. We keep working unsolved cases. A prostitute was murdered here several years ago. We did the investigation; we had a pool of suspects which we narrowed down. And I firmly believed that we discerned the identity of the individual responsible for this woman's death. Our opinion, of course, is not sufficient for arrest. We continued working the case, and eventually, thanks to DNA, we now have sufficient evidence to make an arrest. In short, the fact that a woman is a prostitute does not lessen our dedication. [Due to] the fact that the woman is a prostitute, her sphere of human interaction is far more broad and secretive than, for example, an unemployed homemaker or nine-to-five office worker. This makes identifying suspects more difficult."

The best protection for a fearful prostitute when the serial killer prowled Spokane was incarceration in the Spokane County Jail or at the Geiger Correctional Facility. "I spoke to a woman in jail today," said Everson in January 1998, "a longtime clinic visitor; she'd been arrested on drug charges. I told her, 'In a weird way, I'm glad you're here.' She replied: 'So am I.' "

"I know a very possible suspect in these murders," insisted another female inmate. "I mean, this guy could very well be the killer, okay? I want to talk to a detective, you know, and like right away."

January 21, 1998

"The guy that got me pregnant could be the guy, the murderer," insisted the woman on January 21, "and I'll tell you why. Darla Scott, Laurie Wason, and Linda Maybin—all three of these women owe him drug money. He was always saying that he was going to kill these bitches for not paying him his money.

"He has a history of violence," she told Detective

Connelly, "and I've seen him with a Glock nine millimeter, and a small revolver." She also told Connelly that the suspect carried around pictures of a dead woman. "These are regular photographs, not Polaroids, and they are of one individual," she said. "All this stuff was in a briefcase that also had passports with various names on them. The guy is HIV positive and he may have an ex-girlfriend from Seattle. I think also that he may have recently been released from prison. He drives a black-and-gold Buick Riviera that is located in a car lot at Perry and Illinois."

"I asked her if she was friends with Linda Maybin," Connelly recalled, "and she said that she was and that she had seen Maybin on a Friday night, but had no idea of the date. She stated that she saw her get into a white four-door domestic vehicle. No further information on a possible driver."

Asked about other possible suspects, the informant mentioned a man called Doug, "a white male in his mid-to-late forties, short brown hair, glasses, five-six to five-seven, who was obsessed with Laurie Wason. He smokes a lot of crack and drives many different cars. He's known to have quite a temper. He is supposedly from out of town, but we see him in town about three to four days per week."

"Then there's that cop that drives a 1990s Ford—blue with an extended cab. It's clean and has a gray interior. The guy doesn't smoke, and he followed me for two days before picking me up. Then, after he picks me up, he gives me money but didn't ask for sex. He said he just wanted to help me with my needs, so I told him that I needed money and he gave me fifty dollars."

Detective Connelly asked her why she believed the man was a law enforcement officer. "Well, he wears a baseball cap that says SPD on the front of it," she replied. He never displayed a badge or law enforcement ID. "I asked him his name," she said, "but he wouldn't give it to me."

"I showed her photographs of all the Spokane Police Department officers," reported Connelly. "She didn't recognize anyone as the subject." Detective Connelly and her fellow investigators seriously considered the possibility that the serial killer was a current or former police officer. Several victims were shot twice, known as "double tapping," and officers are trained to shoot twice to make sure they hit their target.

Another reason for suspecting a policeman was that the victims had been shot from the side. "Streetwise women don't let people be on their blind side," said Detective Brian Hamond. A killer cop, however, could easily get a working girl into his car. Fear of arrest alone would be enough to compel her cooperation. "We kept saying, 'This is a cop. This is a cop,' " said Detective Minde Connelly.

"I always thought it was a cop," said Cathy A. "Someone like Sergeant Moore, who's tough on us, or maybe some other vigilante who decided to clean up the streets by throwing out the garbage—and by garbage, I mean people like me and my friends."

"We checked the list of off-duty weapons used by city and county law-enforcement personnel," confirmed the task force. "We did find a .25-caliber Raven, the exact type of weapon used in several of the homicides. The Raven was test-fired, but the ballistics didn't match.''

January 22, 1998

The following day, Detectives Connelly and Miller returned to Geiger Correctional Facility. "We went there in order to interview some females who had been identified to us as possibly having information regarding the string of homicides. We were also advised," Miller recalled, "that these women were willing to talk to detectives about these incidents."

Arriving at 1:00 P.M., Connelly and Miller arranged interviews with four women—two women each. "These interviews were conducted in a visiting-room area at Geiger," Miller said. "When the first woman came in the room, I introduced myself and she immediately told me that she was willing and, in fact, eager to share any information she might have regarding these homicides."

"There's this one guy," she said, "who's white, in his thirties, and he told me that he had just got out of prison last spring or early summer. He's about six feet, very thin, approximately one hundred forty pounds, a scruffy beard, balding, and has real bad teeth. I've never seen him with a gun, but I know he has a knife."

She further told Detective Miller that this man was a crack head and a drugger. "By that, she meant that he smoked crack," Miller explained, "and did IV drugs, probably heroin, and he has track marks on his arm. She stated he can be violent, and on one occasion, he pulled a knife on her when she was joking with him."

"I called him a crack whore," she said, "and that really pissed him off big time. Okay, you know I work on the track, right? Well, every time I see this guy, he's always alone. I think to myself that he is really nuts. I don't know his full name or where he lives. . . ."

She actually didn't have definitive information for Detective Miller regarding this particular suspect beyond her evaluation that he was nuts, skinny, ugly, easily offended, and that other girls on the track didn't care for him, either.

"Early in my conversation with her, I showed her some pictures of recent homicide victims. She told me she knew Laurel Wason, Shawn Johnson, Darla Scott, and she also knew Jennifer Joseph. She freely told me that all these girls, with the exception of Joseph, were pretty much hard-core drug users who all had a habit of ripping off their johns pretty regularly. Again, she said the one exception to this was Jennifer Joseph, whom she described as being new at the time of her death and was relatively clean. She had no knowledge of Jennifer using any drugs, and she did not know of her ripping off any johns. The second suspect," reported Miller, "was known to her only as Doug—a name we had heard before—a white male in his early forties."

"He comes to town a lot and stays in motels," she said. "Mostly, I know of him staying at the Holiday Inn Valley Suites. He's real generous and buys a lot of dope and smokes it with the girls."

When Miller asked if she had personally dated Doug, she replied, "Yeah, but I thought that it was a little strange that he would pay me to more or less spend time with him, smoke dope with him, but we've never had sex." She also told Detective Miller that when Doug is in town, he always drives rental cars.

"When I asked her why she felt that he might be responsible for these homicides, she told me that she felt this because, according to her, Doug is in love with one of the girls who works on East Sprague. This girl gets into a lot of arguments with some of the other girls and is not very well liked. According to her, once someone gets into an argument with the girl he loves, that 'someone' turns up dead."

"Him? Oh, not a chance," offered another woman familiar with Doug. "He is a wimp. I mean, he's a nice guy, but he just lets the women lead him around by the nose, does whatever they want, spend his money, mostly just likes to have 'em around, ya know, doesn't even have sex, I don't think. Mostly, he likes the company. I've never heard of him hurting anybody."

"At one-thirty P.M., January twenty-second, I interviewed a woman who had brown eyes, brown shoulder-length hair, and a tattoo of a rose on her chest," recalled Miller. "She also had a scar on her left hand, and her upper incisors were badly decayed."

"I've known Linda Maybin for about two years," she said, "but during this past winter, we became close friends. The last time I saw her was on November nineteenth at 8:30 P.M. I don't think she's dead. I just think that she's layin' low and making hay, or got her nose to the grinding wheel, or whatever that expression is.''

After Miller completed his two interviews, one of the staff members pulled him aside. "We've had a death threat over the phone."

"She had the threat recorded on her voice mail," Miller recalled. "She played it for me, and it sounded like a female's voice. She stated: 'Someone's going to die.' ''

The entire facility of 480 inmates was aware that detectives were coming out specifically to speak with these women, all of whom were known East Sprague prostitutes. Because so many prostitutes were incarcerated at Geiger, the inmates referred to the women's wing as "the East Sprague Wing."

"I don't think Linda Maybin is dead, either," opined one incarcerated woman familiar with Maybin. "I think she's just on the road with a trucker. She'll be back, ya know, sooner or later. But, ya know, don't wait up all night or leave the light on for her, ya know what I mean?"

A significant vigil for "Spokane-area women who have been killed or are missing" was planned for February 12 , from noon to 1:00 P.M., in Riverfront Park, on the steps behind the Spokane Opera House.

"Organized by Concerned Women of Spokane, members of the community will talk about their loved ones and the investigation into a serial killer," explained Lynn Everson. "I hope that there's a new awareness in our community that these are mothers and sisters and daughters and friends," she said. "It makes me sad that the community is not more outraged."

While Everson and her associates planned this brief public memorial, task force detectives worked through an avalanche of leads, suspects, tips, and witnesses. Among them was Young B., Heather Hernandez's man, who had abruptly left Spokane in August 1997.

"I went to Fresno from here," he explained to Detectives Connelly and Miller on January 27, 1998. "Then I went to Phoenix. Actually, I've been back in Spokane for about a month." The interview with Young B. took place when the fellow was easily accessible—having returned to Spokane, he managed to secure short-term occupancy at the Spokane County Jail.

"Heather and I had been together for about one and a half to two years. We don't have any kids or anything, and it was normal for her to leave me for a couple of days at a time."

Hernandez and Young B. met in Phoenix the previous summer. According to Young B., Hernandez was very particular about her clientele. "She wouldn't date black guys or druggers," he said. "She didn't have a pager, never carried a purse, usually wore a bra, used LifeStyle condoms, and generally worked on East Sprague between Pittsburgh and the Kmart. She would just walk back and forth, waiting for tricks, and then usually take them into a parking lot.

"She preferred working during the day," he explained, "but she would work at night if she needed to." Asked if she carried a weapon, he answered in the negative, then stated that Heather Hernandez often did "trick fucking." When asked to explain this, he said that if the man was not appealing to her, she would often use her chin or thigh and pretend that she was performing sex with the customer. "That may not be honest, but if the guy is satisfied, what difference does it make? At least Heather never ripped off her customers. She never robbed anybody. She wasn't that stupid. I mean, that's a good way to get killed.

"The last time I saw Heather was on a Thursday, about two weeks before her body was found," he said. "I gave her thirty bucks for court and that was it. I never saw her again."

Connelly and Miller showed Young B. pictures of Jennifer Joseph, Shawn Johnson, Darla Scott, Laurie Wason, and Shawn McClenahan. "He was able to identify Jennifer Joseph as 'the cute little Chinese girl that was working the street,' but he didn't actually know her," reported Connelly. "He made positive identification of Hernandez, but had no knowledge of the other females that were shown to him."

During the course of this interview, Detective Miller asked him if he would take a polygraph regarding Hernandez's homicide. "He immediately stated that he was not involved in the homicide," said Miller, "and he would freely take a polygraph regarding it. At that time, I scheduled the polygraph for the following day, January twenty-eighth, at eight-thirty A.M."

Young B., who was released from jail after the interview, told Miller that he would be there for the polygraph on the following morning. "On the twenty-eighth, I was in Tacoma," Miller recalled, "but Detective Heinen had been informed of the polygraph and was waiting for the fellow to arrive.

Upon my return from Tacoma, I learned from Detective Heinen that Young B. did not appear for the polygraph. I attempted to contact him at the telephone number he had given us, and I talked to a male who answered the phone there who told me Young B. wasn't there at the time that I called. I left my name and phone number and asked that a message be given to him to call me."

On that same date, at 2:00 P.M., Detective Connelly spoke with a prostitute incarcerated at Geiger Correctional Facility. During Connelly's prior visit, the woman mentioned an individual whom she considered a most likely suspect.

"I had never seen this person before, and I ain't seen him since," she told Connelly. "I was picked up by this guy at Riverside and Pittsburgh. He seemed okay 'cause he was calm, and that is usually a good sign. I told him to drive over by Michaels craft shop. Well, first he parked right under a camera. When he saw that, he moved the car. Anyway," she explained, "he said he wanted a blow job, and I told him that was forty bucks. I always ask for the money first, but he said that he wouldn't pay me until I did it because he had been ripped off by other women who took the money but didn't give him what he paid for."

"The woman told me," recalled Connelly, "that at this point, the suspect became quite agitated, and the two of them argued about the transaction. Then the suspect took a firearm from between the seats and pointed it at her."

"When he slipped in the clip," she told Connelly, "he said something like 'Let's see how you feel when I get this loaded.' Well, I jumped out of the car and ran. When I turned around to see if he was comin' after me, I saw him standing with the gun pointed at me over the top of the car."

This woman, familiar with Darla Scott, Shawn McClenahan, Laurie Wason, and the missing Linda Maybin, was shown a photomontage by Detective Connelly. "She viewed the photomontage," recalled Connelly, "and pointed immediately to the number two position and stated, 'That's him.' She confirmed this once again when asked if she was certain." Detectives knew the man's identity. They also had already eliminated him as a suspect.

The next interesting and highly suspicious collection of photographs requiring task force attention featured a half-naked woman posed with an erect penis in front of her face—a face immediately recognized by Detective Miller.

February 4, 1998

"Spokane Police Department officer Julie Reisenaur came to the task force office today," noted Detective Miller, "with fifteen photographs that had been turned over by the photo department of Pay 'n Save Photo Department. Most of these fifteen photographs featured one particular white female. In some of the photos, this white female was clothed. In others, she was naked from the waist up, exposing her breasts. Two other photographs depicted this white female's face with an erect male penis directly in front of her face. One other photograph depicted a naked Native American female with a naked white male. They were both in front of a mirror, and he was taking the photo while standing on a chair. This female was bent over in front of him, holding his erect penis in her hands.''

Detective Miller recognized the white female as someone whom he had previously arrested, albeit several years earlier. ''I remembered arresting her on a couple of occasions for prostitution in the late 1980s,'' said Miller. ''We obtained a mug shot of her, and confirmed that it was, indeed, her that was depicted in these photographs. While doing that, we also learned that she had an outstanding felony warrant. Crime Analysis was contacted, and her photograph was put in the daily file with a request that she be apprehended.''

The following morning, February 5, Officer Carr told Miller that the woman was arrested overnight and was currently in jail. At 2:00 P.M., Miller met with the photogenic and exhibitionist female.

''I explained that I was with the task force that was investigating the recent homicides of females from the East Sprague corridor. She immediately told me that she would help in any way that she could. I made it clear to her that I wasn't concerned with her prostitution activity or even her drug activity recently on East Sprague, but that I was concerned with maybe any information she might have on who this killer was. I then asked her if she was aware of any people in the East Sprague area that she thought of as suspects. She immediately told me that there was one person that she had thought of. She did not know this man's name, but said that he was a white male, age forty-two to forty-eight years. She described him as being a big guy and by that she meant he had a large, thick chest. She had never actually seen him standing up, but said that he appeared to be a big man. He had brown hair, which she described as straight, and he drove a newer red pickup. She said it appeared to be a very new, probably mid-size pickup."

"I don't know his name," she said, "but he has tattoos all over his body. I seen this guy out on the East Sprague track for the last couple of years, and I even started to date him once. But what happened was that I had gotten into his truck, and he was sitting there with his"—she groped for the word most appropriate when speaking to law enforcement—"his penis erect and . . . exposed . . . and asked me to have anal sex with him. I immediately ran from the truck."

"She then restated that this male is often on East Sprague, and always has his penis out and exposes it to the women. She claims he always has them look at his penis, and while they're doing that, he says to them that he would like to 'stick this up your ass for three hundred dollars.' "

"That's pretty much his normal request," she explained. "He always offers to pay three hundred for anal sex."

Miller then asked her about the rather explicit photographs that had been turned over to him. "Oh, those," she replied happily. "I remember the photographs, sure. We took those out in High Bridge Park, for the most part."

When Miller asked her the identity of the turgid photographer, she would only identify him by his first name. "Hey, he's a regular customer of mine, super nice guy, very gentle, polite, and fun. He's about forty-eight or fifty, and I would never believe for a minute that he would be involved in anything mean or violent."

She also acknowledged that the photographs of her with the erect penis were of her and this customer. "When I described the other photographs featuring a Native American female," said Miller, "she had no idea who that might be." One more unidentified body.

"Can you identify the women in these photographs?" It was Detective Miller asking Eric, a Washington drug dealer familiar with the dead and the recently disappeared, a question to which Miller already knew the answer.

"I can't recall her name," said Eric of Darla Scott, "but I know that she is one of the twins. I used to do drugs with her and have sex with her. She had a good personality, but she wasn't that street-smart. She was addicted to rock and had a habit of ripping off her johns. I'd say the last time I saw her was in the summer of '97."

He immediately identified Laurie Wason by her first name, stating he met her approximately eight years ago. "Our relationship was generally having her ride along sometimes on my drug deals, and she would also purchase drugs from me. She was generally at the dope house on Pittsburgh. Laurie wasn't all that street-smart because of all the drugs. The last time I saw her was August 1997. She was pretty strung out.

"Now, this is Sunny," he said, pointing to Sunny Oster. "I met her about a year ago in Seattle. Then I saw her for the first time in Spokane in June or July 1997. At that time, she was working the streets as a prostitute and doing dope. Sunny hung out at the South Pittsburgh address and did crack cocaine. She's very street-smart, that one. Yeah, we've done dope together and sex, too.''

Eric quickly identified Linda Maybin by her first name and said that he had known her approximately eight to nine years. "I just got to really know her in these past three years. Mostly, we had sex together and did drugs together. Maybin is street-smart, that's for sure. She has a thing for crack and alcohol—she mostly drinks beer and bourbon. She had several regulars, but I think she would even rob them if she had the chance. Now, if you're asking me about these girls because you think maybe I killed 'em, I'll tell you right now that I didn't ever hurt any of these women. If you want me to take a lie detector test, I will anytime you want.''

Eric took the test. Eric passed the test. Eric submitted blood for analysis. One more suspect crossed off the list; the killer remained unidentified. Within two weeks, another body was found in rural Spokane County.

February 8, 1998

"The body was found Sunday afternoon by a member of the public in western Spokane County. At this time, we cannot make a determination if it's related to the task force," said Captain Doug Silver, co-commander of the force. "An autopsy later this week should reveal the person's sex and cause of death.''

For the next four days, all was silent concerning the grim discovery. Then, almost immediately fol-

lowing Lynn Everson's February 12 touching trib-
ute to the fallen women of Spokane, the homicide
task force issued a press release acknowledging that
the body found in rural Spokane County on February 8 was, due to certain characteristics, assigned
to the special homicide task force.

The "certain characteristics" remained confidential: three plastic bags covered her head; one
gunshot behind the left ear ended her life.

"On February eighth, Deputy Hudson had
responded to a found body located just off the east
side of the road at one mile north of Baker on
Graham," recalled Sergeant Jeff Tower. "I had
previously been notified about the body and had
contacted detectives who were responding."

"Three people had been walking horses and
dogs when one of the dogs began sniffing around
something on the west side of the road under a
clump of trees," Deputy Ron Hudson explained.
"The woman went over to see what the dog was
doing, and she saw what she thought were some
clothes strewn on the side of the road. She then
saw a foot and a hand and realized that it was a
body. The horse started acting up. She helped pull
it away and went back to her residence."

"From there," continued Tower in his own
report, "she called her husband; then she called
in the report. Deputy Hudson requested her to
not leak any information related to the body. She
relayed this request to her husband and to the
other people present when the body was discovered. I helped Deputy Hudson secure the scene.
Detectives Grabenstein and Madsen arrived, as did
Captain Silver."

"I was contacted at my residence by Captain Silver," Rick Grabenstein recalled, "and he advised that a body had been located. At the time, the gender of the body was undetermined, and it appeared that the body had been at the location for some time. Silver requested that I respond to the scene and advised that he would also contact another detective to assist."

Grabenstein arrived as darkness descended. "I made contact with Sergeant Jeff Tower and Deputy Ron Hudson, who were at the scene. Sergeant Tower pointed out the location of the body. . . . The body was in a ditch on the west side of the road, a short distance west of the edge of the roadway, with the head to the northwest and the feet to the southeast. The body was facedown with the left arm extended to the west, and the right arm folded beneath the midsection."

The left arm was devoid of flesh from approximately the shoulder to the wrist, and a portion of the left hand was missing. "Animal activity appeared to be the cause of the condition," reported the detective. "Discoloration from the beginning of putrefaction and exposure was visible, but except for the left arm, the body appeared substantially intact."

The body was clothed in gray jeans and what appeared to be a long-sleeved black sweater, with damage in the left-sleeve area, and there was a green piece of material showing beneath the sweater, which was pulled up somewhat in the back. "It could not be determined at that time if the clothing was a brassiere or a shirt," said Grabenstein. "There were no shoes or socks on the body. What appeared to be a plastic bag—white with some red lettering or logo—covered the head. Some grass and weeds overlaid the body, but it did not appear to have been intentionally buried or hidden. The impression was that the body had been rolled down the moderate slope from the roadway in a short period of time with little regard for the final resting place."

The left shoulder and one side of the head were lying in shallow water. The immediate scene, noted the detective, was unremarkable. "There were no footprints or tire impressions in the immediate vicinity along the edge of the roadway, except for horseshoe prints. There was little else visible at the time that could be immediately identified as evidence."

A decision was made to secure the crime scene until morning. Reserve coordinator Dan Ritchie, scheduled some reservists to guard the scene for the night and at 7:15 P.M., Grabenstein cleared the scene, leaving Deputy Hudson in charge.

"Captain Silver and the detectives wanted very little attention drawn to the scene," Hudson recalled, "so the road was not blocked off, and a perimeter was not established. Reserves were placed at the scene to protect it and to gather the license plates of any vehicle coming by throughout the night."

Detective Minde Connelly received a telephone call the following morning, February 9, at about 8:20 A.M. from the homicide task force office. "I was reached at my residence," she confirmed, "and was requested to respond to the Public Safety Building in reference to a body discovered at approxi-

mately three-thirty P.M. the previous afternoon at
a site eighteen miles from the Maple Street on-
ramp and I-90 westbound at Graham Road.''

At 9:50 A.M., Connelly arrived at the scene and
began making notations. ''The area is rural, with
pasture and pine trees. Standing water and ponds
are also present. At the time of the processing of
the crime scene, the roadway, which is made of
gravel and dirt, was wet. The body was located
between telephone marker poles W82 and W83.''

A thorough and detailed processing of the site
began in earnest. Again, due to extensive garbage
and refuse in the area, it was difficult to discern
which items were associated with the crime, and
which were completely unrelated. Beer cans, a
green rubber glove, a cleaver, and numerous other
items were all bagged and tagged for identification
and fingerprint analysis.

''Two brown AirStep shoes were located near
the deceased victim,'' Connelly reported. ''The left
shoe was south of the victim. The right shoe was
just north and west of the victim. This shoe was
located in standing water. Both shoes were a size
six. Also taken from the site were samples of the
vegetation covering the body. This was collected
for future submission to the Washington State Lab
for hair, fiber, and other trace evidence examination.''

February 9, 1998

Relatives of murder victims Shawn McClenahan
and Laurie Wason held a press conference during
which they pleaded with the killer to end the body

count. "Please turn yourself in so the killings can stop and the families no longer have to suffer," said Kerri McClenahan, sister of victim Shawn McClenahan.

Margaret Streeter, the name of one woman missing and feared killed, was removed from the constantly changing list after her safe whereabouts were established. "Officers are asking three remaining missing women to come forward so they can be removed from the list of possible victims," said Spokane police. The three still-missing women were identified as Linda Marie Maybin, thirty-four, missing since the end of November, Jessica Ann Fitzgerald, twenty-three, missing since early December, and Sunny Gale Oster, forty-one, of Tacoma, who was last seen in Spokane in mid-October.

On February 10, at 9:30 A.M., Ident Supervisor Carrie Johnson obtained positive identification of the deceased victim through fingerprints. The victim's identity was confirmed as Sunny G. Oster, white female, born August 7, 1956. One hour later, Detective Connelly contacted King County. "I requested a chaplain to make notification to Sunny Oster's family regarding her death," Connelly reported. "A teletype was also sent. A chaplain contacted me and advised that he would make notification."

Later that day, at 4:30 P.M., Connelly had a follow-up conversation with Oster's family. The media had already contacted them, but they declined any interviews. "I asked if they would agree to not releasing Sunny Oster's name in the immediate future," said Connelly. "The family agreed with this, as they also did not wish to release her name."

"Her father had a feeling that she was dead, but I kept telling him to wait and see," Cecelia Oster said. "This does put closure on it." The bereaved grieved in private; the task force remained temporarily silent. Beyond the minimal message released to the press on February 12, 1998, further details remained confidential.

Ray Holmes, owner of the Colonial Motel, on Pacific Highway south, between Tacoma and Seattle, knew Sunny Oster. He was saddened and, in his words, "astonished" to hear of her death. "I remember one time when Sunny came in here with a black eye and a busted lip. I said, 'Sunny, just go take a room and sleep for a couple days.' It's like the death of a cancer victim. You might expect them to die, but it's still a shock," he said. "All of a sudden, you can't talk to them anymore and it hits you that they are really gone. Sunny was just too friendly for her own good."

"When I heard Sunny was the latest victim, I wanted to personally kill the motherfucker," said Oster's cousin Dorothy Werttemberger of Walla Walla.

Werttemberger devised her own approach to stopping the serial killer—one both unorthodox and decidedly dangerous. Her ill-advised plan was to retrace Sunny's predeath path to the serial killer's clutches. "I was willing to give my life if, in the process, he could be stopped."

Much as an airliner carries a black box or a hiker utilizes a GPS, Werttemberger would be wired for instant tracking anytime she hit the streets. "Sure, I was willing to work as a prostitute," she confirmed. "And my hope was that he would pick me up just as he did Sunny. Before I went up there, though, I wanted some information that I couldn't get from traditional sources. I knew that there was a guy here in Walla Walla named Jeff Reynolds who used to be what they call a 'distance reader'—a psychic who helps law enforcement find bodies, kidnapped kids, and that sort of thing."

It was common knowledge that Reynolds worked on the Ted Bundy case, among others. He had also pinpointed the exact location where Seattle kidnap victim Heidi Peterson's body would be found, and did so exactly one year prior to its discovery.

"He stopped doing that ESP stuff, for whatever reasons, and became a true-crime writer instead," said Werttemberger. "I figured I had nothing to lose by looking him up and asking him if, as a relative of one of the victims, he'd do me a favor."

She found Jeff Reynolds sitting in the Pastime Café on Walla Walla's Main Street. "I asked him if he still did that stuff, you know—'Do you find dead people?' And I'll always remember his immediate reply: 'Yes, every day on American Movie Classics. Last night, I found Don Ameche inventing the telephone, and Clifton Webb inspiring the sousaphone.' "

Surprisingly, Reynolds was totally unfamiliar with the Spokane serial killer case. Werttemberger told him about Sunny and her murder, then asked if he could tell her anything. "I wanted to know if he could give me an insight into the killer that I would not find out otherwise," said Werttemberger.

"The guy can't get it up," said Reynolds. "There is some sort of sexual dysfunction. Most often, he doesn't get or can't get an erection. He spends time with the victims when they're dead; that's when he can do it. He likes 'em best after he's killed them. He doesn't kill em and dump 'em right away. I see a workshop. It's private, safe, comfortable. It's like a machine shop, or metal shop, not a wood workshop. There is metal—stainless steel or aluminum? I can't tell, but there are metal shavings. He likes having the women spread out there after they're dead. Some of these guys are like that—they don't feel that they have control until the victim is dead, so they kill the victim relatively early on. Once the victim is dead and under control, then they can do whatever they want. Usually, when all is said and done, they will leave the body or bodies in a purposeful or humiliating position or condition. For example, instead of burying the body so no one ever finds it, he dumps it somewhere like garbage or stacks some old tires on top of it just to be rude.

"Now, what is it his victims have in common? Well, it seems to me that his most recent victims are all women who would, if given the opportunity, rip him off. Now I'll tell you something that may sound really weird," Reynolds told her. "There is always a woman with him other than the victim. By that, I don't know if there is a *physical* woman with him or only in his mind, but there is a woman—and I'll tell you what she looks like. She is heavyset, dark skin, dark hair; she smokes; she wears skirts that are too tight and too short for the size of her thighs. Oh, and she wears dark nylons—dark as in dark brown rather than black. She could be Hispanic, Italian, or simply a brunette. It is as if she's connected—there, but not there. He does it, knowing that she's linked. If I ever get a chance to meet the guy, my one question will be 'Who's the woman?' ''

"In the process of our conversation," said Dorothy, "he made it clear that I could be adding an unwise and irritating element to the investigation—making the task force responsible for my irresponsibility—and perhaps jeopardize what ever progress they were making in the case. After all, as Reynolds pointed out, the task force was not revealing everything they and/or the FBI knew about the case, the crimes, the habits and proclivities of serial killers who pick on prostitutes."

February 21, 1998

The homicide task force took to the skies for two complete days, flying over the killer's dump sites. "The helicopter was equipped with special infrared sensors that detect heat changes on the ground," explained Cal Walker. Considering the advanced state of decomposition in which some of the bodies were found, it was highly probable that the killer had more victims stashed away near the dump site. Detectives hoped the equipment might pick up heat generated by a decomposing body.

"The most popular method of murdering prostitutes is strangulation," wrote Investigator Gary Trent of the Washington State Attorney General's Office. Trent shared two important documents with the homicide task force. The first document contained statistics on the methods most commonly used to murder prostitutes in the state of

Washington. Eleven percent of all female homicides in Washington State were prostitutes. Of those, 65 percent died by combinations of strangulation, bludgeoning, and/or stabbing. Only 8 percent died by gunfire from a small-caliber (.22 or .25) handgun. Prostitutes dying as the result of small-caliber gunshot wounds to the head were so uncommon that the odds were overwhelmingly indicative of one person with one significant pattern of homicidal behavior.

The second document was the work of Supervisory Special Agent Larry Ankrom, a member of the FBI's Child Abduction and Serial Killer Unit. "Ankrom researched the postoffensive behavior of certain murderers and reported that many of these killers are likely to visit the grave sites of their victims," stated Walker. "In fact, Ankron personally interviewed offenders convicted of child and serial murders, and these offenders acknowledged that they later returned to either the victim's grave site or the site of the murder."

As an example, Ankrom cited the case of serial murderer Thomas Dillon. Prior to his arrest and conviction, surveillance was established at the grave of victim Jamie Paxton. Thomas Dillon was photographed visiting Paxton's grave. After his arrest, Dillon confirmed that he had indeed visited Paxton's grave on more than one occasion during the year.

This technique, according to Ankrom, did more than confirm suspicions related to known suspects. In the San Francisco investigation into the murders of Angela Bugay and Amber Swartz Garcia, gravesite surveillance resulted in the development of a previously unknown suspect—a suspect who later was charged and convicted.

"In another investigation," Walker recounted, "an individual known to the victim's family, and not previously considered a suspect, was observed during surveillance at the victim's grave site. This individual was ultimately arrested and charged with the murder."

Walker envisioned utilizing Ankrom's research in a well-coordinated effort to bring the killer out into the open. "There have been two previous memorials for the serial killer's victims," noted Walker. "One was in a church, and the other in a popular public location. This time, let's hold a highly publicized memorial right at the killer's dump site. The memorial service for the victims will receive extensive media coverage," said Walker. "We know that for a fact. FBI interviews with serial murderers clearly show that most of these guys are really into media attention. Based upon all the research," he explained, "there is a strong likelihood that the killer will follow coverage of the memorial, and it is also very likely that he may actually attend the memorial himself." The research also indicated excellent odds of the killer visiting a previous dump site or coming to the memorial primarily to pocket another memento, or keepsake.

Acquiring souvenirs is common practice for many serial killers, and that could explain why many of the Spokane victims' personal possessions—shoes, purses, and jewelry—were not found with the bodies. Oregon serial killer Jerry Brudos, for example, kept photographs of his victims, several items of their clothing, a collection of stolen lingerie, and a molded paperweight made from the cast of one of his victim's breasts.

According to former FBI agent John Douglas, killers will often present the souvenir—particularly jewelry—to a family member or significant other. The opening of the film *Kalifornia*, in which Brad Pitt plays a serial killer, shows Pitt's character dispassionately killing a couple by dropping a large rock through their windshield. Examining the death and destruction caused by his simple act of dropping the rock, he takes the dead woman's red shoes and gives them to his girlfriend as a gift.

"Not all serial killers take trophies," acknowledged Walker. "David Berkowitz, the 'Son of Sam,' didn't take trophies, but he did go to the grave sites of the victims." Should the serial killer decide to attend the memorial, visit the site, or snag a souvenir, the homicide task force would be ready.

FBI criminal-profile experts liked the idea, and Sergeant Walker's idea would entail the most elaborate surveillance operation in Spokane history. County crime-victim coordinator Daneka Keith agreed to help Walker organize the event for June 3, 1998. In the meantime, the intense pavement-pounding investigation of the victim's associates and lifestyles continued, and costs to Spokane County continued rising.

March 3, 1998

The Spokane County Sheriff's Office budget received a $300,000 increase to help solve the serial killer case. "The money will fund three detectives, a sergeant, and a secretary to replace employees working to solve the murders," announced the county commissioners. "The money also will be used to buy equipment and pay for travel for homicide investigators. The investigation of other crimes has suffered because so many staff members are working on the city/county task force trying to solve the murders."

March 12, 1998

At approximately 8:48 A.M., Detectives Miller and Connelly interviewed an unhappy resident of the Spokane County Jail. "The purpose of this contact was to interview her concerning our investigation of the homicides," recounted Miller. There was a deeper motive for the interview than mere questions and answers. The killings, some theorized, were being done at her direction and insistence as revenge for insults, real or imagined.

"Detective Connelly actually did most of the interview," reported Miller. "We first asked the woman if she would consent to talking with us, and she stated that she would despite being initially a little reluctant."

"I've got the flu or an ear infection, and it hurts like hell. I mean, my head is killing me," she complained. Connelly asked if she was familiar with the missing Linda Maybin. "Oh, sure. Me and Linda know each other real well. Linda told me that she was from either North or South Carolina. She's got a kid that lives, I think, on the Colville Indian Reservation, and also some other children living in Oroville, Washington."

She indicated that Maybin was at least part Native American and that she last saw Maybin at an address on South Pittsburgh on what she believes was the Friday before Thanksgiving 1997. "I spoke to her on the phone the following day, which would have been the Saturday prior to Thanksgiving. At that time, she told me that she would catch a cab and come and meet me up on Lacrosse Street, but she didn't call a cab—instead, she left with some guy in some car. I haven't seen her since."

"She told us that Linda Maybin was a heavy drinker," Connelly reported, "and that Maybin also did crack cocaine, but she didn't think Maybin was into doing heroin. We then showed her a photograph of Shannon Zielinski. We already knew that she was familiar with Zielinski, but we wanted to see her initial reaction to Zielinski's photograph."

"Sure, I knew Shannon. We got high together with a bunch of other people at the Bel-Air Motel just before she was killed."

"She was then shown photographs of Jennifer Joseph, Heather Hernandez, and Shawn Johnson. She did not know Jennifer or Heather, but maybe she had seen Shawn Johnson around, but did not know her.

"We showed her a photo of Darla Scott," said Connelly, and she immediately recognized her. "The last time I saw Darla was in late September. I never actually knew her all that well, and we were never really friends, but we both ran in the same Spokane 'Crack Crew.' I wasn't surprised at all when I learned that Darla had been killed. There were a lot of people who had grudges with Darla.

As for Laurie Wason," she continued, "I didn't know her all that well, but I seen her around. Actually, I don't even know her name; I just seen her face before."

When shown Shawn McClenahan's photograph, she immediately smiled. "Oh, yes, she was my friend. We became quite close when we were in jail together. It was kind of strange—I mean, we never really knew each other that well when we were outside jail. She said that she was gonna stay with her husband, although she called him a sick motherfucker. I think the last time I saw McClenahan was sometime around October 10, 1997. I remember this date because that's my birthday and I think it was either shortly before or shortly after my birthday that I last saw Shawn McClenahan.

"Sunny"—she immediately reacted to Oster's photograph—"yeah, I knew her real well. I actually knew Sunny from Tacoma. The two of us had done dope together up there."

At length, detectives asked the woman if she knew that she was a prime suspect in the homicides—that other women believed that the murders were being committed at her command. She smiled. "Yeah, I've heard that, too. I'm not that all fucking powerful," she said. "I know who made that story up—they say that because they're jealous." The grinning suspect agreed to take a polygraph test. The severity of her ear infection, however, made the immediate taking of the test impossible. "Nah, I ain't killed any of them. Hell, they were friends of mine. I don't kill people, anyway, especially not people like me. Maybe you want to talk to Tobias Stakhouse."

The Washington State Court of Appeals had recently granted Tobias Stakhouse, convicted in the 1996 murder of a Sprague Street prostitute, a new trial because two jury members were biased against him from the beginning. "They should have been excused," ruled the Court of Appeals. The victim was beaten, then stabbed nineteen times in the neck and head.

"Oh, yeah, that's right," she offered sardonically, "this killer uses a gun. Oh, well, I guess you just better go back and work your first step all over again."

March 20, 1998

First Step Services, the clean-and-sober club offering open arms to Spokane's addicted, disenfranchised, and homeless, was served notice to either pay its water bill of close to $500 or have the water shut off. "It's just the latest of many problems," said owner/operator Darold Johnson. "It's just been a circus. We've been behind before, but not like this." Johnson had juggled bills and sacrificed his time and resources to give hope and shelter to individuals whom many deemed unworthy of redemption, and a serial killer perceived as easy prey.

This depressing news came atop an appeal to increase punishments for prostitutes by Spokane City Council member Phyllis Holmes. Referring to prostitution as a health issue, Holmes said that she would like to "look into increasing the penalties for prostitution." She talked about the used hypodermic needles and condoms left behind in areas with heavy prostitution, such as near Sprague and Altamont.

Lynn Everson, known as both "the Condom Lady," and "the Needle Lady," favored another approach. "Sweden passed a law, I believe a few years ago, that did not make the selling of sex illegal. It made purchasing sex illegal. The money from fines has been used to help get men and women out of prostitution, to provide them with counseling, education, and job training. Because of the financial inequities between worker and trick, tricks almost never suffer from being arrested, whereas workers are humiliated, pay fines, and spend time in jail or prison."

Local prostitutes, however, found both approaches equally appalling. In their view, arresting clients and/or shaming them in public is little more than a moral crusade thinly disguised by the misconception that sex workers need to be rescued, with or without their consent.

"Clients are a prostitute's livelihood, for heaven's sake. Our clientele is not comprised of predators. The real predators are those who pretend to be clients in order to rape, beat, rob, or arrest prostitutes. Thieves and thugs target prostitutes because they know that we can't go to the police and that police don't take our allegations and injuries seriously. Police and court officials think prostitutes don't make credible witnesses. They refuse to pursue our charges because we 'won't show up for court,' " a local working girl explained.

"If you want an example of how our lives are valued," offered one disconsolate sex professional, "consider what happened when they caught those

Susan Savage, recently returned to Walla Walla, was much loved and respected in the small Eastern Washington community. At 22, she was the first known female victim of Robert Yates, Jr. *(Courtesy Walla Walla County Sheriff's Office)*

Patrick Oliver, Robert Yates, Jr.'s first acknowledged victim, and his only known male victim. *(Courtesy Christopher Oliver)*

Patrick Oliver's car (door opened by law enforcement), sighted parked alongside the road not far from the Wickersham Bridge. *(Courtesy Walla Walla County Sheriff's Office)*

Yates' Ruger Security Six .357 caliber hand gun with a six-inch barrel, Serial #150–50785. This is believed to be the weapon used to murder Savage and Oliver. *(Courtesy Walla Walla County Sheriff's Office)*

July 1975 employee photograph of Robert Lee Yates, Jr., taken at the Washington State Penitentiary the same month he killed Susan Savage and Patrick Oliver.
(Courtesy Walla Walla County's Sheriff's Office)

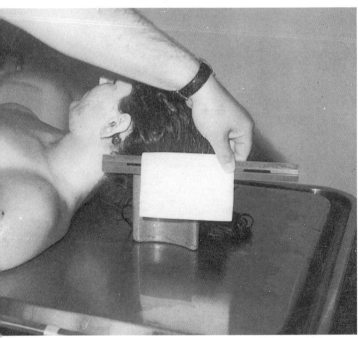

Autopsy photo of Susan Savage, clearly shows the bullet hole behind her left ear. Twenty-five years later, this would be recognized as a "trademark" of the Spokane Serial Killer.
(Courtesy of Walla Walla County Sheriff's Office)

The scene where Shannon Zielinkski's body was found.
(Courtesy Spokane Homicide Task Force)

Shannon Zielinski, 38, hated wearing shoes, but was last seen
wearing distinctive leather boots. They were found near her body
on June 14, 1996. *(Courtesy Spokane Homicide Task Force)*

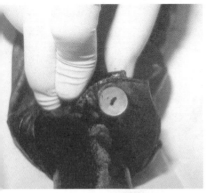

The missing button from Jennifer Joseph's blouse, found under the seat of the white Corvette that belonged to Robert Lee Yates, Jr. (Courtesy Spokane Homicide Task Force)

The severely decomposed body of Jennifer Joseph was found in an alfalfa field near Mt. Spokane. (Courtesy Spokane Homicide Task Force)

The fibers found on Jennifer Joseph's shoe matched the carpet fibers in the white Corvette once owned by Robert Lee Yates, Jr. (Courtesy Spokane Homicide Task Force)

The area where Heather Hernandez' body was found.
(Courtesy Spokane Homicide Task Force)

Detectives found a trail of blood leading
from the parking lot to the decomposed
corpse of Heather Hernandez.
(Courtesy Spokane Homicide Task Force)

The blood stained Mickey Mouse shirt found on the body of Darla Sue Scott, November 5, 1997. *(Courtesy Spokane Homicide Task Force)*

Darla Sue Scott, 29, was found dead near Hangman Valley Road. Two plastic bags were found in her shallow grave. *(Courtesy Spokane Homicide Task Force)*

The task force covered the site of Darla Scott's body with a protective tent, and posted guards, until the scene could be processed in daylight. *(Courtesy Spokane Homicide Task Force)*

HELP US CATCH OUR KILLER

YOLANDA SAPP	NICKIE LOWE	KATHY BRISBOIS	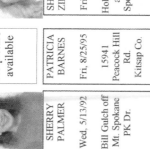 SHERRY PALMER	No picture available — PATRICIA BARNES	 SHANNON ZIELINSKI
Thurs, 2/22/90	Sun, 3/25/90	Tues, 5/15/90	Wed, 5/13/92	Fri, 8/25/95	Fri, 6/14/96
4150 E. Upriver	3200 E. Upriver	12400 E. Trent	Bill Gulch off Mt. Spokane PK Dr.	15941 Peacock Hill Rd. Kitsap Co.	Holcomb Rd. and Mt. Spokane PK Dr.

JENNIFER JOSEPH	HEATHER HERNANDEZ	DARLA SCOTT	MELINDA MERCER	SHAWN JOHNSON	LAURIE WASON

Tues, 8/26/97

Forker and Judkins Rds

1800 E. Springfield

Wed, 11/5/97

12600 Block Hangman Valley Rd.

Sun, 12/7/97

South Tacoma

Thurs, 12/18/97

11400 Block Hangman Valley Rd.

Fri, 12/26/97

Near 14th and Carnahan

SHAWN MCCLENAHAN

Fri, 12/26/97

Near 14th and Carnahan

SUNNY OSTER

Sun, 2/8/98

16000 S. Graham Rd.

LINDA MAYBIN

Wed, 4/1/98

14th and Carnahan

MELODY MURFIN

Tues, 5/12/98

600 S. Napa
**

MICHELYN DERNING

Tues, 7/7/98

218 N. Crestline

CONNIE LAFONTAINE ELLIS

Tues, 10/13/98

1700 108th St. South Tacoma

** Missing believed to be a victim of the serial killer.

Poster (Courtesy Spokane Homicide Task Force)

Shawn L. Johnson was found dead, December 18, 1997 off Hangman Valley Road. Semen found in her body genetically matched Robert Lee Yates, Jr. *(Courtesy Spokane Homicide Task Force)*

Detective John Miller investigates the site where Laurel Wason's body was discovered. *(Courtesy Spokane Homicide Task Force)*

Diagram of the interior of the 1979 Ford van owned by Yates indicating where evidence was uncovered. *(Courtesy Spokane Homicide Task Force)*

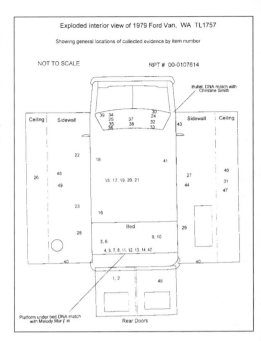

Exploded interior view of 1979 Ford Van, WA TL1757

Showing general locations of collected evidence by item number

NOT TO SCALE

RPT # 00-0107614

Bullet, DNA match with Christine Smith

Platform under bed DNA match with Melody Murfin

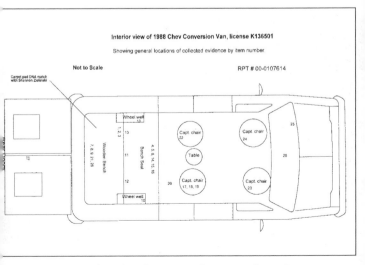

More evidence found in the 1988 Chevy van driven by Yates.
(Courtesy Spokane Homicide Task Force)

Laurel Wason, 31, and Shawn McClenahan, 39, were found head to head on December 26, 1998. Robert Lee Yates, Jr.'s DNA was found on both bodies, and debris atop the bodies came from Yates' backyard. *(Courtesy Spokane Homicide Task Force)*

Sunny G. Oster, 41, was found February 8, 1998, in a wooded area in Western Spokane County. Three plastic bags covered her head. *(Courtesy Spokane Homicide Task Force)*

inda Maybin, 34, was found dead April 1, 1998, only fifty yards from the Wason and McClenahan crime scene.
(Courtesy Spokane Homicide Task Force)

he non-indigenous plant trimmings covering Linda Maybin's body and strewn about the site matched vegetation in Yates' backyard.
(Courtesy Spokane Homicide Task Force)

The body of Michelyn Derning, 47, was found
July 7, 1998. *(Courtesy Spokane Homicide Task Force)*

Michelyn Derning's remains lay under this
discarded hot tub cover.
(Courtesy Spokane Homicide Task Force)

Investigators remove the cover.
(Courtesy Spokane Homicide Task Force)

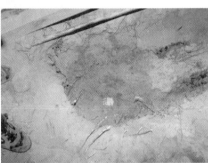

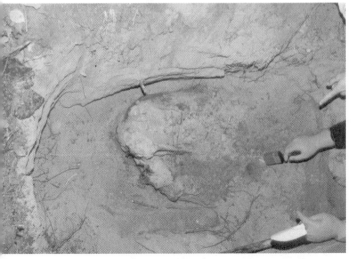

Melody Murfin, missing since 1998, was unearthed after Yates made his plea bargain deal with the Spokane County Prosecutor. (Courtesy Spokane Homicide Task Force)

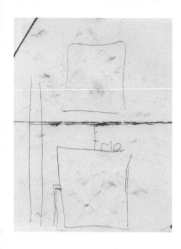

Robert Lee Yates, Jr. drew this map to the secret burial site of Melody Murfin – his own backyard.
(Courtesy Spokane Homicide Task Force)

The personal file cabinet of Robert Lee Yates, Jr., searched by the homicide task force.
(Courtesy Spokane Homicide Task Force)

Robert Lee Yates, Jr., on the day of his arrest April 18, 2000.
(Courtesy Spokane Homicide Task Force)

two men in British Columbia who murdered Pamela George."

Pamela Jean George, a twenty-eight-year-old mother of two, was beat to death by Steven Kummerfield and Alex Ternowetsky. Justice Malone instructed the jury that the defendants should not be convicted of first-degree murder because Ms. George "was indeed a prostitute." The jury found the men guilty of manslaughter; Malone sentenced each to 6 and a half years. Ternowetsky was granted day parole in August 2000; Kummerfield was granted full parole the following November, having served less than four years.

"They got about three and a half years for murdering Pamela. They took her life. Because she was a prostitute, I guess it was okay to murder her. After all, what's one more dead woman?"

Killers of prostitutes have more than a 50 percent chance of getting away with murder in Canada. Fifty-four percent of prostitute murders between 1991 and 1995 remained unsolved at the beginning of 1996. The unsolved rate for all other murders in Canada is 20 percent.

The private nature of a street prostitute's activities can make the identification of a killer very difficult—all the more so when that person is a stranger.

March 28, 1998

"We've had nine hundred twenty tips since November," said Captain Doug Silver. "We are still in the business of putting together vast quantities of information. We want as much information as we can get. Someone out there has the information that will help solve this."

The only new information regarding prostitutes to hit the newsstands was the announcement that Spokane school administrators banned the book *Rainbow Jordan* from middle schools. The book, used for several years by English teachers in a unit on conflict, tells the story of a prostitute's daughter. Administrators deemed the book "too mature" for middle schoolers. Removing *Rainbow Jordan* from required reading in classroom curriculum was well within the decision-making responsibilities of the school board. Removing the book from middle school libraries, if actually undertaken, would violate the United States Constitution, as ruled by the United States Supreme Court in *Board of Education* v. *Pico* (1982).

In short, the board of education can say what books are used or not used in curricula, but they do not have the authority to remove books from middle school libraries. "[The students'] selection of books from these libraries is entirely a matter of free choice," ruled the Supreme Court. "The libraries afford them an opportunity at self-education and individual enrichment that is wholly optional. [The school board has] discretion in matters of curriculum . . . but here, they attempt to extend their claim of absolute discretion beyond the compulsory environment of the classroom, into the school library and the regime of voluntary inquiry that there holds sway."

The First Amendment places limitations upon the discretion of a school board to remove books from their libraries. "If there is any fixed star in

our constitutional constellation, it is that no official, high or petty, can prescribe what shall be
orthodox in politics, nationalism, religion, or other
matters of opinion," ruled the United States Supreme Court. "If there are any circumstances
which permit an exception, they do not now occur
to us."

   Thankfully, no effort was made to ban the local
Spokane newspaper that announced the discovery
of another murdered prostitute that very same day.

CHAPTER EIGHT

April 1, 1998, 5:00 P.M.

"A human body," the sheriff's radio told Detective Henderson, "has been discovered near Fourteenth and Carnahan Streets." Henderson knew the location—the dump site where he viewed the decomposing remains of Shawn McClenahan and Laurel Wason. "I was present as part of the initial scene investigation of two female homicide victims found at almost this exact same location last December," said Henderson.

5:15 P.M.

"While I was en route, one patrol unit arrived on the scene and advised that the initial report had been confirmed. He was contacting witnesses there. When I arrived, I first checked that a crime scene perimeter was being established. Deputy Brad Gilbert had set up an east perimeter at the

intersection of Fourteenth and Carnahan. The
body had been determined to be located just off
Fourteenth, approximately halfway between Carnahan and Havana Streets.''

The body was lying in the undeveloped section
just off the roadway. "An adult couple and a child
were walking along Fourteenth Street this afternoon," reported the detective, "when they noticed
what appeared to be a partially concealed body just
off the south side of the road in a relatively deep
ditch. They reportedly did not disturb the scene
further before calling. I assisted the officer in plac-
ing crime scene tape to mark the perimeter lines.''

Henderson reviewed the scene and surrounding
area for any evidence that could be disturbed or
changed if not attended to immediately. "Also
since it was close to sundown, I took some photographs to document the scene before it got dark.
The weather conditions otherwise were clear,
sunny, dry, and warm, approximately fifty to sixty
degrees.''

This newest site was approximately forty to fifty
feet to the east of the McClenahan and Wason site,
in the same ditch, which runs generally parallel to
the roadway. "A couple-foot-high mound of dirt is
in such a position that you needed to be able to
look over it to see down into the ditch. Thus, the
body site was not readily visible from the roadway.''

Henderson saw a lower leg with a smaller-sized
white tennis shoe on the foot. "It appears that blue
jeans were also part of the clothing on the body.
The position of this body appeared to be parallel
to the road with the head end toward the west.
An extremity bone was exposed, and some small

portions of clothing. The majority of the body was covered by leaf and vegetation debris. It appeared this debris had been dumped down into the ditch from the roadside onto the body, most likely to conceal it. The body was probably totally covered or concealed initially.''

Several small swatches of torn clothing were scattered about in the immediate area, and a larger portion of what appeared to be a red sweater-type material was several feet south of the ditch. "Animal scavenger activity most likely caused those findings," noted Henderson, "and may have also been responsible for the body being partially exposed. No other apparent evidence was detected in the immediate vicinity during this cursory exam.''

A half-gallon whiskey bottle, a ZIMA bottle, and a variety of trash surrounded the body. Vehicle tire impressions were evident on the dirt shoulder, including a several-foot-long fresh tire track showing some tread pattern. Some older cloth material, looking like a blanket, was found partially covered with dirt and vegetation, and somewhat embedded into the ditch wall.

"The blanket-type object," said Henderson, "looked to have been there for quite a while, and it could not be determined at this time if it had any connection to the body or not.

"Other findings made in the vicinity included a red- and black-striped piece of material, possibly from a shirt, that was found in the field area south and west of the body. An old shoe was east of the body more than fifteen yards away and south off the roadway. An additional small group of worn bones were discovered more than twenty yards

south of the body site behind a large rock out-
cropping. These did not appear connected to the
body, and whether they are human or animal could
not be determined at this time.''

There had been more development work done
in this wooded area since December, Henderson
noted. "This included clearing of the area, plant-
ing utilities, and cutting in a couple of roads. Some
heavy machinery tracks were evident along both
roadside shoulders of Fourteenth near the body
site. This would have had to have been done since
our last scene investigation here in December 1997.
Thus, it is evident that there has been at least some
people frequenting this area since then.''

Detective John Miller arrived at the scene, and
Henderson showed him his findings in preparation
for the more extensive search and body recovery
that would take place in daylight.

"I was called at home at about five forty-five
P.M.," Miller recalled, "and informed that a body
had been located on Fourteenth, west of Carnahan.
This location was very near the two bodies found
on December 26, 1997. I responded to the scene,
arriving at approximately six-fifteen P.M. Other task
force members, Sergeant Lundgren, Detective
Connelly, and Detective Grabenstein, also responded to the scene. It was determined that due
to the hour, not much could be accomplished that
evening, so it was decided that we would return the
following day to process the scene. County reserve
deputies were called and assigned to secure the
scene throughout the night.''

After leaving the scene, Miller stopped and
talked to the people who found the body. "They

told me that as they walked on Fourteenth, westbound from Carnahan, they observed a running
shoe lying in the ditch. When she looked closer at
the shoe, she realized the shoe was on the end of
a foot and leg protruding from a large pile of leaves.
Both claimed they immediately realized they had
found a body and they both walked away from it
and did not disturb the body. The female witness
told me that she has been looking more closely
than she normally would have in the area since
she was aware that this is about where the two
bodies were found in December."

That same day, Miller contacted Linda Maybin's
family and advised them that a body had been
found, but not identified. "I told them that they
would be called after identification was made,"
Miller said.

On Thursday, April 2, Detective Miller returned
to the scene with other task force members to
retrieve the body and to process the crime scene.

"At that time, one foot and portions of the left
side of the body were all that were visible," remembers Rick Grabenstein, lead detective on the case.
"Leaves covered the remainder of the body."
Other personnel present and assisting in scene processing were SPD detectives Miller, Connelly, Marty
Hill, and Carr, identification officers Combs and
Rowles, forensic scientists Jenkins and Schneck
from the Washington State Patrol Crime Laboratory, SPD corporal Sahlberg, and forensic pathologist Dr. George Lindholm.

"The body itself was only partially visible," Grabenstein noted. "The left foot clad in a white tennis
shoe with teal marking and a white sock was visible,

along with a short portion of the left lower leg and a short portion of blue-jean pant leg. An area just above the belt line in the left abdominal area was also visible with apparent animal degradation in that area. The left side of the chest area was also visible and had also been attacked by animals, with a portion of the ribs exposed. The body is lying somewhat on the right side, but generally face-down. Also visible is the left arm, which is basically devoid of flesh except for the hand. It is extended above and to the left of the head. The left side of the skull was visible, but was skeletonized apparently by animal activity. A hole is also visible in the skull, which appeared consistent with a bullet wound.

"The body was clad above the waist in a zipper-front outer garment similar to a sweat jacket. There was also another red sweater-type garment, which has been apparently torn by animal activity, with portions of the red material strewn about the area. Otherwise, the body was covered with leaves."

The Washington State Patrol Total Station was set up, and detectives began searching the area immediately around the body site for other evidence. All evidence located was marked with a flag and a number placard, then photographed and recorded as to location with the Total Station.

"The following articles," Grabenstein reported, "were collected and recorded as evidence:

1. Piece of red fabric similar to the inner garment
2. Piece of white plastic from a plastic bag
3. Piece of red fabric similar to the inner garment
4. Piece of blue jean material
5. Piece of red cloth similar to the inner garment

6. Two pieces of red cloth similar to the inner garment
7. Brown plastic bag with Albertsons grocery store logo
8. Two pieces of red cloth similar to the inner garment
9. A red-and-black-striped shirt
10. Piece of green plastic, possibly from a plant nursery pot
11. Dried flowers around the body believed to be hydrangea
12. White cloth sheet or similar article
13. Vegetation sample from near the body
14. Vegetation sample from near the body
15. Vegetation sample from near the body
16. Seven samples of vegetation on the body
17. Fragments of white plastic
18. Piece of red fabric near the head of the body
19. Pieces of white plastic
20. Mass of vegetation collected near the head of the body
21. Piece of wood from the leaves covering the body
22. Piece of red fabric
23. Piece of red fabric
24. Green twist-tie located amongst the leaves on the body
25. Vegetation near the victim's head
26. Entomology specimens including:
    a. Fly strip
    b. Insects preserved in alcohol
    c. Mass of eggs or larvae

April 3, 1998

"I attended the autopsy of the unidentified deceased victim at the Forensic Institute at 9:35 A.M.," reported Detective Connelly. "The deceased victim appeared clothed with a red top, a dark jacket, blue jeans, socks, and tennis shoes. Two plastic bags were on the victim's head. They were torn and had pieces missing. This may be because of animal infestation."

The two plastic bags were each knotted separately. The outer white plastic bag was adorned with cheerful assurances of SERVICE, VALUE, and SATISFACTION. The knot was under the right portion of the neck. The inner white plastic bag, also knotted under the right portion of the neck, had the distinctive red markings and blue inscription of UNITED CEREBRAL PALSY.

"The body had no underwear, bra, or jewelry," noted Connelly. The left arm was void of skin and muscle, bones exposed, and the victim's ribs showed through her badly decomposed torso. A portion of the skull was exposed, devoid of hair and skin, making the bullet entrance hole above the left ear obvious. "No exit wound was present. A projectile and two fragments were located in the brain matter. The right thumb of the victim was used for identification purposes. The body was identified as Linda Maybin."

"I cannot bear to think of her last moments," later commented Maybin's mother, Jean Fisher, "but choose to think of her as the affectionate little girl who drew so much love from others and gave so much love in return. These memories are mine and they will sustain me."

The deceased was wearing blue jeans, but the fabric covering the seat of her pants was completely decomposed. Protruding from Linda Maybin's exposed buttocks was a pink condom.

"Enclosed is one sealed package containing a used condom," wrote the Spokane County sheriff to Dr. Barry Logan of the Washington State Toxicology Laboratory, in Seattle. "The condom and its contents are evidence in a murder investigation, which is one of a series of murders that are believed to be related under investigation by the homicide task force here in Spokane. The contents of the condom are believed to be seminal fluid deposited by the suspect in these murders.

"In our endeavors to identify the perpetrator," said the sheriff, "we would like to determine what, if any, prescription medications, prescribed or illicit, might be present in this sample. The type of drug, rather than its concentrations, are most important. If concentrations can be determined, that information could be helpful, additionally, we would request that you attempt to identify any drugs present in this sample, using the following guidelines."

The first priority was any prescription drugs, second was any common drug of abuse, and the third priority was any additional information that could be learned from the sample.

"We realize that the probability exists that none of the above may be possible," acknowledged the sheriff, "and that a negative result does not necessarily preclude the presence of any particular drug due to the nature of this sample. We would just appreciate an attempt to develop any information possible."

Both the task force and the prosecuting attorney

discussed the probability that all of the sample might be consumed during these procedures. "We were prepared," confirmed the sheriff's office, "to deal with any consequences of the total destruction of the sample."

"Yes, we utilized every possible scientific tool available to us," confirmed the task force. "And we also firmly believed that the killer was someone that moved amongst the victims without suspicion. He was someone they knew, someone they trusted. The only way to discern the associations in these victims' lives was to meet people face-to-face, on their turf, in their space, and see what cooperation you can get, what you can find out, what patterns emerge."

"There's more than a pattern," suggested one talkative prostitute to Detective Miller. "There's a goddamn trail leading directly to a butt-ugly ass-hole truck driver that was doin' both Darla Scott and Shawn McClenahan. They met him in the Kmart parking lot on East Sprague."

"She told me she had met with and spoken to this man, but she had never dated him," recalled Miller. "She never dated him because she had what she termed 'a creepy feeling' about him. She stated she recalled that this man was hauling crushed cars because they had a conversation about it, and she remembered telling him she had hated hauling that type of load herself because you had to keep stopping and checking the chains on the load to make certain it was secure. She described him as a WM, fifties, fat, and always sweaty when she spoke with him. She also claimed that this man would flash a lot of money and would brag that he 'could get any slut anywhere.' "

In addition to this truck driver, the outspoken hooker described another suspect. "There's this white male in his late forties or early fifties that I was warned about," she said. "I've seen this guy a couple of times. He drove a van with a couple of brown or tan stripes on it. I never actually dated this guy, but I once sat in his van."

"She claimed that while in the van he opened his glove box for an item," recalled Miller, "and she thought she saw a semiautomatic handgun in the glove box. She stated the man never pulled the gun out, displayed it, or threatened her in any way."

She told Miller that she would think more about this person and try to come up with a better description. She then told Miller about an apartment complex frequented by both Darla Scott and Shawn McClenahan. "She stated these apartments were directly across the street from Kmart and that it was an apartment with approximately five units," reported Miller. "According to her, both Darla Scott and Shawn McClenahan spent time in two of the units there. One unit, she said, belonged to an older white male who, she believed, allowed prostitutes and young runaways to stay with him. She described this older male as being 'weird' and thought he traded favors for sex.

"On April 8, 1998, Detective Ruetsch and I visited those units," recalled Miller. "There were supposedly two units in the building where the women would often stay for the night."

Entering the exceptionally tidy apartment, detectives were impressed by the eclectic nature of the interior's decor. "It should be noted that immediately upon going into the small two-room apartment, we were aware of several unusual items. A Christmas tree with decorations on it on the table in the room, Christmas lights in the apartment, and the entire apartment was cluttered with knick-knacks, figurines, movie posters, signs, et cetera. Every space in the apartment was filled with something. It was cluttered; however, it was very tidy and clean."

The resident told the detectives that he had formerly worked for the city of Spokane, driving a truck for the litter-control department. "We went around the city collecting trash and items which had been discarded," he explained. "Over the years, I've collected stuff that I liked that others tossed out. That's where a lot of this stuff comes from."

Most prominent of all displayed items were the brassieres. "A couple of them were actually hanging from the ceiling, intertwined with jewelry and mobile-type things," said Miller. "There were also bras on the backs of all of the kitchen table–type chairs and around the table with the Christmas tree on it. The bras were stretched on the backs of the chairs. I would say there were easily between eight to ten bras on display in the apartment. As we stood up and looked around the apartment, Detective Ruetsch specifically asked if they were trophies of some sort."

"Well, I guess you could call them that," the curator of the makeshift bra museum answered happily. "Some of these bras belonged to women

I've known, and some of them may have been left here by some of the different working girls. Although, they usually left with more clothes than they came with—most of it not their size, not their style, and not belonging to them.

"Listen," said the resident affably, "I've known plenty of prostitutes, and I've let them stay here in the apartment from time to time, and I didn't charge 'em a dime, and I didn't make sex part of the deal. I'm an alcoholic. Alcohol ruined my life. Because of that, I felt sorry for these girls who were, for the most part, drug addicts."

"He had compassion for them," Miller recalled. "Oftentimes the girls would show up at two or three in the morning and they would be cold and sick, and he would let them crash in his apartment until they felt better. He claimed that some of the girls even used his apartment for their mailing address."

"At one time," the resident confirmed, "the girls were coming and going pretty regularly from my place, but recently I stopped letting them stay here. They didn't exactly develop an attitude of gratitude. Even though I was nice to them and tried to help them, they have literally robbed me blind."

He told detectives that he had lived at that apartment for approximately six years and his rent was $280 per month. He had retired from the U.S. Army and lives on $440 per month. "The other half of my retirement pay goes to my ex-wife," he said. "I don't own any firearms, if that's your next question."

"I asked him if he ever dated, or was intimate with, any of these girls," recalled Detective

Ruetsch. "He laughed and said, 'Actually, not very often.' "

"Oh, I may have been intimate with one or two of them on occasions, but that would have only been when I was really, really drunk. Like I said, the arrangement for the girls to stay here did not include sex."

He denied any involvement in, or knowledge about, the killings. "I have no idea at all who's responsible for the murders," he said. The detectives had him look at several photographs of murder victims and missing women. "He looked at each one individually," recalled Miller. "He said a lot of the girls look familiar, but he couldn't put names to faces or give us the dates of the last time he saw them.

"I asked him what other apartments the girls visited," Miller reported, "and the other one he was familiar with was number nine. He told me that the girls went there often. Then I asked if he was aware of any of the girls contacting truck drivers in the Kmart parking lot ,which was directly across the street from his apartment."

"Several girls would meet with several different truck drivers in that parking lot," he replied, laughing heartily. "When these eighteen-wheelers roll in with their trailers attached, it's like when the Beatles arrived at Shea Stadium—you know, fans all waiting and screaming and waving, jumping up and down. Okay, that's an exaggeration, but the girls would be right out there waiting for them when they rolled in."

Ruetsch and Miller then visited another unit in the same building. "The results of that interview were somewhat similar to the one I had with the first resident," reported Miller. "He easily admitted that he knew several of the working girls on East Sprague and stated they used his apartment to crash in when they were cold and tired. He looked at several photographs and stated he recognized Linda Maybin and Shawn Johnson as having been at his apartment. He was very unsure as to time frames and the last time he had seen either one of them. He told me that he had stopped letting the girls come to his place for the same reason as the other fellow—the girls were stealing from him relentlessly."

"They took my socks, my underwear, and my pants. Although I was nice to them, they robbed me blind. I've lived here approximately three years, and I got nothin' to do with the homicides, and I don't own no firearms."

Detectives Miller and Ruetsch walked from the Sprague Street apartments shaking their heads in mild amusement at the well-kept, if peculiar, Brassiere Museum. Looking around the East Sprague neighborhood, they could see all manner of evidence—evidence for sociologists. The old neighborhood wasn't what it used to be.

For over one hundred years, East Sprague Avenue attracted every type of individual, family, race, ethnicity, and occupation. A concrete ribbon of transportation bordered by business, industry, and remnants of immigrant lifestyles, East Sprague offered recent arrivals to the "Inland Empire" upward mobility and lateral expansion.

Homes, schools, taverns, auto-wrecking yards, synagogues, adult bookstores, churches, restau-

rants, car lots, and outbound call centers for tele-
marketing companies can all be found in, or near,
East Sprague. In the late 1990s, residents of Spokane's East Central neighborhood, feeling vulnerable, called a public meeting "to generate ideas on
how to make East Central a safer place."

Bickering broke out. Anger, anxiety, and frustration consumed the meeting. One after another,
residents voiced dismay over the neighborhood's
primary characteristics. The major concern among
more than one hundred neighbors who met at the
East Central Community Center was prostitution.

Rosa Dimico, an eighty-one-year-old widow interviewed by the *Spokesman-Review,* predictably said,
"This used to be a good neighborhood, but no
more."

Hoping to rid the neighborhood of prostitution,
residents of Spokane's East Sprague Neighborhood Association decided to target a new group
for harassment—automobile drivers and potential
prostitution customers. Street signs reading PROS-
TITUTION AND DRUG-DEALING AREA would mark
areas where sex and drugs are for sale.

"The owners of cars seen driving in the area
would have their license plate numbers recorded
and turned over to the police," said one person
proudly. Another man, a veteran of World War II,
seemed horrified more at the solution than the
problem. "I would hope the police would throw the
damn list back in their face. This is not goddamn
Hitler's Germany. I didn't fight the damn Nazis
for that kind of gestapo crap to go on. What's the
next suggestion? Loading up all the undesirables
in a boxcar and ship 'em off to a concentration

camp in Idaho? Or maybe do like the Soviet Union where they would send them off for 'treatment'?"

"Trying to starve us off the streets by scaring away our clients is inhumane," said Nancy, a local Spokane prostitute with two young children to support. "I heard about this latest brilliant idea. How are we supposed to survive once this source of income is taken away? Instead of taking away our one source of income, it would be smarter to make programs such as employment counseling, skills development workshops, and drug treatment available for all who need them."

"One good thing about having all these hookers on East Sprague," commented one wag, "is that as long as we have enough of them to keep feeding the serial killer, the rest of us are safe."

East Sprague was not the only aspect of Spokane life undergoing upset and aggravation. A new chief of police would take over in August 1998; a new sheriff would take charge of Spokane law enforcement on January 1, 1999.

In the wake of disputes with county commissioners over required quarterly budget updates in 1997, Sheriff John Goldman decided against seeking a second term. "For many years, my family members have put their own interests aside," he said. "The demands of a long political campaign and a second term in office would require even more sacrifice on their parts. The choice was obvious."

Another possible factor influencing his decision was a $20,000 pay cut. The sheriff's annual salary, due to budget restraints, was reduced from $90,000 to $70,000 effective at term's end.

Goldman served the department for almost thirty

years, and he recently earned a master's degree in criminal justice. "I may decide to teach after my term is over," said Goldman.

Two candidates for Goldman's position immediately surfaced. On the Democrat side was James Finke, a Spokane County deputy with twenty-three years' experience in the department. Representative Mark Sterk, a sitting Republican member of the state legislature, and a Spokane police officer, had already announced his candidacy.

Sterk's credentials for the position were undeniably impressive. He joined the Spokane Police Department Patrol Division in May 1974. Ten years later, he was promoted to sergeant. His experience included stints as administrative assistant to patrol division commander, assistant director of Training Spokane Law Enforcement Regional Center, trainer for WRICOPS in Washington, Idaho, Montana, and Wyoming; from 1995 through 1998, he was elected to the Washington State House of Representatives. While in the state capitol, Sterk worked tirelessly on a number of important committees, including the Law And Justice Committee, Education Committee K–12, Transportation and Budget Committee ($3.7 billion budget), Washington State Organized Crime Task Force, Washington State Criminal Justice Commission—Officer Training/Education, and K–12 Special Education/Mainstreaming Study.

Goldman's tour of duty as Spokane County sheriff included dramatic battles against separatist groups turned domestic terrorists. Over the years, dozens of these movements had built separatist compounds, settlements, and training grounds—

some of them across the state border in Idaho. Many groups adhered to far-right and white supremacist ideologies, such as the Christian Identity religion, and had stockpiled weapons. Some analysts believe these groups reflect the increasing alienation, fear, and hostility in America; these mind-sets have driven them to isolate themselves from society and government.

There is nothing illegal about isolation. However, converting legal guns into fully automatic weaponry, "legalizing" stolen cars, forging money orders and cashier's checks, bombing buildings and robbing banks, are another matter. Goldman led Spokane County's law enforcement response against domestic terrorist bombings of several buildings in Spokane County. So intense and malevolent were the activities of domestic terrorists, white supremacists, and anti-Semitic hate groups in the Spokane area, that Goldman and his detectives became part of FBI history.

The FBI formed a domestic terrorism task force, including the Spokane sheriff and the Spokane chief of police, to track antigovernment and white supremacy groups in Washington, Idaho, and Montana. "At least three dozen federal, state, and local officers from the three states will participate," said the FBI.

The agents and officers, including Goldman, signed an FBI secrecy oath, making them averse to discussing the group's activities. One thing immediately confirmed was the direct linkage between Coeur d'Alene, Idaho, and Spokane, Washington.

"This is the first time in the history of the FBI

that two field offices have come together to form a
task force to look at an ongoing criminal problem,"
said an FBI spokesman. "It means an FBI agent in
Coeur d'Alene working on a terrorism investigation won't have to get a supervisor's permission
to call an FBI agent in Spokane, thirty-five miles
away."

In 1996, when Detective Grabenstein investigated the murder of Shannon Zelinski, North
Idaho terrorists called the Phineas Priesthood deto-
nated bombs and robbed banks in Spokane
County. They met at America's Promise Ministry,
a Christian Identity church in Sandpoint, Idaho.
Another group, Aryan People's Republic, left a trail
of crimes from eastern Washington to their white
supremacy enclave in Oklahoma. Chevie Kehoe,
their leader, allegedly bombed Spokane City Hall
and was linked to five murders.

The white supremacy groups, never known for
their multiculturalism, didn't appreciate Sheriff
Goldman's law enforcement efforts or his ethnic
heritage. Goldman, according to the Aryan Nation,
"is a traitor suited only for a rope, [and] is a para-
sitic Jew to begin with."

"We are at war against the Jew-controlled federal
government and the idea of a united world—a
world in which blacks, Jews, and other minorities
are treated as equals," a captured Phineas priest
boasted to the press. "We are at war with the Jews,
Niggers, Catholics, Mexicans, and anyone who
wants to take America away from white Protestant
Christians and turn it over to the United Nations.
Make no mistake, this is war, and any military man
or sincere clergyman will tell you that God uses

war to cleanse the earth from wickedness. When it's time for a war, God allows certain evils to be exterminated, and I'm here to tell you it's a privilege to engage in God's wars. The righteous are called by God's law to exercise holy violence against the wicked, thereby manifesting God's wrath.''

The concept of "holy violence against the wicked" was also considered the possible motivation behind the serial killings. Detective Rick Grabenstein, who served on both the antiterrorism task force and the homicide task force, acknowledged that many people seriously considered that "the killer could be using twisted theology as justification for murder."

"Taking women who are prostitutes indicates some type of symbolism or some type of fulfillment of his fantasy," suggested former FBI agent Patricia Kirby.

"The fact that Spokane's killer was shooting his victims in the head lent credibility to this theory," confirmed Grabenstein.

Few serial killers shoot their victims. Most serial killer victims are strangled, stabbed, mutilated, or beaten to death. His bizarre religious rage, were that his motive, could manifest itself in sexually assaulting the victims.

"The killer may believe he's on a mission to clean up the streets," Kirby said. "If you had a perfectly clean body and no sexual assault, that would mean, no doubt, this guy is on a mission. Execution is part of their punishment."

Neither Kirby nor the public knew that victims were sexually assaulted, and repeatedly so. They also were unaware that these sexual violations were committed after the victims were murdered. The Spokane killer, whatever his or her motivation, was a necrophiliac—one who has sex with the dead.

Former FBI agent Kirby and other experts admitted that they had no more solid insight into the killer's motivation and identity than the detectives did on the homicide task force. "There's always the human factor to consider," Kirby acknowledged. "This killer may be the one who does everything that no one would suspect."

Equally unsuspected was that Chief Terry Mangnan would be stepping down in May to join the FBI. The chief of police position paid $87,000 per year, and there were plenty of applicants—twenty-five men and one woman—for that position.

National law-enforcement experts advised that Spokane's next police chief should be "a candid consensus builder with a small ego," be adept at delegating authority, share credit when things go well, take responsibility when things go wrong, and "always involve the community when making policy."

Deputy Chief Paul Conner of the Las Vegas police was one of six finalists for Spokane's chief of police. "Becoming a police chief has been one of my lifelong dreams," Conner, fifty, told reporters. "I'm obviously very happy with where I am now, but I also view the opening in Spokane as an opportunity to advance my career."

In Las Vegas, Conner oversaw the Investigative Services Division of the Metropolitan Police Department, which consisted of 417 employees and had a budget of $36 million. He also presided over the department's Use of Force Board, a citizen and police committee that reviews incidents involving the use of deadly force and recommends disciplinary action. He also supervised the Detective Bureau, the Clark County Detention Center, and the Human Resources Division.

Conner traveled to Spokane for a review of the six finalists. The assessment involved three days of interviews, public hearings, tests, and background checks. "It's real exciting for me and a lifetime professional goal," said Conner, a twenty-six-year veteran of the Las Vegas Police Department. "The job is also especially appealing to me because my wife is from Spokane."

Other finalists for the position were Newport News, Virginia, police commander Alan Chertok; Orange, California, chief John Robertson of Yorba Linda; Whitman County, Washington, sheriff Steven Tomson; Lincoln, Nebraska, police captain Joy Citta; and Spokane undersheriff Michael Aubrey.

The new Spokane chief of police, selected after a search process costing $30,000, was Alan Chertok, former number-two officer in Newport News, Virginia. City Manager Bill Pupo termed the hiring of Chertok as "the right decision at the right time."

"Police work is pretty simple," Chertok told an interviewer. "Initially, you treat everybody with the respect you would give your mother. And then you take the bad guys to jail . . . That's police work— go out there and get the bad guys."

When January 1999 arrived, both the sheriff's office and the police department would find themselves embroiled in problems unforeseen. In the meantime, amidst terrorist threats and possible severe budget cuts, the homicide task force waged a war against public complacency. For the first time, in May 1998, detectives put physical evidence from the serial killer investigation on display.

"Look at these shirts. Please, look at them."

The crowd at the public forum looked at what appeared to be bloodstained T-shirts. "These items were found in mid-April at the Linda Maybin site, which was also the Wason and McClenahan site," explained a task force detective. Anyone who knew anything about these garments was urged to speak up, come forward, or call CrimeCheck.

"These were the first pieces of physical evidence shown to the public, and we displayed them hoping that they would generate more tips," said Sheriff Goldman. "We want to keep this tragic series of events in the mind of the community. Officers need to keep receiving a flow of tips from the public, hoping one provides the key."

Rita Jones of Spokane did not attend the public forum. She had something far more pleasant on her mind—her dream car. She had just acquired for $8,875 a beautiful and well-maintained white Corvette from Robert Lee Yates Jr. Not having a garage of her own in which to store it, she entrusted it to a relative employed in the property room of the Spokane Police Department.

Investigating the murder of Linda Maybin, detectives assiduously reviewed field reports. Two recent incidents involving Maybin immediately came to the foreground. In one, Maybin was having a physical altercation with a man in front of a video store. When the cops arrive, neither one of them wanted the assistance of law enforcement. In the other, more recent incident, Maybin and a young man were found parked in what could not exactly be called "lovers' lane."

"I had just stepped out of a convenience store," he explained to detectives, "when she approached me and asked if I wanted 'some company.' She wasn't exactly wearing a baseball cap, but some type of hat that was tipped toward the back of her head. She had on a loose-fitting jacket and jeans, and she was carrying a Crown Royal velvet bag. Well, I guess I'd say her general appearance was filthy. And she smelled bad, too. I told her that I wasn't interested in having any kind of sex with her, but I was happy to give her a ride. We were headed down East Sprague and I offered to take her to a shelter, or other homeless facilities, but she declined."

As they approached the Sprague/Helena area, he was directed by her toward Trent from Sprague and up near the grain elevators. "She had a bottle in her coat and she kept drinking from it, and talking a million miles an hour, just sort of babbling, and asking me for money all the time. I kept telling her that I wasn't going to give her money."

The couple was stopped by the grain elevators for, in his words, "about three seconds" when a patrol car pulled up. "She kept that bottle of whiskey or scotch underneath her coat while talking to the cops. She did the talking, and lots of it. She was hyper as hell, talking away like crazy. They finally let us go; I dropped her off and was glad to be rid of her. I didn't know her name or who she was or anything until I saw her picture on the news as being one of the murder victims.''

The young man, whose fingerprints were already on file, also provided a full palm print and a blood sample. One more suspect with DNA and finger-prints in the database.

While Goldman pleaded for continued tips, Walker's plan for an elaborate surveillance/memo-rial was coming together. When the press release hit Spokane media, surveillance teams were already in place near Hangman Valley Road where Shawn Johnson's and Darla Scott's bodies had been dis-covered.

"We had people in the woods twenty-four hours a day for a week," said Sergeant George "Woody" Wigen of the sheriff's office. Wigen pretended he was a dog-walking neighbor, trotting along with his terrier. Other officers hid in the bushes. "They were outfitted in camouflage so they'd blend in with the natural environment," said Walker.

The officers, disguised as indigenous plant life, crouched in the underbrush for twelve-hour shifts. Keeping an alert vigil for suspicious dump-site visi-tors, officers sipped soda and ate Twinkies. True to their high standards, they carefully observed all trash disposal and recycling protocols.

Undercover cops in plaid pants wielded nine irons and carried concealed weapons as they put-tered about Hangman Valley Golf Course in little motorized golf carts. Other officers were stashed away in innocuous-looking vehicles. Peering out through peepholes, zoom lenses captured images of passing cars' license plates.

Motion detectors were set up near the dump site, should the killer sneak back in darkness. Deer and other wildlife, unaware of the elaborate plan, kept officers awake all night with their nocturnal activities.

The press and public had no knowledge of the memorial's second-tier purpose. The victims' families were also not aware that the hills were alive with law enforcement. "If I could plan an event like this that would assist law enforcement and, at the same time, provide closure and comfort for the families," Daneka Keith said, "that was okay for me."

"We really tried hard to invite Darla Scott's twin sister, Marla, whose lifestyle was much the same as Darla's," said Sergeant Walker. "We drove all over town trying to find her." Members of Scott's family did not attend the memorial, nor did some other victims' families. Kathy Lloyd, Shawn McClenahan's sister, who attended the memorial, said that she understood why other family members did not participate. "This pain is such a horrendous pain," she said.

Sheriff Goldman, speaking to the modest crowd gathered around a memorial wreath, told mourners and concerned citizens that the victims were not forgotten. "The task force is working tirelessly to find their killer," he assured them. "We will bring the person responsible for these crimes to justice."

"I handed out roses to family members," commented Keith to the *Spokesman-Review*'s Bill Morlin, "and to sit there and know he had just dumped her [body] there . . . it was more sad than eerie, I guess."

"The most recent body, that of Linda Maybin," commented Detective Grabenstein, "was found in early April, and there was speculation that the killer may have left the area, but we couldn't afford to work under that assumption."

"I know the task force is working very hard," said Kathy Lloyd. "Somebody out there knows something. I hope people keep calling in tips."

Hoping to lure the killer with additional souvenirs and trophies for his collection, the memorial wreath was adorned with pictures and personal items of the victims. "We watched the site for three days after the memorial," said Walker, "hoping the killer would return to the site to snag another trophy. He didn't. Eventually, I went back out there, packed up the wreath, and put it in the trunk of my car."

"It's too easy for the public to become complacent and think that it's all over with," said Darla Scott's friend, Arthur. "Just because no new bodies have been found doesn't mean that the killer has changed his mind about homicide. And even if he moved across state, does that mean it's okay for him to kill women over there? Plus, you know, he can always come back. Sooner or later, he's gonna get caught—he damn well better."

Monday, June 15, 1998

Captain Doug Silver, head of the homicide task force, was understandably aggravated. "We haven't really had any solid leads since December," said

Silver. "I'm worried the killer has changed his habits or his location. It's bad to have a serial killer. It's worse to have one that moves around."

The task force diligently pursued each possible path of investigation, processed the crime scenes with exemplary attention to minute detail, created computer databases of suspects and victim interrelationships, and even compiled a list of registered owners of white Corvettes in eastern Washington.

"We then cross-referenced that list with the names of people who had been stopped by police in the area frequented by prostitutes and formally identified in field reports," said Doug Silver. One name among many was that of Robert Lee Yates Jr., but he was only one of several people who had both a white Corvette and had been identified in the area of Sprague Avenue. The homicide task force had collected thousands of leads, many of them volunteered from the public. "Every tip is kind of its own little mini-investigation," said a task force spokesman. "We have prioritized them. Hopefully, we'll solve this case before we go through the whole list."

That very day, another decomposed corpse was found on a dirt road near Mount Spokane, thirty miles northeast of the city. The body had been exposed to the elements for so long that it was in a near skeletal state. An autopsy revealed that the victim was a short woman with light hair, but the cause of death was not discernible.

Meanwhile, investigators continued looking for Melody Ann Murfin, forty-three, four feet eleven inches tall, 120 pounds, a known associate of the killer's previous victims. Despite Murfin's disappearance and the disturbing discovery of skeletal remains, Spokane's summertime prostitutes were exhibiting more skin and less apprehension.

"Prostitutes are easing their way back onto street corners; they figure the killer may have left town or was caught," said Lynn Everson. "Few of them sit shivering and scared in their apartments anymore; the fear is instead a constant general unease for women on the street. This bothers me," she said, "because prostitutes are in the greatest danger in summer, when so many women are working the streets that it could go unnoticed if one—or seven—disappeared."

Michelyn Derning, forty-seven, a former executive secretary with an unpleasant past and a promising future, vanished on July 3. When Derning didn't show up for a planned holiday weekend trip to Priest Lake with Gregory Landis, he wasn't overly concerned. "She was a free spirit," said Landis. "She was always taking off and doing crazy things."

Gordon "Swede" Olund found Derning's naked body four days later in a vacant lot at North 218 Crestline. Stripped of clothing and personal possessions, Derning's corpse was clumsily concealed under a smattering of broken branches and an old hot-tub cover.

A tanned and trim product of southern California surf and sunshine, "Mike" Derning was once the quintessential golden girl. Exceptionally athletic, she was accomplished at snorkeling, surfing, and scuba diving. In her heyday of vitality, she and her son, Ryan chased seagulls on the beaches of Oceanside, California.

Derning's health and happiness slowly ebbed

away following her mother's death from cancer in 1991. She tended to her mother's needs for several years, and following that traumatic emotional uprooting, Derning drifted down to despair, addiction, and a shattered self-image. In 1997, after a devastating period of drugs and homelessness, she came to Spokane to be with her dear friend, Landis.

She worked at a variety of jobs, including ranch hand for Melissa Wallace, owner of Seven Springs Ranch. "There was such fear in her eyes when she came to me," said Wallace, "but that changed." The natural benefits derived from an honest day's work, fresh air, and good friends soon vouchsafed their influence upon her soul.

Faith gradually edged out fear. Although the future was not blinding in materialistic brilliance, it was several shades lighter than the darkness upon darkness that compelled relocation to eastern Washington. "If I don't go there," she told her family, "I'm going to die."

Derning seriously considered returning to school for her nurse's license, and she joined a loving and supportive church congregation in Spokane Valley. "Michelyn had a tree of life growing inside her heart," said Pastor Gary Hebden of Valley Open Bible Church at a memorial service in her honor. "She was a giving person who loved life. Today, our hearts are heavy," Hebden said to the crowd of about thirty mourners. "She was trapped in something, [and] has joined a long line of women who have been vulnerable in life."

"Michelyn wouldn't want any vengeance on the man who killed her," Melissa Wallace said. "She'd ask us to pray that maybe there won't be any more victims." The congregation silently prayed for Derning and her killer. "We will commit ourselves to pray every day until this violence stops," Hebden said. "Let us be at peace, without fear. May the one or ones who are responsible be found out."

Michelyn Derning's body was buried next to her mother's in Oceanside, California. Spokane police detectives did not see her peacefully laid to rest, they saw her under an old hot-tub cover.

Detectives Gilmore, Hollenbeck, and Connelly did the crime scene investigation, with assistance from Ident Officers Carrie Johnson and Deb Rowles. "Recovered at the scene from the victim's hair was a .25 auto casing, CCI brand," stated the official report. "No purse, wallet, or money was recovered."

On July 9, 1998, Dr. George Lindholm and PA Randy Shaber performed the autopsy. Cause of death was determined to be a gunshot wound to the head. No projectile was recovered. Oral, anal, and vaginal swabs were obtained.

Detective Marty Hill questioned several Pantrol employees, including Robert Lee Yates Jr., after Michelyn Derning's body was found near the east Spokane business. Yates did not say or do anything to draw attention to himself. He was just your average generic Joe, one of the workers, the understated, the quiet, the efficient—the deadly.

The serial killer was back, acknowledged Spokane police. "He has resurfaced after three months to murder his eighth victim," said a police spokesman. "Evidence at the scene was similar to evidence found at the scenes of the other murders."

One item of dissimilarity was that Linda Maybin

was missing for almost four months, but Michelyn Derning was found only a few days after her death. This added credence to the theory that the compulsion to kill would suddenly overwhelm the murderer, causing him to impulsively snuff out a woman's life with little or no planning or premeditation. The compulsion to kill overwhelmed him again one month later. His victim: Christine L. Smith. Unlike the others, Smith lived.

CHAPTER NINE

August 1, 1998

Between midnight and two o'clock on the first day of August, 1998, Christine Smith met the Spokane serial killer. Unlike the other prostitutes lured into one of his vehicles, Christine Smith escaped with her life.

Smith charged a standard rate of $40 for oral sex. She had regular satisfied customers, but was willing to open her schedule to accommodate new clients. On August 1, 1998, Smith asked Robert L. Yates Jr. if he was the serial killer.

"I'm a respected National Guard helicopter pilot, and the father of five children," he said. "You have nothing to fear." Christine Smith joined him in his 1970s-era van, accented with an exterior yellow/orange stripe. Inside were bucket seats, interior wood paneling, and a raised bed for their comfort and convenience. Atop the mattress, Yates revealed his flaccid member and Smith began performing oral sex.

Despite her best efforts at earning his return business, seven minutes of fellatio failed to induce an erection. So intense was her concentration on successfully completing the task at hand, she didn't realize that the sudden pain in her head was the result of being shot.

Smith, fighting to stay conscious, thought he had violently hit her on the head out of frustration or perhaps as punishment for not getting him aroused. Yates demanded his money back and attempted to take it by force. Smith, now fearful and traumatized, could feel blood dripping from her head.

"I jumped into the front seat and out the passenger door," she recalled. "I ran as fast as I could to St. Luke's Rehab Center." It was there that Smith summoned assistance from security, who gave her a ride to Sacred Heart Hospital, where she was treated for a half-inch-long cut just above and behind the left ear in the left mastoid area, requiring three stitches.

"He didn't get my money because it was in my pocket, but I left behind my purse," said Smith, "which contained makeup, address books, keys, and jewelry."

"She's living proof that unpredictable head can save your ass," said Florence, an East Coast hooker transplanted to eastern Washington. "Obviously, Christine altered her rhythm all of a sudden—which is always a good idea, anyway—when he pulled the trigger. If Smith were performing mundane, boring, thoroughly predictable oral sex, she'd be one more dead body dumped by the side of the road, in an empty lot, or down by the river like poor Yolanda Sapp was back in 1990.''

The name Yoland Sapp has become a famous part of Spokane's homicide history. On a cold February morning, at 8:30 A.M., the homicide division of the Spokane Police Department responded to a call from the 4100 block of East Upriver Drive. Sprawled over an embankment near the Spokane River was the nude body of a black young woman later identified as twenty-six-year-old Yolanda Sapp.

The unclad victim was shot to death, the entrance wounds indicating a small-caliber handgun as the murder weapon. The only items found with the body were Sapp's black wig, multicolored blanket, a white towel, and a green military-style blanket. "Either the killer took care in cleaning up after himself," recalled detectives, "or killed the victim at a different location and then transported the body after death."

Yolanda Sapp was not an unfamiliar name to Spokane Police. Sapp, a known drug user who had a history of prostitution arrests, was last seen alive on the 3200 block of East Sprague. "When I saw her on the street," a freelance coworker told police, "she was wearing black jeans, black slip-on flat-soled shoes, black panties, a black T-shirt, and a beige rabbit-fur coat."

Sapp's personal taste in accessories included nine jangling wrist bracelets, a silver chain necklace, and her wedding rings. All were missing from her body, as was her ever-present denim purse.

The victim's hair and fiber samples were taken during autopsy, as were oral, anal, and vaginal swabs. Despite thorough investigation, there were no suspects and no traditional motive. Frustration faced investigators at every turn, and potential leads led nowhere. Less than a month later, another body was found.

Sunday, March 25, 1990, at 6:00 A.M., the Spokane Police Department was called to the 3200 block of East South Riverton. A white female had been shot to death, then dumped in the road. Like Yolanda Sapp, thirty-four-year-old Nickie Lowe also had a known history of prostitution—she was last seen the previous day working East Sprague. A .22-caliber bullet, virtually intact, was recovered from Lowe's body during the autopsy, and the medical examiner noted the strong smell of motor oil. Toxicology tests showed the presence of cocaine and cocaine metabolites.

The remarkable similarities between the two homicides did not escape investigators. The same individual almost certainly murdered Yolanda Sapp and Nickie Lowe, but there were no clues to his or her identity or identifiable commonality of motive. After seven weeks without either investigative progress or increased body count, detectives seriously theorized that the killer had traveled to another city. That theory was immediately discarded on Tuesday, May 15, at 7:45 P.M., when the Spokane County Sheriff's Office was informed that the dead body of another nude female was found in the Trent and Pines area near the banks of the Spokane River.

"Judging from the contusions and lacerations to her head," reported detectives, "the victim was beaten with a blunt object in addition to being shot." Recovered from the crime scene were various pieces of women's clothing, a pair of shoes, a bloodstained plastic bag, a cigarette butt, and vegetation samples. "This time, however, we also found tire tracks," said the Spokane County Sheriff's Office, "and the tire's tread patterns were carefully photographed." Almost a decade later, these tire track photographs would prove a major source of dismay to the homicide task force.

The victim was identified as Kathleen Brisbois, thirty-eight. Her profession was no different than Sapp's or Lowe's, nor were the results of her autopsy. Bullets recovered from her body and trace evidence, such as hair and fiber, were sent to the state crime laboratory. Toxicology tests revealed the presence of morphine and cocaine metabolites, indicating that she had used cocaine, and most likely heroin, prior to her death.

"Scott, Johnson, McClenahan, Wason, and Oster also had illegal drugs in their bodies at the time of death," commented Cathy A. in retrospect, "but no one thinks those women were murdered due to their high probability of failing a random drug test."

"He's a drug dealer," said the young man whose pager number was found in Shawn McClenahan's pocket. He was referring to a friend of his, a resident of Ritzville, Washington, for whom he acquired the pager. "He makes frequent trips to Spokane." Detectives made a trip to Ritzville.

It sounded promising: an alleged drug dealer's pager number is found in the pocket of a murdered drug addict. The reputed dealer lives out of town but makes frequent trips to Spokane. He could kill them, dump them, and go home. In truth, this particular young man was incapable of any such behavior. He lived with his sister, didn't own a car, and traveled to Spokane by Greyhound bus. Meeting with detectives in a patrol car outside his sister's home, the young man insisted that he didn't know the murdered women, and he eagerly offered blood samples to prove his lack of involvement in these horrendous homicides. Detectives immediately took him up on his offer. One more suspect cleared.

August 28, 1998

A chunk of human scalp with hair attached was happily carried home by a dog, its upsetting souvenir clutched in its canines. The Spokane task force and a band of about sixty searched a forty-acre piece of land southeast of Deadman Creek near the intersection of Holcomb Road and Mount Spokane Park Drive, but no body was found. They returned two days later. "We're doing a more intensified search," said Sergeant Walker "We used seven or eight dogs," Walker recalled, "but no helicopters or other special equipment was utilized. It was basically a people-and-dog search. The 'scalp' was really a big clump of hair with a bit of decomposing flesh connected to it," he explained. No body was found, and, as Walker noted, "the dog could have carried that home from anywhere—it could have come from miles away in any direction."

September 2, 1998

"The clump of human hair, attached to a bit of scalp, that was found last week does not appear to be linked to the serial killings or any other homicide," announced Captain Doug Silver. "We are still looking for Melody Ann Murfin. Because of the circumstances surrounding Murfin's disappearance, her lifestyle and associates, we are now treating her case as a homicide."

September 24, 1998

A composite sketch of a possible serial killer suspect was officially revealed to Spokane's citizenry at a homicide task force press conference. The composite was actually created on August 27, 1995, following the murder of a Seattle homeless woman named Patricia Barnes.

"Task force detectives closely investigated the Barnes homicide because she had a similar lifestyle to the other victims'," said Doug Silver, "and she was killed in a similar way. It is possible that the man that Ms. Barnes was seen with the night she died may be connected to the cases here," he said. "We cannot say if this case is definitely related to the serial killings, but it is close enough."

Barnes, a homeless woman who frequented Seattle's Pioneer Square, was last seen between 3:00 and 4:00 P.M. in downtown Seattle with a white male who had reddish blond wavy hair, blue eyes, and a muscular medium build. Her naked body was found wrapped in a sleeping bag and dumped

in the woods not far north from the King/Pierce
County line.

"We consider this a very good lead," said Silver,
and the response was immediate. "More than one
hundred residents called before noon with information, [and] telephones in the task force's headquarters at the Public Safety Building continued
to ring throughout the afternoon. I've taken five
or six calls myself," Silver said. "We've gotten everything from the specific—'I know who that person
is'—to the general—'I saw that guy yesterday.' "

"That guy in the picture," said one woman on
the telephone, "I think I seen him, and he tried
to date me. I don't mean ask me out to the opera,
I mean I was working—you know what I mean, as
a prostitute."

"About two weeks after two of the bodies were
found," she continued, in person, "this guy drives
up to where I am, right, which is about at Sprague
and Ray. Anyway, he's a white male, thirty-six to
thirty-seven years old, short blond hair, slightly red,
basically short, and a little curly in back. He had
a medium build, but I couldn't estimate a height
because he was sitting down. He was very clean
cut," she said, "and was clean shaven. He was driving one of those full-size utility vehicles like a
Bronco or a Blazer. It's older, but in nice condition
and well cared for. It was brown and had tinted
windows.

"There was this gun rack on the inside," she
explained, "and that was on the driver's side on
the sidewall, not the back wall of the vehicle."
There was a rifle about at the level of the driver's
head, and across the rear driver's side window.

"When I saw the gun, I decided that I wasn't getting in the damn car, ya know? He said that the gun never bothered anybody before, but I still refused to get into the vehicle. Now, here's the real weird part," she explained to detectives, "he turned off his lights and drove away. Ya get that? He turned off his lights and then drove away. I mean, isn't it weird that he turned off his lights? He didn't turn 'em off when he stopped to talk to me, but he turned 'em off when he drove away. I'd never seen him before, and I've never seen him since."

If the man she saw was the same man seen by Barnes, then perhaps he was the same man last seen with Connie LaFontaine Ellis, a strikingly lovely and well-groomed woman whose life, it seemed, was singled out for tragedy. At age thirty-five, her life was over.

Originally from North Dakota, Connie LaFontaine Ellis was found by Pierce County deputies in a Tacoma ditch on October 13, 1998, only days after task force detectives questioned a suspect in her home state of North Dakota. The man was a prime suspect in three deaths and two disappearances in Lewiston, in the 1970s and 1980s. "Task force investigators interviewed the man after receiving a tip that he might somehow be involved in the serial killings," said Captain Doug Silver. "The man was ruled out as a suspect following his interview with detectives. This isn't unusual. We do those kinds of interviews almost every day."

The body, due to extreme decomposition, was not immediately identified. Two weeks later, the

Pierce County medical examiner announced that the victim's name was Connie LaFontaine Ellis.

October 30, 1998

"It's like we're starting from scratch, like we just found the body today," said Deputy Ed Troyer, Pierce County spokesman. "Pierce County authorities plan to release LaFontaine's photograph to the Puget Sound media in hopes that somebody saw her get into a car or walk away with someone shortly before she disappeared. But detectives aren't sure when that was. Nobody even reported her missing. She was last seen about a month before her body was found."

"We are still working with authorities in Pierce County," said Silver. "Their investigators are very busy. The lead investigator on the [LaFontaine] case has a lot of other things going on. It has been hard for us to get in touch with them."

"They are chasing a serial rapist who has attacked fourteen women during daylight hours," explained Deputy Troyer. "They're also investigating several other homicides. LaFontaine's murder has been assigned to a detective, but it will be up to Spokane authorities to investigate it as a serial killer case. We're not going to join the task force," he said. "We'll work with Spokane. We're sharing everything we have with Spokane, but they have all the information on [the serial killer] at this point, understandably. They've been working on it since the beginning. Basically, they're the lead on this thing. Obviously, if it gets to be a bigger deal for us here, we may do something differently."

"Task Force detectives found nothing here in Spokane that would connect her to drugs and prostitution locally," said Silver, but LaFontaine Ellis had other strong ties to Spokane.

Connie LaFontaine, member of the Turtle Mountain Chippewa Band, grew up on the tribe's North Dakota reservation, atteneded a Native American boarding school in Flandreau, South Dakota, and moved to Spokane when she was eighteen. Her mother, separated from her father, also moved to Spokane and lived there until her death.

"Connie wore her reddish black hair stylishly short and her clothes were immaculate," said longtime friend Nancy Raya-Martin. "She wore a size two and was never caught without lipstick and eye shadow. She was beautiful."

"She was a lovely young girl—warm soft voice, sunny smile," recalled Carolyn Samuels of Spokane's American Indian Community Center. "I met Connie after she and her family moved here. She was excited about moving to the big city and attending beauty school. Connie did fine for a while." She eventually became a licensed cosmetologist on March 3, 1997. "She got mixed up with a man who was abusive," said Samuels. "Things got from bad to worse."

"Connie started getting into drugs when she moved to Tacoma in 1992," lamented her father, Emil LaFontaine. "She was shooting heroin and was in and out of rehab." While in Tacoma, Connie LaFontaine married Rick Ellis. After they divorced, she traveled regularly between Tacoma and Spokane. According to Emil LaFontaine, she returned to North Dakota in the summer of 1995 to attend her mother's funeral.

"We last saw Connie in 1996 when her eight-year-old son, Randy, died of a heart condition in Seattle," said her father. "That's when she lost it." This was not the only child's death to devastate Connie LaFontaine Ellis. Another son was lost to sudden infant death syndrome. "I don't think Connie cared about life too much after that," her father said. "I usually heard from my daughter every week, but lately her calls had been less frequent. I hadn't heard from my daughter in a while. She called here about a month ago and I wasn't home."

Her one vice was heroin, and her father always considered addiction as a side effect of life in the city. "You don't really know what kind of things the city can do to you when you live on the reservation," he said. "I always wondered how she could stand living that life."

Connie LaFontaine Ellis's distinguishing characteristic was her impeccable grooming. No matter what her financial situation or personal problems, she always presented herself in the most pleasant and positive manner. She was also known as a kind, loving, and sensitive person whose life was one of suffering and disappointment. Just prior to her death, she told a friend that she was planning a move to the Spokane Indian Reservation to enroll in a training program. She also thought of returning to North Dakota to be with her father, daughter, and grandchildren.

Ellis, addicted to heroin, supported her habit by prostitution and was a regular on Tacoma Way South, Pierce County's equivalent of East Sprague.

Not far from McChord Air Force Base and the Fort Lewis Army Base, Tacoma Way South was known for its strip clubs and adult bookstores.

"She was really nice. I used to see her all the time," said Wendy, a twenty-nine-year-old prostitute who knew her as "Indian Connie." LaFontaine, whose arrest record in Tacoma and Pierce County included charges related to drugs, indecent conduct, and prostitution, pleaded guilty in 1992 to burglarizing a Tacoma home. She and her then-husband, she confessed, stole five guns and a TV/VCR, which they pawned for drug money. Sentenced to eight months in jail, she agreed to enter a drug rehab program instead. She only stayed in the program for two days.

"Ms. Ellis is a serious heroin addict who supports her habit through prostitution and small drug sales," wrote community corrections officer Christina Maleney in 1993.

"Sometimes you take the wrong turns in life," Connie's father said, "but I never thought she'd get killed like this. Just like that, some guy takes all the hope, all the love you have for your daughter, off the face of the earth."

The way LaFontaine was murdered matched the Spokane serial killer victims. As with the eight serial killer victims, she was shot in the head. "A ninth woman, Melody Murfin, is thought to be a victim of the killer, even though her body has not been found," said Sheriff Goldman. "Investigators are not ready to call LaFontaine victim number ten. There has to be a very methodical analysis of the evidence, crime scene, and other factors—possibly by an outside agency—before that can happen."

Not long after the identification of LaFontaine's body, investigators from Spokane's homicide task force met face-to-face with their Pierce County counterparts. "Task force members spoke with the detective assigned to the LaFontaine case," confirmed Pierce County sheriff's spokesman Ed Troyer.

"We're going to talk about the need to cooperate and so on," said Undersheriff Mike Aubrey prior to the meeting. "This isn't a sit-down between the detectives to compare notes. This is about improving communications."

"We want to remind them what we're looking for," said Sheriff John Goldman. "Now, with this other body, there's more relevance."

"The task force also may ask other agencies, including the Washington State Patrol and FBI, to join the hunt," added Alan Chertok, the, new Spokane police chief. "They have some assets we may be able to take advantage of. For example, the state patrol could make one of its airplanes available to help shuttle detectives back and forth to the west side, and the FBI has a serial killer unit that may be able to provide more resources and expertise."

"There are several west side connections to the serial killings in addition to the latest body," explained Sergeant Walker. "Melinda Mercer, who was shot to death in South Tacoma last December, has already been linked to the Spokane serial killer. Sunny Oster, another victim, had recently moved to Spokane from the Tacoma area shortly before her body was discovered."

One link of which detectives were unaware was

that Robert Lee Yates Jr. was in Tacoma the weekend that Connie LaFontaine Ellis disappeared. Had they known, it really wouldn't have made much difference. Robert Lee Yates Jr. was not under suspicion.

November 10, 1998

At 1:25 A.M., Officer Reynolds of the Spokane Police Department watched the driver of a Honda Civic, license number 918AJH, pick up known prostitute Jennifer Robinson at the corner of First and Crestline.

"I agreed to give him a blow job for twenty dollars," recalled Robinson. The man with whom she made the deal was Robert Lee Yates Jr. Reynolds pulled them over. Robinson, not wanting to lose her oral sex customer or her personal freedom, quickly devised a story off the top of her head. "Tell them that my father works with you and asked you to find me, pick me up, and bring me home," Robinson said to Yates. "I'll back up your story." With Robinson confirming Yates's explanation, Officer Reynolds had no choice but to let them go.

If Yates planned on killing her, he wisely changed his mind. Two days later, at 6:00 P.M., there was a knock at Yates's front door. It was the Spokane police.

November 12, 1998

The police arrived at the Yates residence, five miles south of East Sprague, in response to a

domestic dispute. In an argument with his nineteen-year-old daughter, Yates physically threatened
her. Yates was potentially charged with misde-
meanor assault, and the matter would be dropped
as long as Yates didn't commit any crimes. He
didn't tell police about his string of recent homicides or his attempted murder and robbery of
Christine Smith.

On the same day that Spokane police visited the
home of Robert Lee Yates Jr., Captain Doug Silver
of the homicide task force admitted dismay over
the number of deaths since the task force's formation almost one year earlier. "I do believe we will
catch this person," said Silver. "Detectives have
cleared about half of the three thousand tips
received in the past year, and the rapport between
investigators and prostitutes has improved. We're
making progress. There are still a number of people who are in the 'persons of interest' category,
meaning they could become firm suspects."

Detectives would not disclose further information or theories they held regarding the killer.
"Anything we would share with the public would
mean sharing it with the serial killer," commented
Detective Grabenstien a few years later. "After all,
he was part of the public. There is no reason to
tell him what we knew and what we didn't know."

"It was decided very early in the investigation not
to reveal too much for that very reason," confirmed
the task force. The biggest, best-kept secret of all
was that the task force had the killer's DNA isolated
since July and his palm print since March.

"It used to be that you couldn't recover fingerprints from plastic bags," explained Detective Fred

Ruetsch, "but now scientists have a new high-tech way to recover fingerprints called vacuum metal deposition."

Ruetsch learned of this new technique, originally discovered in the manufacturing of antiglare glasses, while watching the Discovery Channel one night after work. "I couldn't wait to tell the other members of the task force about it the next day," Ruetsch confirmed.

Equally excited by the prospect of recovering the killer's fingerprints, the task force sent Detective Rick Grabenstein to Costa Mesa, California, to meet with Steve Todd, owner of Vacuum Metal Deposition.

"No matter how old they are, fingerprints leave behind oil or mineral deposits," explained Todd. "I put the plastic bags from Spokane inside a four-foot by five-foot vacuum cylinder in my lab. We turned on the machine and watched as the atmospheric pressure in the chamber reduced to one-millionth of the air pressure in the room, reducing the number of atoms in the chamber. A microscopic atom becomes the size of a baseball."

Any fingerprints are immediately highlighted in the process, which utilizes small amounts of gold dust and zinc dust. "The gold dust coated the chamber and the plastic bags," recalled Grabenstein, "and the zinc dust highlighted the fingerprints."

"The contamination [from the fingerprints] alters the surface of the items in the chamber," Todd explained. The process revealed a partial fingerprint and a full palm print from one of the plastic bags removed from the head of Shawn McClenahan—the palm print of the serial killer.

As for DNA, the Washington State Patrol Crime Laboratory conducted an examination of sperm recovered from McClenahan, Wason, Scott, Oster, and Johnson. "The DNA typing results . . . were compared to possibly find a common genetic profile," reported forensic scientist, William A. Culnane on July 6, 1998. Culnane found a common genetic profile. "An individual with this profile could have contributed DNA to all of the listed samples."

"We had the killer's palm print and his DNA," said Grabenstein. "We just didn't know who he was."

November 17, 1998

Sheriff-elect Mark Sterk, who would command the task force effective January 1, 1999, delineated what he saw as the task force's strengths and weaknesses at a special press conference. "I think they're doing their homework," said Sterk. "One of the things that I really was impressed with is the fact that they are going out and researching other serial killer task forces to learn from them what should be going on. They've done a good job of cooperating with other law enforcement agencies across the state, sharing information but also secreting information that needs to be secreted at this point in order to maintain the integrity of the investigation."

The sheriff-elect also wasn't shy about voicing his concerns. "The one thing that I was always concerned about is that the administration was getting in the way. I think that, at times, the administration has come in and changed the direction of the investigation, instead of letting our trained people do their jobs. I'm going to rely on the people we have sent to the training, who are the professionals in this area, to tell me how this investigation should be going. I feel like I'm more a resource person. I will go out and get you what you need to do the job. Obviously, I will make the policy decisions about how many people are in the unit, but I'm not going to go in and tell our professionals how they should be doing their job."

When asked how the task force would catch the killer, Sterk did not hesitate in his reply. "I think that basically this guy is going to make a mistake. And when he does, we have to have the people in the position to notice the mistake and be so immersed in the case that they realize this is a real lead to the person that's doing the homicides.

"I think we need to narrow the focus," said Sterk. "The first thing you'll see is a link analysis being done. We'll be dumping the information into the computer and doing a very extensive link analysis. I really do want to know who these [victims and suspects] have been associating with, who are the common interests between these people. Once we find that out, we'll start working on eliminating suspects from the case. I do believe we've had contact with this person. We just need to go back through the databases and find out who he is."

The task force morale, according to Sterk, had been "up and down." Detectives Miller and Connelly had left the task force for other assignments, and Sterk referenced them without mentioning their names. "There have been times when certain information has been released on the case that has kind of devastated the investigators. They felt like it shouldn't have been and it hurt the process. . . . I've seen at least two detectives leave the task force because of it.

"Other cases sit on the back burner," acknowledged Sterk, noting the influence the serial killer case was having on other crime-solving efforts. "Probably the biggest thing that's suffering right now is property crimes. We can't get to the burglaries. We can't get to the thefts. We can't get to those kinds of things. When you pull detectives off those kinds of cases, you just don't get to them.

"I want detectives to concentrate," reiterated Sterk, "on finding potential links between the victims and their killer, whose name likely is in police arrest records. I'm not sure if he's from Spokane, but I am convinced we have had contact with him. Either the sheriff's office, Washington State Patrol, or Spokane police have had contact with this guy, and he is in our database."

Sterk also voiced his intention of relieving Doug Silver of his obligations as commander of the task force, replacing him with Lieutenant John Simmons, head of the Major Crimes Unit. "Not only for the task force, but detectives as a whole, it's time for a little different perspective. I would also like to add four new detectives to the task force— two from the sheriff's department, and two Washington State Patrol major crimes detectives."

There were two points on which everyone agreed— the task force had moved with astonishing

quickness and flexibility to establish trusting rela-
tionships with Spokane's prostitutes, and it had
treated the victims' families with compassion and
respect.

"I admire the members of the task force and
feel they have a horrendous job to do," said Kathy
Lloyd, the sister of Shawn McClenahan. "They've
always taken the time to speak with me. And I feel
that communication is crucial in this situation."

"Catching the killer," said Captain Doug Silver,
"may be a combination of luck and legwork." The
task force was legwork-intensive. The luck part
seemed to elude them. "I'm sure we have dealt
with the killer before," insisted Mark Sterk, making
the task force his number one priority. "We'll find
him."

November 30, 1998

Ten dead women begged the citizens of Spokane: HELP US FIND OUR KILLER! The women,
including Yolanda Sapp and Shannon Zelinski,
were all possibly linked to the Spokane serial killer,
and all looked down at motorists from billboards
and into automobiles from the sides of buses. "We
know there's a need to raise community awareness
about these killings that have really been dragging
on our community for a while," said Executive
Director Allen Schweim of the Spokane Transit
Authority. "Offering this space is just one thing
we can do."

The task force worked closely with the Spokane
Transit Authority and local businesses in the design
and placement of the public service billboard. "We

didn't want the public to forget these women or the fact that the killer was still amongst us," said Sergeant Walker.

In the year since its formation, the homicide task force had doubled from four detectives to eight, and the investigation's geography expanded to Tacoma. The murder of Melinda Mercer was officially linked to the Spokane serial killer; the relationship of Connie LaFontaine Ellis's homicide was still undetermined.

"Over fifteen hundred tips have been cleared by the detectives working this case," said Captain Silver, "and we've confirmed nine victims and are investigating the deaths of seventeen others for possible links."

December 1998

While fresh leads dwindled for the task force, orders were drying up at Pantrol, Inc. Robert Lee Yates Jr. needed a new job quickly. Unless he did something fast, the Yates family would not have a happy new year. He shared his feelings about this situation with Aloha Ingram, a prostitute whom he dated on a monthly basis in 1998.

"I dated him regularly until he was hired at Kaiser Aluminum in December 1998 as a replacement worker," recalled former prostitute Ingram. She met him in the winter of 1997 when snow covered the ground; Jennifer Joseph and Heather Hernandez were already dead; Darla Scott was missing. Yates picked up Ingram and a friend at the corner of Second and Division, then drove to the Shilo Inn to have sex with both of them.

"We ordered pizza and had it delivered," recalled Ingram. Her friend fell asleep before the pizza arrived, and she slept through Yates and Ingram having sex. "He talked about his family, sports car, and job as an Army National Guard helicopter pilot," Ingram recalled. "He said he used his job as an excuse to be gone overnight. I asked him if he, as a military pilot, didn't face drug tests, he casually replied: 'Not as a rule.'"

At Kaiser Aluminun, Yates worked as a carbon setter. "It's a physical job," said Larry Strom, vice president of the Mead Union Local. "It's typically a young man's job." The temperatures are over 100 degrees, and Yates wore several layers of clothes, steel-toed boots, and required ear and face protection.

"Me and him were cool," said Tim Buchanan, the man at Kaiser with whom Yates took his coffee breaks. "He played like a leader role, or father role," Buchanan said. "He got along with all of us. He seemed like he was a very family guy. He talked about his daughters just like any other kind of average dad. One time, he brought a booklet on how helicopters were made and showed us which ones he flew before."

His new employment was tough and demanding, but Robert Lee Yates Jr. was trained tough and demanding; Yates, Jr. was never one to shirk his duty to God, country ,or family.

The Christmas season returned. Again, there was no comfort or joy for the families of the serial killer's victims. "Years ago, I'd wait for some random call from my daughter," said Darla Scott's mother, Barbara. "She'd always call and say, 'Hi,

Mom.' Now I wait for a call from someone telling me her murder's been solved. This waiting is harder.''

The home of teacher Kathy Lloyd was bright with festive holiday lights, but her heart was dark with depression. ''This is the lowest month for me,'' Lloyd said. ''Shawn was a big hugger. I'd give anything for just one more hug. Sometimes I think I'd like to go join her. I just keep waiting for the pain to go away. I want to know things that I'm not being told,'' Lloyd commented. ''How was my sister killed? How long was she dead before her body was found? Did she suffer before she died? Who killed her and why? I know I'm not going to get any of those answers until someone's caught.''

''This is tough for an investigator,'' admitted Doug Silver. ''One thing an investigator likes to do, and is accustomed to doing, is solving crimes. Unfortunately, things haven't panned out yet. The possibility exists that we could stumble onto our serial killer in any number of ways. You always hope for that.''

An unexpected witness, a stroke of good fortune, perhaps even divine intervention, could bring successful closure to the task force's diligent investigation. ''But, like we said initially, we're probably looking at a three-to five-year process.''

Part of the process was the utilization of evidence-analyzing software. Tips and leads were entered into databases and were then searched for commonalities. ''Any thread could be the one that unravels the mystery,'' said Silver.

As of Christmas 1998, the Spokane police and sheriff's departments spent close to $500,000 on personnel costs and over $12,000 on travel. "We're not just going to stop the money," County Commissioner Phil Harris said. "Some things are more important than money."

Per Sheriff-elect Mark Sterk's request, the Washington State Patrol agreed to assign an additional detective to the task force in January. "The morale on the task force remains high," said Captain Steve Braun, task force co-commander. "I think things are going extremely well, considering the breadth of the investigation and the amount of information they are dealing with on a daily basis. This is unlike any case that we've ever had here before. We firmly believe that this isn't a Spokane problem. It's a state problem; I see that as another challenge in the coming year, along with building better communications with detectives on the west side of the state."

"And they think *they* had problems," commented Cathy A., longtime Sprague Avenue prostitute. "Things were bad enough for us as it was. Most prostitutes don't work the street, and most prostitutes aren't drug addicts, but I happened to be both, and so were plenty of other girls. Life was hard enough without having to worry about some damn psycho serial killer."

"We're seeing some pretty desperate women out there," said Lynn Everson. "This is a terrible time of year for women and prostitution. If they are addicted to drugs, there is no holiday from that. I also wait for the Spokane community to rise up and demand justice for the serial killer's victims."

"If Lynn is waiting for Mr. and Mrs. Spokane to give a rat's ass about drug addict-hookers, I can tell her exactly when that's gonna happen," remarked one streetwalker sarcastically, "the same day that the compassionate Christians of this fair city joyously arise to fund that women's shelter she's always talking about."

"One response to the serial killer's presence in our community was to open a shelter that accepts any woman that comes to the door without regard for chemical use, mental-health status, or lifestyle," said Everson a few years later. "It's called Hope House and was opened by a group of people who believe that every woman deserves a safe place. Those of us who worked on opening the shelter had no experience with shelters, but all of us had experience with working with women out in the streets and believed that this was critical to our community."

Critical for the victims' families was word of significant progress in the investigation. "It's hard, hard to wait for word every day," said Darla Scott's mother. "I just hope someone's still out there, searching."

The task force was still searching, and in December 1998, Detective Marty Hill compared the tire photographs taken on Tuesday, May 15, 1990, near the body of Kathleen Brisbois, with tire tracks found close to Michelyn Derning's body. They matched. "Similar tracks were spotted in an unsolved murder from Kitsap County," confirmed Sergeant Cal Walker. "We delved into it pretty hot and heavy, and our crime lab technicians identified the tracks as Goodyear Eagle GTs." These tires, Eagle GT, are standard on police squad cars. "The end result," remarked Walker with a sigh, "was that supervisors reminded patrol officers to not park close to crime scenes."

Accusations and suspicions were rampant, and the belief that the killer was a rogue cop remained ripe on the streets. "One pimp thought Fred Ruetsch and I were viable suspects," said Walker. One Spokane citizen, confusing correlation with causation, wrote to the task force noting that the killings stopped when Police Chief Mangnan resigned after eleven years with the police department to join the FBI.

Police Chief Alan Chertok would mention this in an offhand manner while speaking at a local high school in 1999, fueling a mounting fire of discontent and precipitate a major crisis in the Spokane Police Department. As for the Spokane serial killer, he also had problems—financial and sexual.

CHAPTER TEN

"I noticed that we were running out of money," said Linda Yates, "and I complained about his frequent withdrawals from ATMs. For the first time in our marriage, he started telling me to get a job." Her husband, commandeering cash for crack and companionship, needed a second source of income, and wanted a reliable erection.

Yates had problems with impotence, a fact never mentioned by his prostitute companions. Those who experienced it firsthand wound up facedown. Perhaps, he told his wife, he should pursue a prescription for Viagra. "I told him, 'It's okay. You're probably tired and I'm tired.'" Sex, however, was Yates's obsession. "I found magazines featuring orgies and lists of people interested in group sex, and he asked me if I fantasized about making out with another woman."

When Linda noticed credit card receipts from Al's Spa Tub Motel, she wanted to know who he took there and why. Yates told her that after grueling twelve-hour shifts at Kaiser, he used the motel's hot tub to relieve his aching muscles. In truth, Al's Spa Tub Motel was where he took one of his regular prostitute dates.

"He picked me up at Trudeau's Marina on East Sprague, then drove down Division Street to Al's Spa Tub Motel, chatting freely about his daughters," recalled Julie, who dated him several times in 1998. "What is this dude's wife thinking? He's out half the night. He's getting two hundred and up out of the cash machine. Where's the money coming from?" The money was coming from the ATM, and the cash from the ATM came from the Yates family savings account.

"In terms of tricks on the street, he was not that different," said Lynn Everson in retrospect. "Men drive a variety of cars, everything from broken-down pickups to Mercedes . . . Lincoln Continentals. A number of those cars have child seats in the back, and many of those men—as it seems to me that Yates was—have sexual addictions in that they are frequently out on the prowl, driving around looking for women. There seems to be a lot of that, and there are repeat customers. It is a very hidden activity in that it is shameful to many men that they do that. Many of them drive family cars."

"The credit card bills confirmed my suspicion that my husband was having affairs," said Linda Yates. "The bills showed he'd been going to the motel for at least a year. I was raised with old-fashioned values: when you marry, you marry. Apparently, he didn't take it seriously like I did."

Yates's daughter Sonja also had her suspicions about her father's lifestyle outside the home. "I found my father's address book one day and started calling the numbers of women whose names I didn't recognize," she later told reporters. All the women denied knowing Robert Lee Yates Jr., and Yates told his daughter that the women were selling him head gaskets and other automotive items.

"I think people get the impression that a serial killer is someone you can spot a mile away," said Keith Kirkingberg, a chaplain at the Spokane County Sheriff's Office. "That only adds to the burden of the wife, because when they say, 'I have no idea,' folks are saying, 'Oh, come on, how can they not know?' "

Linda Yates later acknowledged that there were clues. "Especially when he said he was going hunting and he was dressed up nice and had cologne on," she told NBC's *Dateline*. "You don't go out hunting with cologne on. Who goes on a 'hunting trip' wearing cologne? He always had answers to everything," she said.

"There are a lot of women who don't really know what their husbands are doing," said Ann Rule, former Seattle policewoman and accomplished true-crime author. "The average woman will imagine everything, including 'Is my husband gay?' or 'Does my husband have another woman?' before she thinks, 'Is my husband a serial killer?' "

"The women I hear from are women who have suspicions they just don't want to believe," Rule said. "The men were gone odd hours, coming home dirty, wet, nervous, sleepy, drunk, smelling funny, without an explanation. . . . All of these women heaved sighs of relief when I told them there were so many wives with the same stories whose husbands didn't turn out to be the Green River killer."

According to experts, it's not fair to judge the wife of the serial killer. After all, if it is someone no one would ever suspect, the wife would never suspect him, either. The wife is not stupid, ignorant, or completely submissive. There may be such a division in the killer's personality that the social veneer that separates one life—husband and father—from the other life—crazed murderer— never weakens, crumbles, or intersects.

To successfully blend in with society, many violent serial sex offenders develop a thick superficial veneer of personality that is entirely disassociated from their violent criminal behavior. "Violent serial sex offenders are successful criminals," states forensic scientist Brent Turvey. "They are intelligent enough to avoid detection and persist in the repeated commission of their crimes. They live in our society with little or no leakage as to their true nature. Many are married or in a relationship."

The more intricate the fantasy, the more the victim is regarded as a mere object, and the more distance is then mentally created between the violent criminal behavior and the superficial veneer of personality. "The behavior of the serial sex offender deliberately avoids detection, indicating that the offender knows full well that the behavior is not acceptable to society," says Turvey. The normal behavior of the violent serial offender in social contexts is deliberate, and it is judiciously practiced. All people display more emotional transparency with family members in the home than they do with coworkers on the job, but for the serial sex killer, veneer is more extreme and the idea is to keep the two "lives" or "worlds" absolutely separate.

By 1999, the two worlds of Robert Lee Yates Jr. were merging into one. Prior to New Year's, he brought home the ultimate souvenir—a corpse. With great attention to aesthetic detail, he buried the body of Melody Ann Murfin in his backyard, directly under his own bedroom window. On March 2, a dog belonging to Joe Rohrback also brought home an unusual souvenir from an evening romp in the woods near Preston, Washington—a human hand.

"We're treating the case as a possible homicide," confirmed the King County Sheriff's Office, "but the cause of death has not been determined." The King County medical examiner identified the body, found in what appeared to be a rural dumping ground two miles from the dog's food dish, as that of Jennifer Diane Justus, twenty-six. Reported missing from the Seattle area by her mother in November, Justus had a history of prostitution, drugs, and theft in the Seattle area. "We'll check into it," said Doug Silver of the homicide task force, "but right now, there's nothing linking her to Spokane." Justus, despite fitting aspects of other victims' profiles, was not deemed the serial killer's eleventh victim.

March 17, 1999

Spokane prostitute Cheryl Sickerman stood at her usual corner at First and Scott awaiting her next customer. A 1985 Honda Accord slowed down, the

driver nodded, and when the car stopped, Sickerman got in.

With her usual friendly professionalism and
pleasant demeanor, Cheryl recited the enticing
items on her sexual menu. He ordered oral sex.
"Cheryl dated the driver of Washington license
507JKN on March 17, 1999," recalled her boyfriend, Joe Lockridge. Concerned about the serial
killer, the considerate Lockridge kept track of every
customer's vehicle description and license plate
number. If Cheryl didn't return within a reasonable amount of time, he could call the police with
an accurate description of the customer's car.

Sickerman returned heady, unharmed, and
twenty dollars richer. The customer, Robert Lee
Yates Jr., didn't harm a hair on her head. Perhaps
he was exhibiting remarkable control. Perhaps he
had "caught his limit." Or maybe the meshing of
worlds scared him. The well-veneered wall separat-
ing social conventions from his sexual predator
deviations was evaporating like the morning mist
back home on Whidbey Island. "One minute, he
could be real easygoing," recalled his wife, "and
then go into a room, come out, and be a totally
whole different person."

The majority of Spokane police officers wanted
a different person as chief of police. This internal
conflict proved destabilizing and dispiriting to the
police department; it distracted the smooth func-
tioning of the homicide task force, which, on January 8, officially added Connie LaFonatine Ellis to
the victim list.

There were, thankfully, no new bodies uncovered after the holidays. There were also no new

clues. An experimental investigation, based upon the contents of Linda Maybin's stomach, only revealed her last meal was vegetarian Chinese.

April 14, 1999

The affluent home of Dr. Joseph S. Taylor was raided by task force detectives who seized bed-sheets, pillows, and a 9mm pistol. They also searched Taylor's 1990 red Toyota SUV.

The case against Taylor, subsequently abandoned, began in February when a twenty-five-year-old prostitute told police that a man abducted her at gunpoint, forced her to the floor of his Toyota 4Runner, and threatened to kill her while he drove to his house.

"When we got there," she told detectives, "he raped me and pistol-whipped me." Police didn't have a warrant until April because the victim didn't know the address, and couldn't recognize the house. Patrolling the general area searching for clues, an investigator spotted Taylor's 4Runner in his garage.

The woman, however, refused to cooperate further with authorities, and would not testify in court against Dr. Taylor. "Without her testimony, the case against Taylor is too weak to take to trial," said a task force spokesperson. "We need more from a witness than just a report. She's declining any contact with law enforcement at this point, and without that, we can't get answers to some unanswered questions. The statute of limitations in such cases is ten years," the source added, "so things could still happen."

Taylor's attorney, Carl Hueber, was pleased that his client was never actually arrested or charged. "These allegations were very serious and were thoroughly investigated," Hueber said. "I'm pleased that Doctor Taylor was cleared."

April 17, 1999

Kelly Conway, 23, suffered from diminished mental capacity, was easily manipulated, and last seen at the Helen Apartments with 300-pound Stanley L. Pietrzak, a convicted child rapist, the night before she vanished.

"I strangled Conway," bragged Pietrzak to fellow tenants. "I cut off her head and hands, and burned her body in the basement furnace." Investigating Conway's disappearance, Detective Terry Hammer found 1,300 charred pieces of human bone in the apartment building's furnace. Forensic anthropologist Sarah Keller pieced together the skeleton, and true to Pietrzak's bragging, the hands and head were missing.

"Detective Hammer also found human hair hanging from a pipe in the furnace room," said Cal Walker. "Scientists matched the DNA samples from the hair with a pap smear taken from Ms Conway at a Spokane hospital."

At his murder trial, Pietrzak admitted beheading, dismembering, and burning Conway's body. He insisted, however, that she was already dead when he chopped of her head. "I still kick myself time and time again for not telling authorities," said Pietrzak.

"For a while, he was our prime serial killer suspect," said Walker, "but his DNA did not match the serial killer's DNA."

With decomposed hands found in a dog-food-dish, and charred bones found in a basement furnace, 1999 was off to a depressing start. As for Police Chief Chertok, things were going from bad to worse. From every indication, Chief Alan Chertok faced revolution within his department and harsh criticism from every direction.

The local police officers union termed him "an ineffectual leader," and interdepartmental personality clashes made local headlines. City Manager Bill Pupo reprimanded Chertok early in 1999 when the new chief got into an argument with a uniformed patrolman regarding jumper cables.

"The allegations [against me] are part of a concerted effort by police department insiders to drive me out of Spokane," said Chertok. It was no secret that Chertok, selected after an extensive nationwide search, was not the man favored for the position by the 285-officer department. Deputy Chief of Police Roger Bragdon was "one of our own," but he was eliminated from consideration because he did not meet the city requirement of a bachelor's degree.

"Some members of the force are challenging me because of the initiatives I've talked of implementing," Chertok insisted, "including a possible revamping of the way patrol officers are deployed." The Lieutenants and Captains Association disputed Chertok's comments. "No individual member of this association is aware of any substantial changes made by or planned changes initiated by Chief Chertok in the police department."

"I may just jump into the airplane and go flying," said Chertok, speaking of his Cessna 182M Skylane. "It's a good time to do it." With critics and officers snapping at his boot heels, Chertok took an unscheduled holiday to fly the comparatively friendly skies. His landing, however, was bumpy.

Steve Tucker, prosecuting attorney, was already investigating remarks made by Chertok to a Ferris High School classroom—remarks about the serial killer investigation.

"All officers—except those on the task force chasing the serial killer—are forbidden from talking about the serial killer case," stated the Spokane Police Guild, representing over two hundred local police officers. "Any member represented by the Spokane Police Guild would be disciplined for violating this order."

"I opened my mouth as wide as I could and jammed my foot into it," said Chertok lightheartedly, but detectives were seriously evaluating whether or not Chertok jeopardized the case. "The Ferris incident was simply a gaffe that has since spun out of control. I was talking about the serial killer case. I told the students that the task force had received thousands of tips from the public, including at least one about Mangnan."

"I don't think Chertok meant to imply that Mangan was a suspect," Terren Roloff, a spokeswoman for Spokane District 81, said to the press. Roloff confirmed that "the kids said they thought Chertok was joking about Mangnan."

"The detectives were attempting to dispel rumors about Mangnan and to protect Chertok's credibility," said Sheriff Sterk, who acknowledged that what

Chertok said was simple fact—tips about Mangnan did come in, but they were never taken seriously. "My comment about Mangnan wasn't meant to be taken seriously," said Chertok, "and I think the entire incident is being blown out of proportion."

"The investigation began after a parent of one of the students in the class wrote a letter to the sheriff's department about Chertok's comments," Sterk later explained. "Sergeant Cal Walker was dispatched to interview that parent and student." It was Bill Pupo who asked that Sterk expand the investigation to the rest of the students.

"With great reluctance, I agreed," said Sterk. "I was hesitant because my agency works with the police department on a daily basis." The investigation's findings were then forwarded on to Spokane County prosecutor Steve Tucker. "That's strictly routine," Sterk said. "For the record, I don't think any criminal charges will be coming out of this."

The Lieutenants and Captains Association, unfavorably disposed to Chertok, faxed a press release directly from police headquarters. "The chief of police should be above reproach in matters concerning credibility. This is not the case with Chief Chertok, as questions regarding his credibility continue to be raised."

"I have no plans to resign," said Chertok. One day later, May 27, Chertok resigned. "The chief has submitted his resignation and I've accepted his resignation," City Manager Bill Pupo said. "Chertok received a $65,000 severance package and agreed not to sue the city." Deputy Chief Roger Bragdon was designated acting chief.

What the task force found most disconcerting

about the Chertok incident wasn't the comment about Mangnan, it was Chertok's revelation to the students that the task force had the killer's DNA. Of course, no mention was made of this comment in anything for public consumption.

June 7, 1999

Lynn Everson's dream of a shelter in downtown Spokane that didn't discriminate against chemically dependent homeless women became a reality in the first week of June. The shelter accepted single women without children, and they didn't have to be clean, sober, upstanding members of the community. It wasn't mandatory that these women be in near-perfect physical shape and radiating good health. The women did not have to be in tip-top physical health and compulsion free to qualify for a night safe from the serial killer.

The serial killer wasn't feeling particularly safe himself. Burning the receipt doesn't erase the transaction, and some tracks can never be covered. Impotence, financial disaster, erotic obsessions, and an ever-increasing reliance upon crack, meth, and heroin were self-evident indications that Robert Lee Yates Jr.'s life was out of control.

He knew something was definitely wrong in September 1999. The most obvious indicator wasn't the number of dead women he'd tossed down gullies, dumped like garbage, or lovingly interred in his backyard. He knew something was wrong because the Spokane homicide task force wanted him to come down to the office and answer a few questions.

"Yates was considered a person of interest because he was connected to East Sprague prostitutes, but he was in a class of hundreds of other 'persons of interest,' " said Cal Walker. "Each and every one of these people that we contacted were approached much the same way," he explained. "Essentially, what they were told was simply that their lifestyle made them a suspect in the series of prostitute homicides, that we weren't interested in pursuing drug or prostitution-solicitation charges against them, and we were giving them an opportunity to clear themselves as a suspect through a DNA test."

The task force didn't want to make the error of chasing all its best leads and overlooking others. "We had databases detailing known sex offenders, and one that contained the identities of people linked to East Sprague through traffic offense or criminal behavior," said Walker. "A significant problem was that these databases were incompatible with each other, and we kept changing data systems and software, and every time we did that, we had to enter the information all over again."

When Sergeant Cal Walker assigned tips to task force personnel, he picked a mix of the top two priorities. "If we had only been looking in our number one tips, Mr. Yates might still be on the streets today," said Walker. "Yates was in our 'twos' category. Eventually, Yate's name came up on the list. He was simply the next one to be interviewed."

Males by the hundreds were summoned to task force headquarters, questioned, and asked to provide a blood sample. "We were getting five to six voluntary blood samples a day," said Walker, "and with the demand for DNA testing constantly rising, you know there's a backlog. The lab can only do so much. Also, there is not yet a comprehensive DNA data bank. But every conceivable suspect was asked to provide a sample of their blood. Giving it, of course, was one hundred percent voluntary and we made sure that everyone we asked knew that it was entirely up to them."

September 15, 1999

Robert Lee Yates Jr. arrived at the Public Safety Building on time, and on edge. Detectives Rick Grabenstein and Dave Bentley asked questions; Yates answered and sweated.

"We asked Yates if he procured the services of prostitutes," recalled Grabenstein, "and he admitted that he used their services occasionally when he was stationed in Germany, but he denied having any association with the prostitutes on Sprague Street here in Spokane."

He also told a story about giving a young prostitute a ride in the rain but turning town any offer of sexual relations. When detectives inquired about the incident with Jennifer Robinson, Yates simply recounted the concocted explanation: "Her father requested that I pick her up and give her a ride home."

"Mr. Yates was very nervous," reported Grabenstein, "and he was unable to provide alibis for two significant dates related to the homicides." Ironically, when detectives mistakenly referred to him driving a white Chevrolet Camaro when stopped by Officer Turman on Sprague in 1997, Yates corrected them. "No, that wasn't a Camaro. It was a white Corvette."

Captain Doug Silver had built an extensive database of Corvettes, including every Corvette in Washington and Idaho. Corvette clubs were contacted and membership roles acquired. "We had the clue of the white Corvette from the beginning, but it's exceptionally easy to give a car a new paint job," said Walker, "and there are plenty of Corvettes in Washington and Idaho."

At the conclusion of our interview with Mr. Yates," said Grabenstein, "we asked him if he would provide a blood sample. He told us that he wanted to think about it. While that was certainly his right, it wasn't a good sign. Also," noted the detective, "it seemed to us that Mr. Yates sweated too much. The next day, we contacted Jennifer Robinson."

"Yes, I remember the incident involving me and him and the police that night," she told detectives. "When the police stopped us, I told him to tell the cops that story about my father—it wasn't true at all. In fact, my father doesn't even live in Spokane, and he never worked with that guy in his life."

September 18, 1999

Three days after the interview, Yates called Grabenstein and left a message that he would not be providing a blood sample. "That placed him in a smaller class of suspects," Walker said. "We were especially interested in anyone who was reticent to submit to a DNA test. Plus, his previous ownership of a Corvette made him of significant interest. We pretty much decided to go looking for the car—and this would not be the first Corvette found and

searched as part of this investigation. We had been
through this process before," confirmed Walker.
"Each time, of course, we hoped that we had found
the right car and the correct suspect. Plus, forensic
investigation takes time—it is very detailed work."

The investigation was taking its toll, emotionally
and physically, on the task force personel. Detectives Fred Ruetsch and Bill Miller both suffered
from insomnia. "I became so obsessed," said
Detective Miller, "I bout of pneumonia. Miller's
health also suffered as his weight increased along
with his obsession. "After my doctor prescribed
high blood pressure medication, I returned to the
major crimes unit in early December."

December 24, 1999

The day before Christmas, the task force received
its much anticipated, long-awaited, and much
dreaded holiday lump of coal—the Spokane Police
Department pulled its five detectives from the task
force. "It's a priority we can't fund," Police Chief
Roger Bragdon said. "We're embarrassed we can't
do that."

None of the detectives wanted to walk out on
the city's most important homicide investigation,
but orders are orders. "There was some anger,
some resentment, some confusion, some armchair
quarterbacking," said Detective Brian Hamond in
retrospect. "When you're deeply engrossed in the
whole thing, it's not easy to just walk away—it's
not an easy thing to do at all."

"The moral for those of us who remained was
pretty low," recalled Rick Grabenstein. "It felt like

the police brass were abandoning what they believed was a sinking ship, another failed Green River killer investigation. It was like they wanted to distance themselves as far and fast as possible. Before this, the moral was really upbeat. Now, we were very concerned that the Spokane County commissioners might disband the task force all together.''

January 7, 2000

The task force tracked down Rita Jones, the owner of what was once Yates's white Corvette. A title records check showed that Yates had owned the Corvette from September 8, 1994, through May 7, 1998.

"Rita Jones told us that the carpeting in the car, according to Yates, had been changed a year earlier," reported Grabenstein. "She consented to a search of the vehicle, during which several fiber samples were obtained from various locations throughout the car," said the detective. "The samples were then submitted to the Washington State Crime Laboratory for analysis. Then we found evidence that the Corvette's carpet had been changed twice over a two-year period, instead of only once. We thought that was rather unusual. I mean, you don't change your car's carpet that often unless it is ruined pretty bad—damaged or severely stained."

"I took several pictures of my wife in the classic Corvette she loved," said her husband, Bruce H. Jones, "before it was seized by sheriff's detectives."

"The vehicle wasn't seized immediately," confirmed Walker. "We took a fiber sample from the car's interior on the seventh of January, 2000, and turned it over to the lab. The task force continued to look at hundreds of other leads. We processed that Corvette exactly as we had the previous Corvettes and other vehicles that we examined for evidence. We had our big break; we just didn't know it yet. The investigation continued on all fronts, even with our reduced resources."

January 14, 2000

Task force detectives interviewed Yates's former employer at Pantrol. "Yates had a number of vehicles while working at Pantrol," he said, "including a mid-80s model Ford pickup, possibly a four-wheel drive, and a van. Although I don't recall the van well enough to describe it, I do know that Yates got it in June 1998." The date that Yates acquired the van was about two months before his encounter with Christine Smith.

February 28, 2000

"We are not about to disband the task force," insisted Sheriff Mark Sterk at the standing-room-only audience of about 250 in the county's Public Works Building. The dramatic public meeting, held on Sterk's forty-eighth birthday, clearly demonstrated that despite the task force's size being halved, its dedication and resolve remained intact.

"We didn't expect this kind of crowd, quite frankly," admitted the pleasantly surprised sheriff before revealing a surprise of his own. "We will make an arrest in this case," he announced emphatically. "In fact, when we make an arrest in this case, and I'm sure that we will, we will be certain that we have the person responsible for killing these women because investigators have conclusive DNA evidence that is an 'exclusive identifier' of the killer."

"I think that's the first time in this state that anyone has even discussed DNA evidence before an arrest was made," Spokane County Sheriff's Corporal Dave Reagan said. "But we had to do something to keep up the public interest in this. It's hard to keep this on the front page without new information."

"The FBI has also joined the search for the serial killer," said Sterk. "We will solve this case when we run across the right person because we do have DNA evidence in the case. The challenge is finding the right person."

"We thought we had the right person at the time we called that meeting," Cal Walker later commented, and he wasn't referring to Robert Lee Yates Jr. In mid-February, Detectives Bentley and Hammer heard of a local businessman who fantasized about killing prostitutes. "He wasn't on any suspect list previously, but that tip made him a man of significant interest."

"We needed covert surveillance help," said Walker, and that meant Sergeant Rick VanLeuven's undercover team from the Career Criminal Unit. "They would follow suspects who refused to give blood samples and collect their DNA from a pop can, or maybe a cigarette butt."

VanLeuven's team shadowed the businessman for three days, following him to restaurants, video rental outlets, and grocery stores. "The first two days he never left behind anything that could provide DNA," recalled Walker. "We weren't going to go up and take a straw out of his drink. It had to be something he left behind. On the third day, however, he met some friends downtown after work. They were having dinner, and at a nearby table were Deputy Mike Drapo and VanLeuven." Undercover deputies Erick Nelson and Lloyd Hixson were outside watching the man's car.

"We sipped on Diet Pepsi and ate appetizers while we watched him," VanLeuven said. "We memorized where he was sitting and everything he used to eat dinner."

When dinner ended, the customers left, and Deputy Drapo guarded the table while VanLeuven talked to the restaurant's manager. "I told him there were a couple of items on the table we wanted for evidence, and paid him $4.35 for it."

"VanLeuven placed a water glass, napkin, set of silverware and coffee cup in a paper evidence bag," said Detective Rick Grabenstein, "and I planned to send it all off to the Washington State Patrol Lab to obtain the guy's DNA. But, the man kept talking about killing a prostitute, and we were worried that he might do it before we got the results back."

"We couldn't take the chance that he might actually commit this crime while we were investigating," Walker said later. "We decided we needed to approach him directly, tell him what we knew and get a blood draw to make sure he wasn't our serial killer."

"We finally just went up to him, told the man

we knew about his fantasy, and that he needed to get a new one," said Walker. "Well, he willingly gave us a blood sample. When we got back the results, it turned out his fantasy was exactly that— a fantasy. He wasn't the killer."

"It was a bit of a letdown for the task force," acknowledged Detective Grabenstein. "We thought we might have found our man." On the other hand, the DNA samples from the serial killer eliminated one more suspect. If the task force detectives hadn't received a tip from the public about the man's fantasy, there was always the possibility that he may have crossed the line and acted on it.

"It was to encourage the public to continue providing tips and leads in the case that Sheriff Sterk called the February twenty-eighth meeting," said Walker, "and FBI Agent Charles Mandigo told folks that this investigation was only the second local serial killer case the agency had ever investigated."

"The FBI conducted interviews with possible suspects in Idaho, Montana, and South Dakota," said Mandigo. [They] interviewed a possible witness in Tennessee, checked the military records of a potential suspect in Missouri, and looked into a similar series of unsolved killings in Germany. The FBI will pursue all possible suspects," Mandigo assured the audience, "including those who work in law enforcement."

"There have been some suggestions," Sterk said, "that we shouldn't invest large financial resources on a case in which prostitutes are murdered." There was no way, said the sheriff, that he could sanction such a disregard for human life. "This guy has killed upward of eighteen women—he's left this community before, I am convinced of it—and he's come back."

"We handed out a sheet showing the eighteen slain women, with the dates each of their bodies were found," recalled Walker. "There was a gap of more than three years between two of the slayings, but gaps of just a few days in others. We hoped that maybe the timeline would jog someone's memory and lead to a new tip that would help solve the case."

"The DNA evidence enabled detectives to eliminate thousands of suspects," said Sterk. "Unlike the Green River case at that time, we had good physical evidence. We believed that the suspect was in our database and that he had been contacted by law enforcement in Spokane before."

"I'm begging you to help out. Let's get this guy stopped," pleaded Steve LaFontaine, brother of victim Connie LaFontaine Ellis. An important aspect of "getting this guy stopped" was not impeding the cash flow to the task force.

"Sheriff Sterk also used this public forum to impress upon the public the importance of funding," recalled Walker. "We faced mounting evidence costs. Over one thousand items of evidence were collected at that time, and processing costs had grown to over two hundred thousand dollars." Citizens were encouraged to contact the county commissioners and voice their support for continued funding of the task force investigation.

"The task force's major complaint was a lack of resources," Sterk later commented. "They needed forensic work done, as well as new computers and an experienced crime analyst, a position for which they never received funding. The most difficult time was when county commissioners suggested breaking up the task force and allocating the funds elsewhere.''

March 17, 2000

The reward money offered in the search for the Spokane serial killer increased to $20,000 when the FBI contributed $10,000 for information leading to the arrest of a suspect. Another $10,000 was already offered by the Secret Witness program. Federal agents confirmed that the FBI was stepping up its involvement in the case. ''We followed up investigations in Tennessee, Indiana, Montana, South Dakota, and a couple of other states at the request of the task force,'' said FBI Special Agent Norm Brown.

Every conceivable clue and aspect of the investigation was given microscopic evaluation, including ragged pieces of paper towels found with the bodies. Even the most mundane item is someone's specialty, and the Fiber Science Group at Integrated Paper Services in Appleton, Wisconsin, wrote the book on paper.

''Enclosed is a paper towel from a roll of towels at a local retail establishment,'' wrote Detective Rick Grabenstein on March 24, 1999. ''I would request examination of this towel to determine if it is of similar composition to towels previously submitted to you. . . . [If so], we would then want the more extensive examination as conducted on the original three towels.''

Grabenstein hoped to identify the brand and origin of the paper towels utilized by the serial killer. Where he bought them, who sold them, and other such details could be of marked significance. "I learned more about paper towels during that investigation than I ever cared to learn," acknowledged Grabenstein. No degree of analysis, however, revealed the brand, manufacturer, or distributor of the "serial killer paper towels."

April 5, 2000

Forensic scientist Kevin Jenkins looked through the eyepiece of his desk-sized light comparison microscope. He examined two fibers side by side, looking for similarities. One fiber was from Yates's Corvette; the other was found with Jennifer Joseph's body. They matched perfectly. Jenkins grabbed the telephone and called Sergeant Walker. "Cal," said Jenkins excitedly, "come to the lab right away."

Walker looked through the eyepiece while Kevin Jenkins provided commentary. "In the world of fibers," Jenkins explained, "two fibers don't match any better than these two." Another group of fibers, although lighter and a slightly different color, were also similar to a fiber recovered during the Joseph investigation.

"As soon as we had the fiber match," Walker recalled, "we set up twenty-four-hour-a-day surveillance on Yates, and started planning how we were going to arrest him. The sheriff was out of town, but we got hold of him right away."

Sheriff Mark Sterk of Spokane and Sheriff Mike

Humphries of Walla Walla are the best of friends. They were together in Colorado for training at the National Sheriff's Institute when Humphries noticed nervousness in his old friend's behavior. "I could tell there was something going on," he recalled, "so we talked about it a little bit. What was happening is that he knew they were getting close to actually making an arrest in the serial killer case; he put a lot of time and effort into it and was eager to get back on the job.

"I was supposed to take Mark to the airport, but on that particular night, he couldn't get a flight out," Humphries said. "So, with extra time together, we talked about his serial killer case, and he told me that they had evidence tying a certain suspect, Mr. Yates, to the slaying of one particular woman, and that an arrest was imminent. He shared some details of the homicides, then said, 'I think this guy was from Walla Walla.' Well, the more he told me about the recurring patterns— the placement of the bodies, and especially the gunshot wounds to the head—the more fascinated I became. I immediately called back to Walla Walla."

Humphries had Detective Skeeters dig out the Oliver/Savage file and do some backtracking. Sure enough, Robert Lee Yates Jr. not only lived and worked in Walla Walla County at the time of the slayings, he owned a Ruger .357, which he purchased from Payless Drug in 1974.

"Upon checking the files," reported Skeeters, "Yates's name was mentioned as purchasing some S&W .357 ammo from Payless Drug on 07-03-1975. This was ten days prior to the shootings. I then checked with the Walla Walla Police Department and learned that Yates purchased a Ruger .357-caliber revolver, bearing serial number 150-50785, from Payless Drug on April 25, 1974. A check with the Washington State Penitentiary showed Yates worked there for a short time beginning in July 1975. It was suggested that I contact a William Brewer, a retired employee of the Washington State Penitentiary, and also the father in-law of Yates, for further information."

On April 4, at 11:45 A.M., Detective Skeeters made contact with William L. Brewer. "He confirmed that Yates did work at the penitentiary for a short time in 1975, that Yates owned several guns. Brewer further advised," said Skeeters, "that Yates had a favorite place up Mill Creek."

Additional investigation revealed the serial number of the weapon and its posthomicide history. Yates sold the weapon to Kesselrings Sporting Goods in his hometown of Oak Harbor, where it was soon purchased by Larry W. Johnston. "When I spoke to Mr. Johnston," said Skeeters, "he told me that he had sold the weapon to a private party by the name of Halvorson in either 1977 or 1978, and he couldn't provide more information than that."

Important information, however, was forthcoming from Sturm Ruger Arms, the weapon's manufacturer. "They provided the serial number of the weapon," said Skeeters. "They told us that it would have five lands and grooves, with a right twist. This would be consistent with the weapon used in this homicide."

Skeeters's dedication led to a quick recovery of the weapon and an immediate analysis. The results, however, were slightly disappointing. "The lab couldn't say conclusively that this was definitely the weapon used to kill Patrick Oliver and Susan Savage," explained Humphries, "and they also conclusively couldn't say that it wasn't the murder weapon. The reason the tests were not conclusive is that a weapon's rifling characteristics change over a period of twenty-five years."

The results were consistent with the type of weapon utilized in the killings. Because of all the supportive circumstances, Humphries said, "We are *assuming* that this is the murder weapon."

April 10, 2000

Detective Grabenstein prepared a search warrant for the Corvette and took it to Judge Michael Donohue of the Spokane County Superior Court. As with all previous search warrants related to the investigation, this one also was kept secret. Dried flakes of blood were recovered from the driver's-side seat belt, the rear deck, under the rear-deck carpet, and from a fire extinguisher holder. Under the passenger seat was the matching mother-of-pearl button missing from Jennifer Joseph's blouse.

"There were several areas on the passenger-side floorboard that appeared bloodstained," reported Grabenstein, "and we noted what appeared to be dried bloodstains and flakes of dried blood on the bottom of the passenger seat." DNA was extracted from three of these suspected bloodstains, and tests revealed that all the blood was from the same person.

"Blood samples had previously been obtained from Jennifer Joseph's parents," Sergeant Walker later commented, "and DNA had been extracted from those samples. Results of the DNA comparisons between the blood from Joseph's parents and the bloodstains found inside the Corvette were matched."

From all indications, detectives finally had the "big breakthrough" they had always wanted. Then, three days later, news came from Michigan that Robert Lee Yates Jr. might not be the only serial killer claiming Spokane victims.

CHAPTER ELEVEN

April 13, 2000

"Spokane was not the only city searching for a
serial killer," said Cal Walker. "Five Detroit prostitutes died violently at the hands of a former navy
fueler, identified as John Eric Armstrong." Detroit
police believe Armstrong's alleged killing spree
may have begun eight years ago in North Carolina
when he joined the navy in Raleigh.

There may be eighteen to twenty deaths worldwide associated with the suspected Mr. Armstrong.
"As the investigation keeps going on, bodies keep
popping up. The numbers keep increasing," said
Officer Octaveious Miles. "There is a similar pattern that ties them all together that creates a trail."

A Detroit radio station announced that Armstrong confessed to killing a Spokane woman, giving rise to speculation that perhaps Armstrong was
not only Detroit's prime suspect but Spokane's as
well. The Detroit killings shared similarities to the

Spokane murders—similar victim profiles and dump sites—but they were dramatically different in method.

The Detroit killer strangled his victims; the Spokane killer shot them in the head. "Spokane's investigators haven't contacted Detroit police yet," confirmed Sergeant Walker on that date. "Every time a serial killer gets arrested, the phone rings off the hook with calls from every agency with outstanding murder cases. We thought we'd wait a few days before making the call to find out if these cases are related." Walker, of course, already knew that the task force was ready to move in on Robert Lee Yates Jr. immediately after the weekend—the weekend that Robert Lee Yates Jr. broke down sobbing.

Saturday morning, April 15, 2000, Linda Yates was told an outright lie. Her husband said he was going to Tacoma to return some military clothing to Fort Lewis. In truth, he was going to Al's Spa Tub Motel for sex with a local prostitute. Linda questioned him about receipts from Al's Spa Tub Motel as far back as December 1999, and she had suspected her husband of having an affair or a series of affairs. Equally troubling was the sudden and inexplicable shrinking of their bank balance.

A $600 difference between Linda's check register and the most recent bank statement triggered anger and confusion. "There's got to be a mistake," she said angrily. That's when Robert Lee Yates Jr., killer of at least thirteen innocent victims, broke down and confessed—confessed a lie.

"Linda, I have a problem," he said, sobbing. "You need to help me." Having a problem was more than obvious—this was no revelation to the distraught Linda Yates. "Sure, I knew he had a problem. I just couldn't figure out what it was."

One symptom was his irresponsible use of the family's finances. He recently attended U.S. Army National Guard high-altitude flight training in Colorado, all expenses paid. In addition, Yates spent another $2,100, telling Linda that he'd purchased presents for the kids and her, and sent them to Spokane via UPS. "They should arrive any day," he assured her. Those gifts didn't exist, and they would never arrive. He confessed that lie and admitted draining the family finances by using ATMs as the spigot of convenience.

His face soaked with tears, Robert Lee Yates Jr. told his wife where the money went—but he didn't tell her the truth. "I have a gambling problem," he said, and Linda didn't know if this was confession or fabrication. Either way, Linda Yates's sympathy account was overdrawn. Her husband cried; she left the room. "He boohooed," she recalled. "I walked out. I knew then that he'd lost his grip. I sensed that something terrible was about to happen."

April 17, 2000

On the night of Monday, April 17, 2000, while the Yates family peacefully slept, detectives had already staked out the Yates household and preplanned their arrest strategy. "They had been there since noon [on] Monday," explained Walker. "They saw Mr. Yates come home from work, watched him play catch with his son, and Tuesday morning, at about six A.M., Yates got into his Honda and started driving to work."

"We followed him to the 7000 block of North Market," reported Deputy Brandon Armstrong, "at which time Mr. Yates's vehicle was pulled over into a church parking lot by uniformed deputies in two green-and-white patrol cars."

It was Detective Rick Grabenstein, arriving a few minutes later with Detective Dave Bentley, who had the distinguished honor of snapping the handcuffs on Robert Lee Yates Jr. "I told him that he was under arrest for the murder of sixteen-year-old Jennifer Joseph," Grabenstein recalled, "and the man didn't seem the least bit concerned."

Detective Bentley sat next to Yates in the squad car's backseat during the drive to the Public Safety Building. "I'm a Vietnam vet, and attempting to bond with Yates," Bentley recalled, "I told him how ground troops sure did appreciate helicopter pilots during the war. He just looked at me, calm as can be, and said, 'I was never in combat.' "

Then, to Bentley's astonishment, the captured serial killer began chatting amiably about his early retirement from the armed forces and his job at Kaiser. "I was shocked," recalled Bentley. "I thought, 'You've just been arrested for murder and you're rattling on about "duh" stuff.' "

Taken in to custody, Yates underwent two hours of intense questioning at the city-county building preceding his formal arrest. At about the same time that Yates was being booked into jail, Kaiser called Linda and asked why her husband wasn't at work.

"He'd left home two hours earlier," she later commented. "I thought I would find him at Al's

Spa Tub Motel." Emotionally preparing herself to catch her husband with another woman, Linda drove to North Spokane. She was further distressed when she didn't find him. "I drove to a Burger King for coffee, pie, and a chance to think," she said.

"When Mrs. Yates exited her vehicle," reported Detective Ruetsch, "we blocked the parking-lot exits. I came up to her and assured her that she wasn't in trouble."

"If this is about Bob," said Linda, "I'm gonna kill him."

That's when Fred Ruetsch told her that her husband had been arrested for murder. Shocked, Linda Yates blurted out the long-held family secret—Robert Yates's grandmother had killed his grandfather with an ax.

"Then," Ruetsch recalled, "Linda asked for her coffee and pie. We were completely convinced that she had no idea at all what her husband had done."

"She was asked to come to the station," said Detective Grabenstein, "that's where she was told that her husband might actually be the serial killer. That isn't something you tell a woman in front of the children. This is the primary reason why Mr. Yates was not arrested at his residence."

Linda Yates and her children were not allowed to return home. Food, clothing, and lodging at a good hotel were paid for by the Spokane Sheriff's Office. "Two detectives were assigned to make sure that Mrs. Yates and her children had everything they needed," commented Sheriff Mark Sterk. "We even picked up their pet cats, Bell and Toby," he said. "It is the least we could do for the family."

Detective Major Bambino of the Washington State Patrol and Detective John Grandinetti were the two assigned to care for the Yates family. "First of all," said Sergeant Walker, "they drove Linda to pick up the kids from school." Daughter Michelle attended Lewis and Clark High School, son Kyle was at Hamblen Elementary, Amber was at her job at a plant nursery. "Sonja Yates lived with her boyfriend and she joined the family later. The other daughter, Sasha, was sleeping at the residence when the search of the Yates home began."

Robert Lee Yates Jr. was booked into jail at exactly 9:41 A.M. on suspicion of first-degree murder. While authorities would not identify the victim to the press, they did confirm that her death was one of the eighteen murders under investigation by the task force. "I have to classify this as a major break in our investigation," said Sheriff's Corporal Dave Reagan. "We are hopeful, but our detectives have been very specific about not linking him to the serial killings this time." His bail was set at $1.5 million.

Yates's home was soon crawling with investigators who'd cordoned off the street, restricted traffic, and blocked prying eyes with utility tarps around the house. A specially trained yellow Labrador retriever, Cascade, was flown in from Miami under the auspices of the Bureau of Alcohol, Tobacco, and Firearms (ATF). Cascade's specialty: explosives and ammunition. The dog's credentials included the Columbine High School investigation in Littleton, Colorado.

While Cascade sniffed the lawn, other investigators searched Yates's personal locker at the Kaiser

Mead Smelter, and others drafted a search warrant for Yates's locker on the Fort Lewis military base. State judges, however, have no authority on federal military installations. There was no way detectives could expeditiously search Yates's locker without his permission. It was deemed prudent not to broach the subject with Yates at that particular time, considering he had only been arrested that morning. An official press release was prepared and electronically delivered to all significant media outlets.

"Members of the Spokane homicide task force announced today that they have successfully arrested the person responsible for this series of crimes. Preliminary DNA results has identified Robert L. Yates as the person responsible for at least one of these homicides of women in the Spokane and Tacoma areas. A specific number of homicides is not being released at this time because there are other investigatory considerations beyond DNA testing."

The announcement stunned Yates's family, coworkers, and longtime friends. Al Gatti, incredulous, attributed Yates's arrest to the investigators' strong desire to solve the killings. "In my heart," Gatti said, "I believe he's innocent."

"He lived two doors down and I didn't know beans about him," said neighbor Jay Nooney. "I saw him working on his car, kind of a muscle car, a Plymouth and a van and a little blue car. He kept pretty much to himself."

"One of the things about him is he was wonderful with those children of his," said neighbor Vina Musgrove on the day of Yates's arrest. "He showed a different side to us, I guess. He was out playing pitch and catch with his son yesterday." Vina's husband, Bill Musgrove, regarded Yates "as a neighborly person. He used to have the nicest-looking Corvette; then he sold it about a year and a half ago."

The extended family of the recently arrested Yates was dumbfounded and dismayed by the accusations that their beloved Bobby was a serial killer. "We, the family members of Robert L. Yates Jr., feel deeply shocked and saddened by the recent allegations directed toward our beloved son, brother, father, and friend," his sisters said on behalf of the family.

"Bobby is a loving, caring, and sensitive son; a fun-loving and giving brother; and an understanding, generous, and dedicated father, who enjoys playing ball, fishing, and camping with his kids. Bobby is the type of person you would want to have for your best friend. We feel deeply for the families who have experienced loss and for the community as a whole. We ask that all judgments be reserved until the timely due process of law has been completed."

Time and process were also imperative for the homicide task force. Specifically, task force detectives wanted to identify people who knew in what grocery and hardware stores the suspect shopped, or had information regarding any storage units or private garages he may have rented. The task force also requested "information about his lifestyle, hobbies, and activities outside his home."

A photograph of Robert Lee Yates Jr. was widely circulated and was featured prominently in the

Spokesman-Review newspaper. The task force set up two hot lines for forwarding information about Robert Yates Jr. to detectives. "One person has been assigned to answer these lines," the public was advised, "so it is likely callers will encounter an answering machine. Callers should leave their name and number and be patient as it may be several days before a detective can contact you."

There was contact, albeit minimal, between the task force, the Tacoma Police Department, and the Pierce County Sheriff's Office. "[The homicide task force] told us that they arrested a suspect for one of the Spokane murders," acknowledged the Tacoma Police Department's officer of Public Information, "and that's about it."

The Spokane detectives were taking no chances, guarding their comments, and making sure that no statements to either the press or other law enforcement could jeopardize their investigation in-progress.

"All I can say is that she was killed many, many months ago," said Sheriff Sterk about the victim. "In the last forty-eight hours, we developed information that heightened our interest in Robert L. Yates in one of the unsolved slayings of a Spokane prostitute." Walker explained that one reason detectives were not releasing the victim's name was because of difficulty in reaching her next of kin. Within days, Yates was linked to several more homicides.

April 19, 2000

"We feel like we've arrested the person responsible for up to eighteen homicides in our community," Sheriff Mark Sterk said at a local news conference. "We're very confident (Robert L. Yates Jr.) is a suspect in twelve of our homicides, up to eighteen. We have other evidence besides the DNA results linking Mr. Yates to the Joseph homicide," said Sterk, "but we do not wish to discuss that evidence at this time."

"Authorities obtained a blood sample from Yates and confiscated seven vehicles that will be thoroughly searched," added Dave Reagan. "A private laboratory has analyzed the blood for DNA markers. In addition, authorities have canvassed seventy-six homes in the neighborhood where Yates lived and intend to canvass thirty more, interviewing residents about the suspect. The cars that were confiscated include vehicles Mr. Yates has used that are driven by his wife and adult daughter, and the vehicle he was driving when he was arrested."

The following day, members of the Spokane homicide task force continued processing the outside areas of the Yates home for evidence and conducted interviews with persons who called the hot line. Canvass of the Yates neighborhood for information regarding his habits and movements was already largely completed.

"Seven vehicles had been seized by homicide task force investigators, and others may be seized in the near future," announced the sheriff's office. "One detective was assigned to process search warrants on the four not already documented for evidence processing, but it is unknown when actual processing of the vehicles will begin."

Detectives began collecting evidence from the outside areas of Robert Yates's home on Friday,

April 21, but did not specify what evidence would be seized. "There is no firm timeline for searching the interior of the home," said Sheriff Mark Sterk, "other than outdoor work must be completed before interior work can begin—We'll comb Yates's home for cloth fibers and other microscopic evidence. We're going to spend at least two weeks, three weeks, in that house," Sterk said. "It's going to take us a long time to go through that house. We have Mr. Yates tied to at least twelve of the homicides, possibly eighteen. Additional charges are expected, and detectives hope to provide a list of those victims with a link to Mr. Yates by Friday. The white Corvette and evidence we found in that vehicle led us to the arrest of Mr. Yates, and through DNA to a number of the other victims in this case," said Sterk.

"If we knew what pushed this guy's buttons early on, it would have helped us solve this case earlier. We didn't know. Police have seized nine vehicles, including the Corvette which Yates sold in 1998," Sterk commented, "and two vans formerly owned by Yates. Another car Yates formerly owned was recovered Thursday in Idaho. Authorities have not yet recovered a murder weapon. Spokane authorities are working with the FBI to determine if there were unsolved slayings in places Yates had lived in the past."

By Friday, April 21, Spokane County Sheriff's Office detectives announced "definitive evidence tying Robert Yates to the murder of nine victims, Jennifer A. Joseph, Darla Sue Scott, Shawn L. Johnson, Laurel Ann Wason, Shawn A. McClenahan, Melinda L. Mercer, Sunny G. Oster, Linda A. Maybin, and Michelyn Derning.'' Melinda Mercer's death, would not be charged in Spokane County because it was a Tacoma Police Department case.

Such firm and unyielding statements implicating Yates as the killer irked Richard Fasy, the public defender assigned to Yates. ''Statements such as these make it impossible for my client to receive a fair trial,'' said Fasy. ''I know it's a big case and the community has a right to know, but Mr. Yates also has a right to a fair trial.''

Investigators awaited laboratory results that they believed would tie Yates to the homicides of Shannon Zielinski, Heather Hernandez, and Connie LaFontaine Ellis, but detectives would still not specify what evidence linked Yates to each specific homicide.

Tragically linked to Yates were his devoted wife, loving children, and numerous members of Yates's extended family. Chaplain Keith Kirkingberg collected class notes and homework for the two Yates children still in school, allowing them to keep current with their studies. While the overwhelmed offspring of suspected serial killer Robert Lee Yates Jr. grappled with a destroyed home, and the demands of homework, other relatives wrestled with the mind-numbing shock of ''Bobby Yates'' being accused of such horrific acts.

''If he did do these things, knowing Bob like I do, he'd 'fess up to it,'' his old pal Al Gatti said. ''If he did do these things, the way I feel about it is, my friend Bob Yates died a long time ago. Because this isn't the same Bob Yates I know.'' Gatti last got together with Yates in January while Yates was in Tacoma for training. ''We had laughs, a good talk," Gatti recalled. "He's been married over twenty-five years. He told me most marriages, they have their ups and downs. He told me, 'Through all those years, Linda and I are the best of friends.' He told me he never imagined love could be that wonderful. He's telling me, 'It's greater than anything I can imagine.' "

"I've had a hard time comprehending that it even happened," said cousin Brian Yates. "It's shocking that anyone could do it, but when it's somebody downstream in your own family, it's very shocking. Even though I didn't know the man that well."

Tragically ironic is the close relationship between the mother of victim Shawn Johnson and Pennie Yates, Robert Yates's cousin. As for her emotional response to the charges against her cousin, Pennie Yates said, "He had a good life and was successful. I think most of us think of his wife and kids. I mean, that's got to be the hardest thing in the world."

Investigators sealed off eight square blocks near Yates's home and took over everything inside the house. Authorities combed through every inch of his property using a "total station mapping" that utilizes lasers and the Global Positioning System (GPS) to create an accurate 3-D map of the crime scene that can later be shown to the jury.

April 25, 2000

German police said they were investigating whether Yates was involved in any crimes while he was stationed in Germany. "It is possible the former

U.S. soldier could be linked to unsolved murders in Germany, although we have nothing concrete as yet," a police spokesman said.

April 30, 2000

The task force uprooted a twelve-foot blue spruce tree next to Yates's home. "They also sifted soil from another site where neighbors said Yates removed a hedgerow and filled in the area with new soil," said Corporal David Reagan. "Yates said he replanted the tree after it was knocked over by a drunken driver."

As the evidence exponentially mounted, Sheriff Mark Sterk requested, and was granted, a prosecuting attorney to work full-time with task force investigators. "The detectives received a flood of information regarding Robert Yates Jr. since asking the public for help regarding his activities outside his home," said the sheriff's office. One new piece of evidence concerned a red or orange 1980 Mustang Ghia. Detectives learned that Yates owned the car, and during the fall of 1997 had it parked in front of the home on Forty-ninth with a For Sale sign displayed. An individual purchased the car for $800.

"Robert Yates had never registered the Ford in his name, making tracking the car extremely difficult," said Sergeant Walker. "Detectives asked anyone who might have purchased the Mustang, or who may have information about the car or the current owner, to call the homicide task force tip lines."

One month to the day after Yates's arrest, Christine Smith contacted the task force. Seeing Yates's photograph triggered a horrific realization: she was the serial killer's only living victim. Despite the unavoidable embarrassment to her parents, she swallowed her pride and contacted the authorities.

Smith advised the task force that Yates might be the suspect who assaulted and robbed her in August 1998. Detectives Bentley and Hill interviewed Smith again on May 12, 2001.

"In March, I was treated at the University of Washington Medical Center in Seattle for head injuries because I was in this car accident," she said. "When they X-rayed me, the doctors said that I had metal fragments in my head—you know, like I'd been shot in the head—and there were still pieces of it in my skull. So what I'm figuring is that he didn't hit me over the head with something like I thought at first—and I always wondered about how and why it was so sudden and severe—but he actually tried to kill me. When he pulled the trigger, he expected me to drop dead face first in his lap."

Detectives obtained signed medical release forms from Smith, and obtained copies of the University of Washington Medical Center medical records, including X rays of the treatment of Smith. Dr. John Hunter and Dr. Timothy Evans both concluded in their reports that Smith had a probable old gunshot wound to the left mastoid area.

A search of the van formerly owned by Yates

revealed bloodstains, a .25-caliber casing on the floor, and a spent bullet above the windshield in the roof track. Smith agreed to the removal of bullet fragments from her head to see if they matched bullets recovered from Yates's victims.

CHAPTER TWELVE

May 18, 2000

No one sang "For He's a Jolly Good Fellow" to Robert Lee Yates Jr. on his forty-eighth birthday. He was charged with eight counts of aggravated first-degree murder, one count of attempted murder, and one count of robbery; the indictment upgraded the previous first-degree murder charge in the case of sixteen-year-old Jennifer Joseph to aggravated murder. The other aggravated murder charges were for the deaths of Darla Sue Scott, Shawn L. Johnson, Laurel A. Wason, Shawn A. McClenahan, Sunny G. Oster, Linda A. Maybin, and Michelyn Derning. The attempted murder and robbery charges concerned the attack on Christine L. Smith.

Meanwhile, authorities were still attempting to get into Yates's military locker. "It's secure. It's locked up. But it's safe and it's documented that no one can get in there for now," said Sheriff Mark Sterk. "Hopefully, we'll get inside very soon."

May 23, 2000

Detectives finally completed their extensive search of the Yates home, and returned family possessions that were taken from the house. The search yielded evidence in the yard matching clippings and detritus found near the dump sites of three of his alleged victims. Having already been charged with eight murders, Spokane authorities then prepared two more murder charges against Yates—the deaths of Heather Hernandez and Shannon Zielinski.

May 26, 2000

Richard Fasy, the public defender representing Robert Lee Yates, Jr. filed a motion to have the case reassigned from Judge Kathleen O'Connor to another Spokane County Superior Court judge. Fasy would not give any explanation for the request. "It involves too many conversations that are confidential for me to appropriately make any kind of comment."

Five days later, Yates pleaded not guilty to eight counts of First-Degree Murder, and was held without bond by order of Judge Greg Sypolt due to the nature of the case, and the fact that prosecutors might ask for the death penalty. Within sixty days, attorney Richard Fasy, put the finishing touches on the death penalty mitigation package—his explanation of why his client should not face the death penalty if convicted.

"Suddenly, and much to the dismay of many people," recalled Sergeant Walker, "the prosecutor cut a deal with Robert Lee Yates, Jr. whereby Yates would never face the death penalty, or face a jury in the Spokane killings.''

Robert Lee Yates, Jr., upon the advice of his lawyer, and in cooperation with the prosecutor, made one of the most controversial and hotly debated deals in homicide history.

On June 30th, 2000 Yates' attorney drafted a letter to Spokane County Prosecutor Tucker suggesting that no trial take place. "A trial would most likely reveal unnecessary and painful details for the families of the victims," wrote Fasy. "The anguish and emotional trauma associated with that public exposure could very well be counter productive to their healing process."

If the prosecution wanted logical reasons to abandon a death penalty trial for Yates, Fasy offered several. "The primary mitigating circumstance that exists," Fasy wrote, "is the willingness of Mr. Yates to cooperate with the State in the resolution of a number of unsolved crimes. I have provided polygraph results which should confirm to law enforcement and the State the full extent of the past criminal activity on the part of Mr. Yates."

In addition to his client's cooperation, Fasy asked the prosecution to take into consideration Yates' military record, including his sixteen commendations and awards, including the Humanitarian Service Medal, the Army Commendation Medal, and the Master Army Aviator Badge.

"Mr. Yates is a husband and father of five children," Fasy continued. "To put him to death would be to victimize his family. As you know, they have already suffered considerably. Since the arrest of

Mr. Yates, they have had to relocate and are now dealing with the emotional trauma associated with this controversy."

"Mr. Yates was molested repeatedly by a neighbor boy at approximately six years of age," revealed Fasy. "This has remained a deep secret for him throughout his life and has certainly contributed to his frustrations and inner sense of shame. While this certainly does not provide an excuse for the actions attributed to him, it does provide some insight into the origins of his pathology."

Only four percent of those sentenced to death are actually executed in Washington state, and Fasy reminded Tucker that in cases that present substantial legal issues, the chances of the death penalty being imposed are significantly less. "Mr. Yates is now forty-eight years old. The average length of time for a death sentence to be implemented is twelve years. At that rate it is unlikely that Mr. Yates would be executed until he is in his advanced years," Fasy reasoned. "The inevitable delays in this case would only increase the frustrations of the family members of the victims, and unnecessarily postpone feelings of closure."

"Mr. Yates has demonstrated model behavior in the Spokane County Jail. The way he has conducted himself is consistent with his military training and discipline. There is every reason to believe that his good behavior will continue within the confines of a prison setting for the remainder of his life.

"Aside from the costs involved in seeking the death penalty," said Fasy, "both the State and the Defense recognize and acknowledge the ambiguities in the death penalty statue in reference to these factors. Case law indicates that 'common scheme or plan' does not encompass serial murders that occur over a one and a half-year time span. There is little or no evidence that the murders were committed in furtherance of a robbery and there is no evidence that they are committed to conceal the commission of another crime. This case could establish a precedent that is contrary to the interests of law enforcement. I would suggest that resolution the plea agreement is the more prudent course of action."

As for potential public outcry, Fasy countered that with his closing comments. "The community will understand the concession necessary to allow for the proper burial of one of the victims, and will be satisfied that the police and our county prosecutors solved all the crimes that Mr. Yates committed."

The deal between Fasy and Tucker was this: Robert Lee Yates, Jr. would confess to 10 murders in Spokane County, two in Pierce County, two in Walla Walla and one in Skagit County. He would also confess to the attempted murder of Christine Smith. "Yates had never been a suspect in the murder of Susan Savage and Patrick Oliver," confirmed Walla Walla Sheriff Mike Humphries. He had also not been a suspect in the 1988 Skagit County shooting death of twenty-three-year-old Stacy Hawn. Yates would answer detectives' questions about the fifteen murders, tell them what he did with three handguns, and he would draw detectives a detailed map leading them to the body of Melody Murfin, forty-one, missing for over two years. In return, there would be no possible death penalty, nor would prosecutors ask him about any other crimes.

"I agonized over the plea agreement," said Spokane County prosecutor Steve Tucker, "but I didn't have enough evidence to prove aggravating circumstances." Under Washington state law, the prosecution would have to prove that victims were killed to cover up a robbery, which was not the case in the Yates slayings. "I agreed to the plea to give peace to the victims' families," he said.

"We were furious," said Detective Rick Grabenstein, and it wasn't only the proposed deal that had detectives outraged. The polygraph results that Fasy said, "should confirm to law enforcement and the State the full extent of the past criminal activity on the part of Mr. Yates," did nothing of the sort.

"We have grave concerns," said Cal Walker, "about the results from Yates' polygraph test. To give the polygraph a nod of approval—we can't do that. We'd be totally remiss to accept those results as reported."

"I saw the polygraph test results," recalled Walla Walla County Sheriff Mike Humphreys, an experienced polygraph test administrator. "I was in Spokane at the task force office that day, and they asked me to take a look. It was ridiculous. It was indicative of nothing—I have never seen a polygraph test administered in which the suspect controlled the entire process. Yates created the questions, and he supplied the answers and the results showed nothing."

Sheriff Humphreys wasn't the only professional with years of polygraph experience to deride the test results. Three other polygraph experts examined the charts at the request of the *Spokesman-Review*. None were favorably impressed, and none reached a conclusion of honesty on the part of Robert Lee Yates, Jr.

"During the June 24th polygraph examination," explained Walker, "Yates voluntarily gave a hand-written statement, confessing to his murders in Washington. Then, the examiner then hooked Yates to the polygraph machine and asked him if he was lying. This is not the way polygraph tests are conducted."

Frank Hovarth, an expert in polygraph deception issues, said examiners must ask questions that are clear, concise and direct. "It would be standard practice to ask a relevant question such as, 'Did you kill any person outside the state of Washington'? For some reason, standard practice was not allowed here," Hovarth said. "I do not know why the examinations (of Yates) were structured as they were. In my opinion, the departure from accepted practice was not justified. It is my view that because of the way the examinations were structured, confidence in the outcomes would be low."

Hovarth, despite couching his professional opinions in utmost courtesy, was clearly displeased with the Yates polygraph. "Even in the event that these concerns are overlooked," he said, "it is my view that the conclusion reached by the examiner in this matter cannot be supported."

Ted Ponticelli, a polygraph expert whose advice was sought in the Charles Manson, Hillside Strangler, and O.J. Simpson cases, was straightforward in his negative appraisal. "It's inferior and, I believe, improperly administered," Ponticelli said, after reviewing the Yates lie detector tests. Such tests typically conclude with a statement of no deception indicated, deception indicated, inconclusive, or no opinion.

"This test is inadequate," Ponticelli said. "There's no opinion that can even be rendered. The questions are inferior, they're inadequate. I have to ask if this test was rigged, maybe not consciously. Maybe he went in there hoping that he's going to end up with truthful results just to satisfy the attorneys.

"There's no doubt in my mind that Yates is a sociopathic personality," said Ponticelli. "Anyone who is a sociopath will produce little or no reaction.

"These charts are uninterpretable, at best. They do not provide enough physiological information to make an accurate numerical evaluation to determine where he's being truthful or deceptive."

"I'd tell the prosecutor not to rely on the results of this test," Ponticelli said. "He's got egg on his face if he relied on these tests."

In Los Angeles, lie detector expert Larry Peelen said Yates' polygraph chart readings were "horrible." The best these charts are is inconclusive, which means zero," Peelan said. "It certainly doesn't mean he was being truthful."

When prosecutor Tucker learned of the overwhelming negative response of experts to the supposed integrity of Yates' polygraph test, he said that he may not have gone through with the plea bargain if he had known the Yates lie detector tests were inadequate.

"This plea agreement is not a good deal," detective Ben Estes told Tucker when the two men met face to face, "The victims and their families are not going to see justice served with this plea bargain."

"There was evidence in the lab that still hadn't been processed," Estes later commented. "I was flabbergasted by how fast he was working to get this plea deal done. There's no way [Tucker] or Fasy had all the facts of the case. It was like, in my opinion, they didn't want us to investigate other crimes that he might have done."

"What about the bloodstains in various vehicles he owned?" asked Sgt. Walker. "And we have a receipt that clearly shows that Yates hired a commercial cleaner to remove a bloodstain from his a motor home—a motor home we still haven't located."

"We had a ton of evidence to process and work to do, and here's Tucker, making a deal with the devil," Estes said. "I thought Tucker was being duped by Yates and his lawyer, and that's what I told him."

"With the enormity of the crimes and the number of victims," said Walker, "I couldn't imagine a better scenario to pursue the death penalty. If you don't use the death penalty in this case, where do you use it?"

The *Spokesman-Review*, based upon extensive interviews with the task force, asserted that "detectives wondered who was influencing Tucker . . . Was it the woman Tucker was dating . . . or was it Fasy . . ."

Fasy and Tucker, friends for years, played golf together at Hangman Valley a week after Yates was arrested. "We agreed on the first tee not to talk about the case," Tucker later commented, also insisting that he and his girlfriend, who worked in the public defender's office, also avoided the topic. "Did my ex-wife tell you how much influence she had on my decisions? I can tell you, I made the decision alone."

According to Tucker, Pierce County prosecutors John Ladenburg also approved the plea-bargain until lead detectives Rick Grabenstein and Fred Ruetsch, both angry over the proposed deal, visited Pierce County detectives and prosecutors. On the very day that Yates was supposed to reveal the secret location of Melody Murfin's body, Pierce County withdrew from Tucker's deal. John Ladenburg, Chief Prosecutor, filed two counts of aggravated murder against Yates. "I considered charging Grabenstein and Ruetsch with interfering in a criminal case," said Tucker, "but decided that would only make things worse."

"Mr. Tucker threatened to arrest me," confirmed Ruetsch, "and tried to get me fired, so I have nothing to say."

Fasy, Yates' attorney, had plenty to say. "I think Pierce County pulled out of the Spokane deal because Prosecutor John Ladenburg was running for election as county executive," he said. "I think Pierce County was getting pressure from the cops."

When Pierce County Prosecutor John Ladenburg first heard that Tucker was considering accepting a plea bargain, he arranged a conference call with Tucker, Yakima County's Jeff Sullivan and King County's Norm Maleng. "I told him point-blank that if he was even thinking about plea bargaining the Pierce County cases, I would not consent to sending those cases to him," Ladenburg said. "Every experienced prosecutor involved in that call told Mr. Tucker the plea bargain was ill-advised and recommended against it. Elected prosecutors were concerned that Mr. Tucker was rushing into a plea bargain even before the investigation was complete."

"Tucker said he worried about the trial costs of seeking the death penalty," Ladenburg said, "but we told him cost could not be a legitimate factor in the death penalty decision. Both Maleng and I offered to send senior prosecutors to Spokane to help with the case."

Pierce County filed its own charges against Yates, seeking the death penalty for the murder of Melinda L. Mercer and Connie LaFontaine Ellis. Yates' Spokane defense attorney, Richard Fasy, saw things much differently than John Ladenburg. "We would not have gone to such elaborate lengths, including the disclosure of incriminating information . . . unless we had been assured that a resolution would remove Mr. Yates from the jeopardy of the death penalty," wrote Fasy. "I truly feel that Mr. Ladenburg broke his promise to Mr. Tucker, and indirectly to us, well after we had committed to a particular course of action."

Tucker met with Spokane detectives and Pierce County prosecutors Gerry Horne and Barbara Corey-Boulet in August, and explained his reasoning behind the plea bargain—Washington state law requires proof that the defendant had "a common scheme or plan."

Tucker did not believe that Yates' hobby of murder met the State's legal criteria. Former Spokane County prosecutor Donald Brockett, who failed to persuade jurors to impose the death penalty on three different occasions, consulted with Tucker, and reinforced his opinion. "I also polled the victims' families," Tucker told reporters, "most of them opposed the death penalty for Yates."

"At no time have I wanted the death penalty for Robert Yates," confirmed Jean Fisher, mother of Linda Maybin. "I do not want the State to take a life on behalf of my daughter, members of her family, friends, or myself." Pierce County prosecutors remained undeterred in their determination to pursue the death penalty for Robert Lee Yates, Jr. "We wondered how there could be any rationale for going easy on Mr. Yates," Prosecutor Gerry Horne later commented.

Tucker and Fasy struck another deal in October. The new deal was identical to the previous attempt with one significant difference: because Yates now faced two murder charges in Pierce County, he refused to talk with detectives about the crimes to which he had confessed, and he wouldn't tell them what he did with the murder weapons.

"That's almost unheard of in plea bargains," Estes said later. "If he was going to plead guilty, he should have been forced to answer our questions about these murders. In my opinion, Steve Tucker didn't do his job." Tucker, or course, saw things differently. "The deal was in the best interest of taxpayers, speedy justice and the victims' families," he said.

Yates' map to the resting-place of Melody Murfin was simplicity itself—it showed the little garden under his own bedroom window. "They way it worked was like this," explained Cal Walker. "Prosecutor Steve Tucker, the defense attorneys, and the task force knew for a fact that Melody Murfin was dead, and that Yates would show us where she was buried her if he didn't have to face the death penalty. Murfin's family wasn't told because we wouldn't know if Yates were telling the truth until the body was recovered and identified.''

"Well, I was being led to the body of Melody Murfin by defense attorneys Richard Fasy, Scott Mason and Jay Ames. Based on everything we knew about Yates, and his past behavior, I thought we'd end up out in the woods, somewhere near where he discarded his other victims' bodies.''

As he followed the attorneys through traffic, Walker couldn't figure out where they were going. "We were not heading toward the woods, not toward Hangman Valley Road—we were heading back to the house of Robert Lee Yates Jr. When their turn signal came on to go northbound on Crestline, I can't even describe how I felt,'' Walker said. "My gut was in a knot, and I just started shaking.''

"Once we arrive at the abandoned Yates home, Mason handed me the map that Yates had drawn in his jail cell,'' Walker said. "Outside the bedroom shared by Linda and Robert Lee Yates, Scott Mason pointed to the spot on the ground and told me, 'You'll find her right there.' ''

Detectives Fred Ruetsch, Rick Grabenstein, Ben Estes and Marty Hill took turns with hand trowels and shovels, exhuming the body of Melody Murfin. "Her head was wrapped in three plastic bags,'' recalled Walker. "It was thirty-four inches down, just a few inches from the home's foundation.''

Detectives Dave Bentley and Terry Hammer went to the home of Wanda Murfin, Melody's mother, who saw the news on television. Three pieces of jewelry found on the body—a musical note earring, a dolphin earring and an eagle pendant—confirmed the identity of the victim missing since Mother's Day, three years previous. "What really bothers me," said Wanda Murfin, "is to think [Yates' wife and children] walked all over her and didn't even know they were doing it."

Major Bambino, a detective with the Washington State Patrol advised Linda Yates of the body in her backyard. "Amber planted flowers around the yard," exclaimed Linda. "She could've dug that body out. I don't know how he managed to bury a body so close to the house without anyone noticing."

"I realized the task force blundered in our earlier search of the yard," acknowledged Walker. "We weren't there looking for a body then, because it didn't fit anything he'd done. He had dumped all the other bodies someplace else—like trash. To think we had spent all that time there and failed to recognize there was a body buried in the yard, well, it was just a mistake."

"Yates buried the body just a few feet from his bed," said forensic psychologist Reid Meloy. "It's a way to control his victim even after death. "You can continue in fantasy the complete domination of her, because she's buried in the ground below you. It can be a sexual stimulus in between killings."

"[To make that deal] he pulled Melody Murfin out of his back yard," said Lynn Everson on *Court*

TV. "She was buried under his bedroom window. That's how he plea bargained here. He told them he could tell them where a missing victim was buried. She was under his bedroom window. She was a mother, and a grandmother, and a very kind person. It again communicates his disrespect for his victims."

Despite the controversy of Tucker's deal with Yates, or perhaps because of it, the Washington State Bar Association Board of Governors named Tucker the recipient of their 2001 "Courageous Award." The board of governors presents this award to the lawyer who displayed "exceptional courage" in the face of adversity. It was awarded to Tucker for his decision not to pursue the death penalty.

Spokane defense attorney, Carl Hueber, also president of the Spokane County Bar Association, submitted the nomination. "My practice is focused primarily in the criminal defense area," Hueber wrote. "I spend most of my days on the other side of the prosecutor's table. I recognize there is a certain irony in this nomination coming from an adversary. However, I think it is important that the bar look beyond their selected roles and acknowledge when someone from our ranks has done a truly courageous act."

"[Robert Lee Yates, Jr.] killed all of these girls but he started bargaining for his life. I don't understand that," lamented Ondraya Anita K. Smith, mother of Sunny Oster. "Where was the bargaining with my Sunny? Where was the bargaining with all of these people? He took their lives. And what in God's name was going through his mind when he did it? What was he thinking? I really want Yates to get the death penalty. And maybe we'll have to wait for Pierce County for that.''

Yates's parents were in Walla Walla when they heard about their son pleading guilty in exchange for not facing the death penalty. They immediately traveled to Spokane. "We spent an hour and a half with him," said his father. "He had not showered in a while. He wore cloth slippers. He cried when he spoke about his five children. He talked about his faith in God.

"I held out hope that my son was innocent, but it wasn't easy," said Yates Sr. "I had talked to the public defender and prosecutor and I had been told by Cal Walker that they had mounds of evidence. I had a feeling that he could very well be guilty. The DNA evidence, it is hard to refute that.''

"When someone dies, there is closure," Cardeller Yates said. "But this will never die. It's always going to be there. There will never be closure.''

"We have the greatest sorrow for the loved ones of the victims," Yates Sr. said. "We are sorry. I know how I'd feel if someone did that to one of my daughters. I understand how the community feels. I think I'm getting used to sorrow.

"He confessed to the Lord, so the Lord knows what he did, and he's asked for forgiveness. Some might call it jailhouse Jesus, but I believe it is truthful.

"I love you no matter what," Yates Sr. told his son, "and I'll stick with you, but I abhor what you've been accused of if you are guilty. But I'll love you and I know you'll be in eternity when Jesus comes a second time.''

"My parents agreed to the plea-bargaining," said Dan Oliver, brother of victim Patrick Oliver of Walla Walla. "Hearing Mr. Yates say in court the words Guilty, Your Honor, to the death of Susan and the death of Patrick did give us a sense of relief after years of speculation and wondering. Now we want Mr. Yates locked in a state penitentiary with minimum privileges for the rest of his natural life. I cannot comprehend the loss and grief my parents have endured. Mr. Yates owes my family a precise explanation of the events that surrounded the killing of Susan and Patrick. We want to know why. Did he know Susan or Patrick? Many questions are unanswered and only Mr. Yates's request can give his answers."

Robert Lee Yates Jr. sat in a Spokane courtroom with a box of tissues in front of him. It was placed there should he break down in tears. He listened dispassionately as his victims' families and loved ones told him exactly what they thought of him. He never once reached for a tissue.

"I never thought that the day would come that I would meet the person who killed my brother," said Chris Oliver. "Today is that day; now is the time. As I sit and look at a face, I see a deceitful, evil, sociopathic, calloused monster that has complete disregard for human life. You've murdered my brother and you don't deserve to live. If you had a conscience, if you had any remorse, empathy, or feelings for anyone besides yourself, you would beg for the death penalty. Robert Yates, this is only the beginning of your day of reckoning. You could postpone your ultimate Judgment. You can't avoid that day."

"On October 13, 2000, Robert Lee Yates Jr. signed a plea agreement wherein he admitted, Count two, he murdered my brother, Patrick Alan Oliver, on July 13, 1975," said Dan Oliver. "The maximum term and fine is life and ten thousand dollars. Life must be cheap in eastern Washington. Mr. Yates deserves to die. Mr. Tucker has been duped by a clever defense attorney in dealing away with the death penalty."

Oliver looked directly at Robert Lee Yates Jr. "Mr. Yates, you were raised as an Adventist. Why did you fail your religion, Mr. Yates? Didn't you learn that murder is wrong? How would you like to find your twenty-two-year-old daughter beneath a sleeping bag and a tire, Mr. Yates? Do you know what dead flesh looks like, Mr. Yates? Do you know what dead flesh feels like, Mr. Yates? Because of you, I know. You have stigmatized your wife and five children who attend schools in Walla Walla, Mr. Yates. You have disgraced the Adventist religion, Mr. Yates. You have shamed eastern Washington, Mr. Yates. And Mr. Yates, you deserve to die now."

One after another, they faced the demon who killed their loved ones. "My name is Heather Smith; Shannon Zielinski was my mother. God will not forgive you, Mr. Yates. You killed my mom."

"Some of the victims were younger than your daughter," Shawn Johnson's sister said, addressing Yates. "Had she taken the wrong road in life, would you have killed her, too? Or would you have helped her? You took that choice from my sister, and I don't understand how he can see his family and we can't see ours. Someday, Mr. Yates, you will have to face the real Judgment Day. And when you do, I hope you get everything you deserve.''

"My name is Darcy Acevedo; my sister is Laurie Wason. Why did you do this? Do you have something against once-over women that are on the streets? It's not that they don't have family members that love them, because everybody has a family member somewhere. The sentence you will receive will never be enough, but to know that you are behind bars, it's easier to come into Spokane. I hope this haunts you for the rest of your life, Mr. Yates.''

"You deserve to die the slowest, most painful death possible. You had no right to take the life of anyone. You ended women's lives that you decided were not important. No one would miss. The day is coming when you will stand before the ultimate judge,'' added Cecelia Oster. "He will read off all the names of the people you have murdered and the families that you've hurt. And then He will give you the punishment that you deserve.''

" 'Useless garbage.' Those two words come pretty close to describing your existence,'' said Sunny Oster's father. "May you rot in hell. Does anybody know what he does to dead girls after they're dead? Does anybody know that he has sex with them after they're dead? Like he did with my Sunny?''

"How could you take my mother and bury her in your yard?'' demanded Melody Murfin's daughter. "And then you and your family walk around my mother for two and a half years. You stole her soul. I don't think you deserve to ever see daylight, ever see your family. You must be tormented in prison for the rest of your life. Tortured. You're a sick monster."

"If he killed once out of passion or uncontrollable anger, we might believe him capable of genuine regret for his action and the potential for his reform," commented Heather Smith, Shannon Zielinski's daughter. "I believe with all my being that anyone who is capable of repeated, premeditated, brutal murder is unequivocally incapable of regretting it, let alone genuinely repenting it. If Mr. Yates feels anything resembling remorse right now, it is undoubtedly remorse at being caught."

Clara Page, Laurel Wason's mother, could scarcely control her pain and rage. "Why did she have to die? You had no right to take her life. And I hope you rot in hell."

"It's very bittersweet to realize, Mr. Yates, that your fingerprint was on the back of my daughter's head," said Shawn McClenahan's mother. "It's bittersweet because I felt that she was saying, 'Here he is. Here is the serial killer.' My family all felt the same way. Kathy and I talked about this many times and—with Terry, too, and Patrick, my son. We all agreed that this was her way of saying, 'Don't worry. It's over. It's done now.' "

When the final family members of Yates's Spokane and Walla Walla victims had given their statements, the next to stand was another of Yates's victims—his own daughter Sasha.

"I'm the eldest daughter of Robert Yates," she said, her voice trembling. "I feel immensely terrible that this has happened. It feels like a dream. I'm still in shock. They didn't deserve this. No one deserves to be killed like that. No one. Thank God

I have my grandfather here with me. I also, like most of the victims, want to know why, what caused this. Because we were raised differently, that you just didn't do that kind of thing. I'm standing here shaking, still thinking about it and imagining their faces. What they went through. These poor families. How they feel about us. How much they probably hate us. The only way I've been getting through this is actually looking to the Lord, because only He can help us and help my father. And I do want you to know, I do love him, even though he did do this."

Sasha Yates turned her sad and tragic gaze toward her beloved father, the confessed sex slayer. "I still love you, Dad, even though you did this. I may not understand why. I may never find out why, the reason behind this. But we've been going through hell, the whole family, all of us. I have a younger brother that's twelve He did not want to talk to my dad because he is so afraid of him now. I'm glad I have my grandfather here."

Her grandfather, Robert Lee Yates Sr., tearfully spoke to the crowded courtroom. "I'm sorry to all the families. You all have broken hearts. Your Honor, I'm so sorry. I want to apologize to the community of Spokane County. I love my son. Thank you."

It was then that Robert Lee Yates Jr. was asked if he had anything to say. "Yes, Your Honor, there is," said Yates, and he began his prepared statement:

Nothing I can say will erase the sorrow, the pain, and the anguish that you feel and I've caused in your lives. I've caused much sorrow. Much pain. You can't know how much pain I know I've caused for all of you and my family. I've taken away the love, the compassion, and the tenderness of your loved ones. And I've submitted in that place grief and bitterness. I pray that God will right the wrongs that I've committed. That justice will bring closure to all who, as a result of my actions, have become victims. I pray. And I apologize to the public, this community, this nation, to law enforcement, to my family, my lovely wife, my children who I dearly love, my friends, and my family. Most of all, to the families and friends of Susan Savage, I'm sorry.

With each name, there came more tears and cries of anguish, but not from Robert Lee Yates Jr. He often had to glance down at the notes in his hand to recall his victims' names.

To the family and friends of Patrick Oliver, I am sorry. To the family of Stacy Hawn—to the friends and family of Stacy Hawn, I am sorry. To the family and friends of Shannon Zielinski, I'm sorry. To the family and friends of Heather Hernandez, I am sorry. To the family and friends of Jennifer Joseph, I am sorry. To the friends and family of Darla Scott, I am sorry. To the friends and family of Sunny Oster, I am sorry. To the family and friends of Shawn Johnson, I am indeed very sorry. And to the friends and family of Shawn McClenahan, I am sorry. To the friends and family of Laurel Wason, I am sorry. To the friends and family of Linda Maybin, I am sorry. And to the family of Michelyn Derning, I am sorry. And to the friends and family of Melody Murfin, I am sorry. And to the friends and family of Christine Smith, I am sorry.

In my struggle, my struggle to overcome my guilt and shame, I have turned to God—or returned to Him. I hope that God will replace your grief with hope and your sorrow with peace.

"His tone of voice . . . I've never heard an apology like that before," said Detective Grabenstein, who sat with fellow task force members in the front row. "It was almost like he was shouting at the victims' families in anger."

"It was not sincere," Ruetsch said. "It was not genuine."

Walker made eye contact a few times with Yates. "He sounded sorry that he'd been caught, is what I thought."

Robert Lee Yates Jr. was sentenced to 408 years in prison. He didn't shed a tear. Later, when Linda told him that the one of the family's cats died, he broke down in tears.

"Looking back," said Detective Rick Grabenstein, "when I clasped the handcuffs on him, after three years of looking for him, you might think I'd have feelings of elation or something—but I didn't. It was just like every other arrest as far as that goes. No, the elation was when we got the match on the DNA—that we knew at last who the serial killer was."

"We tested a heck of a lot of suspects for matching DNA," recalled Walker. "Each one of the suspects' blood draws cost $8.30. The examination of crime scene evidence, blood and hair, came to about $60,000.''

For Detective Fred Ruetsch, the moment of elation was finding the mother-of-pearl button from Jennifer Joseph's blouse under the seat of Rita Jones's Corvette. "When we noticed a dark stain on the passenger's seat belt," said Grabenstein, "Fred said the stain was from a Slurpee—of course it really was blood. Then when the button was found, Fred's attitude changed remarkably.''

"I said, 'That's the same button I remember from one of our cases,' recalled Ruetsch. "I went back to the office, checking our files, and confirmed that the button matched the one missing from Jennifer Joseph's blouse—she was the teenager last seen getting into the Corvette.''

"The county bought Rita Jones's dream car from her for just over $10,000,'' said Sergeant Walker. "Altogether, the Spokane County Sheriff's Office spent close to $2 million on the serial killer investigation, and the Spokane Police Department spent about $730,000 before they pulled out of the investigation. The total cost of catching the serial killer was roughly $2.73 million—and that's not counting the contributions in man power and expertise from the Washington State Patrol, the state attorney general's office, and the work of FBI Special Agent Norm Brown.''

There would be after-the-fact costs as well—the Pierce County Court ruled Spokane's evidence admissible in Yates's upcoming trial in the deaths of Melinda Mercer and Connie LaFontaine Ellis.

The United States Congress approved a $2 million grant that would reimburse the city of Spokane, Spokane County, and the Washington State Patrol over a three year period. The Washington State Patrol, having completed its role in the serial killer investigation, turned its attention to Dr. George Lindholm, the respected Spokane County Medical Examiner famed for finding incriminating clues on victim's bodies.

August 9, 2001

Dr. Lindholm's drug prescriptions led to his arrest following a secret six month investigation by the State Patrol—an investigation prompted by acrimonious allegations by Lindholm's ex-wife, Ronnie Blackwell. The homicide task force, working closely with Dr. Lindholm, knew nothing about the investigation.

"Dr. Lindholm's arrest came as a complete shock," acknowledged Cal Walker, "and it also posed threats to the use of his autopsy findings in the Pierce County trial." In mid-April, evidence linking Yates to the Spokane killings was ruled admissible in Yates' Pierce County trial.

The former Mrs. Lindholm, residing in Alaska, went to the Alaska State Troopers with her allegations immediately following the finalization of the divorce. In turn, she told WSP detectives that she and her ex-husband would share narcotics taken home from the morgue, and would then drink alcohol and smoke pot.

Describing her ex-husband as a "kind and sensitive man," she said that her ex-husband's use of drugs and alcohol had increased over the past three years because he had learned that he had a son, Steve, who was previously unknown to him. Dr. Lindholm invited the son, Steve Anderson, nineteen, to move in with his wife and him. "I love him," Anderson said. "I couldn't ask for anything more in a dad."

The investigation, which included daily sifting through Dr. Lindholm's trash by a State Patrol detective, resulted in a search of his residence, followed by Lindholm's arrest, his resignation as Spokane County Medical Examiner, and his voluntary admission into an alcohol detoxification center.

Drug containers found at Lindholm's house included antidepressants, cough syrup, and Oxy-Contin, a prescription medication for pain relief. Also found were seven marijuana plants and several unspecified prescription bottles.

Ronnie Blackwell told detectives that Lindholm repackaged stolen drugs and hid them in his bedroom, in closets and in bathrooms. During the search, detectives found repackaged drugs in his bedroom and kitchen. Two empty prescription bottles were found in Lindholm's trash.

Lindholm's attorney, Carl Hueber, noted that Blackwell, "according to the court papers, has her own problems with alcohol and drugs. One should probably take the allegations of a bitter ex-wife with a grain of salt."

"Empty pill bottles in Dr. Lindholm's trash doesn't mean he took all the drugs himself," said Hueber. "I don't know if you can conclude from empty bottles that Dr. Lindholm or others were consuming the prescriptions."

Prior to his resignation, Lindholm was under contract with Spokane County to run the medical examiner's office and the morgue at Holy Family Hospital. Spokane County could face liability issues if individuals who were convicted of crimes based on Lindholm's testimony had their convictions overturned. "County taxpayers paid for Lindholm's malpractice insurance as a part of his contract," said Spokane County Chief Executive Francine Boxer. "The county hardly ever escapes litigation in matters like these."

"Of course, Yates' attorneys will certainly use this to his advantage," commented Cal Walker. "The DNA evidence establishing Yates as the serial killer was overwhelming, and much of it was gathered during the autopsies performed by Dr. Lindholm." Within thirty days, defense attorneys in Tacoma took their first step toward disqualifying evidence gathered by Dr. George Lindholm. If defense attorneys could show Lindholm performed autopsies under the influence of narcotics, his medical findings here in Spokane might not be admissible in Tacoma.

Yates' legal representatives immediately challenged the clues recovered by Dr. Lindholm because of allegations against him. In truth. Lindholm's evidence and testimony wouldn't be imperative to convict Yates of the two Pierce County homicides, but his findings could be critical to the prosecution's winning the death penalty. Lindholm performed autopsies on the 10 women whose murders in Spokane County are the backbone of the state's death penalty cases against Yates in Pierce County.

"The jury in Tacoma will hear about the Spokane killings as a way of proving that murders on both sides of the state were part of a common scheme or plan," offered Tacoma Detective Robert Yerbury. If Lindholm's findings were ruled inadmissible by Pierce County Judge John McCarthy, it could be more difficult to show aggravating circumstance necessary in a capital punishment case.

"We may not even have to call Lindholm as a witness," said Pierce County prosecutors. "Spokane detectives have also frozen much of the biological evidence against Yates if defense lawyers challenge the validity of DNA matchups."

November 7, 2001

"The task force that helped capture serial killer Robert Yates will shut down Dec. 31, 2001," announced Spokane County Sheriff Mark Sterk.

"Spokane detectives met with more than 80 detectives from Washington, Oregon, Idaho and Canada," confirmed Sgt. Walker. "We discussed several topics and methodologies, including geographic profiling. In fact, geographic profiling led investigators to within thirteen blocks of Yates' home four months before he was even a suspect."

"One of the things that linked the victims was plastic bags which came from six different stores," said Walker, "several of which are national chains with more than one Spokane location. We wondered if the killer's shopping habits would help aid in his capture, so we consulted a geographic information specialist."

They received a list of Albertsons and Safeways

spread around the county. But the killer also used a bag from Super 1 Foods. The only Super 1 Foods in Spokane County is on Twenty-ninth Avenue on Spokane's South Hill.

"We plotted the locations where their killer dumped his victims," explained Walker, "and there was an overlapping pattern, and the center of those patterns were only blocks apart at Thirty-seventh and Napa, and Forty-first and Fiske. Robert Yates lived about halfway between those two locations.

"Geographic profiling was not actually used in this case to eliminate a suspect," he said, "but it did help us prioritize persons of interest by giving special attention to those living on the South Hill."

December 18, 2001

As Christmas approached, detectives received holiday best wishes from an unlikely source—the family of Robert Lee Yates Jr. "We still have a good working relationship with that family," confirmed Cal Walker. "It's another one of the odd things that came out of this case." In the Christmas message, Linda Yates thanked the officers for the support they gave her family after her husband was arrested.

January 1, 2002

Detectives Grabenstein and Ruetsch returned to the sheriff's major crimes unit. Sergeant Cal Walker was promoted to captain and now oversees the department's new Valley Precinct office. Doug Silver, former co-commander of the task force, retired.

"Records of the task force investigation will be stored in a special cage in the basement of the Public Safety Building," said Walker. "Also in there will be that forty-by-sixty-foot billboard that used to be up on Sprague Avenue. The task force wanted it preserved," he said. "We didn't want it in somebody's rec room, or on the side of a barn."

The task force detectives will attend the Pierce County trial scheduled for June 2002, and several of them will testify for the prosecution. If Yates's guilt is not proved beyond a reasonable doubt, Spokane can still charge him with the murder of Shawn McClenahan, the case with the most damning evidence.

When Yates confessed, Walker told reporters that he can now sleep at night. He may not be so fortunate. Further investigation has revealed that Robert Lee Yates, Jr., despite being the Spokane Serial Killer, was not responsible for the serial murders of Yolanda Sapp, Kathy Brisbois, and Nickie Lowe.

"He's out there, somewhere," said Walker. "He could be in prison, in another city . . ." His voice trailed off, the balance of his sentence remaining unspoken because it went without saying—there is the possibility, albeit remote, that the Riverside Killer is strolling along East Sprague, smiling at the working girls, and contemplating a comeback.

ACKNOWLEDGMENTS AND AUTHOR'S NOTE

This horrific story of homicide, lies, obsession, and postmortem sexual deviancy is one of relentless tragedy, dismay, frustration, inadvertent errors, and eventual victory. The Spokane Serial Killer—Robert Lee Yates Jr.—began his trail of terror over twenty-five years ago in my hometown of Walla Walla, Washington, population 27,000. His victims' families lived not far from my own family, and the pain of those unsolved homicides nagged at our little community for over a quarter of a century. In the late 1990s, he murdered women of high-risk lifestyles in Spokane, Washington. Among them was Shawn Johnson, a graduate of Walla Walla High School, my alma mater, and Darla Sue Scott, former girlfriend of Arthur A., a longtime friend.

Unlike my previous true crime books for Pinnacle, this is not a case which I brought to my publisher's attention. Rather, because of my familiarity with the social and cultural makeup of the locales, and my personal interaction with one or more principal characters, Pinnacle asked me to "take the case."

At first, I was reticent. Due to its high-profile nature, I feared that an exploitive and superficial rendering of the investigation would be in bookstores before I began my initial research. I was correct. The Spokane homicide task force was outraged and insulted by the other author's inaccuracies and allegations. As a result, my arrival at task force headquarters announcing that I was writing a book about their successful investigation initially triggered more serious concern than enthusiastic cooperation. Subsequent meetings with Sergeant Cal Walker, the homicide task force detectives, and Spokane County Sheriff Mark Sterk allayed their fears regarding my motives and approach. Doors were opened, questions answered, and all was revealed.

"It would take more than a year of research and one hundred thousand words to tell this story," said Sergeant Walker. "We made mistakes, of course. Everyone does. But the proof of the investigation is in the outcome—and Robert Lee Yates, Jr. was arrested, charged, convicted, and sentenced to over four hundred years in prison for these murders. He still faces the death penalty for two other homicides in Pierce County."

Condensing such elaborate and complex events, issues, and intense investigative methodologies into a comprehensible narrative would have been impossible were it not for the exemplary cooperation afforded the author by the Spokane County

Sheriff's Office, the detectives of the Spokane homicide task Force, Walla Walla Sheriff Mike Humphreys, Detective Mike Skeeters, and many others too numerous to mention individually, who appear within these pages.

Conversations and statements recounted in this book are adaptations of such as recalled from memory. For purposes of clarity, concision, and continuity, statements and conversations necessitated condensation and emendation. For obvious reasons, the names of many secondary characters have been changed.

The author has made every effort to preserve accuracy of fact and portrayal. Any errors are unintentional. Gratitude is expressed to Andy Sorfleet, Jenette Marlowe, and the Sexual Workers Alliance of Vancouver, for their significant contributions, cooperation, and guidance concerning prostitutes rights.

The investigation into the multiple homicides committed by Robert Lee Yates Jr. saw dedicated professionals, working under adverse and challenging conditions, accomplish a Herculean task. Funding was inadequate; staffing was insufficient, public apathy was palpable, and armchair quarterbacks—including a convicted felon and self-proclaimed "expert" on detection—heaped derision on the task force with tactless and tasteless regularity.

In the end, the task force captured the killer, and the killer confessed. The case was closed. Unfortunately, the twenty-one-bed women's shelter created to specifically shield women who fit the victim profile of alcoholic and drug-addicted prostitutes was threatened with closure the moment Yates was securely behind bars.

"We are nothing but serial killer fodder," commented a homeless Spokane woman. "As long as we can be fed to the sharks, the 'good people' feel safe. Do they think I'm not a real woman because I'm on the street? Do they think I'm not a real woman because I perform sexual services for men who are not getting their needs met otherwise— men who are perfectly happy to pay me for what they should be getting at home for free?"

Happily, Americorps volunteers stepped in and kept the shelter open.

Most clients of prostitutes are convivial regulars who pose no threat, cause no trouble, and commit no felonies. There is, however, that deadly minority who beat, torture, and kill these women specifically because they *can* without causing public outrage.

The answer is not stronger laws against sex workers and their clients. Rather, sex workers should receive the same protection under the law as workers in any other profession. This is the stated goal of the North American Task Force on Prostitution. Founded in 1979, the North American Task Force on Prostitution is a network of sex workers, sex workers' rights organizations, and individuals and organizations that support the rights of sex workers to organize on their own behalf, work safely, and do so without legal repression.

As for Robert Lee Yates Jr., theories abound as to what causes a man to cross the line between fantasy and reality—to act out in the real world of flesh and blood the personal fantasies best kept fleeting and private. According to some homeopathic physicians, the remedy for individuals such as Yates is anacardium, a substance needed by people who have been abused, and/or feel inadequate. It could be that simple; it could be far more complex. Robert Lee Yates Jr. fits the classic definition of a psychopath.

The foundation of all current knowledge on the topic of psychopaths and their behavior is based upon the extensive research—over thirty years—of Dr. Robert Hare, author of *Without Conscience*. It was he who first delineated the relationship between psychopathy and crime, and defined psychopathic behavior.

According to Dr. Hare, psychopaths are "social predators who use charm, manipulation, intimidation, and violence to satisfy their own needs. They are found in both sexes and in every society, race, culture, ethnic group, and socioeconomic level." Although small in number, their contribution to the seriousness of crime, violence, and social distress in every society is grossly out of proportion to their numbers.

Psychopaths can readily be identified by qualified clinicians noting the defining features of the disorder. Among these are repetitive, casual, and seemingly thoughtless lying, apparent indifference to, or inability to understand, the feelings, expectations, or pain of others, and a complete lack of conscience.

Just as the colorblind cannot experience red, blue, green, or yellow, a person without a conscience cannot experience empathy, sympathy, compassion, remorse, guilt, or shame. "Psychopaths," said Dr. Hare, "have no anxieties, doubts, or concerns about being humiliated, causing pain, sabotaging future plans, or having others be critical of their behavior.''

The senses of guilt, shame, and remorse (penitence) are not the same. Guilt is feeling bad about what you have done. Shame is feeling bad about what you have not done—the actions not taken, the standard not attained. Remorse, or penitence, is a combination of emotions. Famous philosopher Adam Smith considered it the most dreadful of all sentiments. He described it as "made up of shame from the sense of the impropriety of past conduct; of grief for the effects of it; of pity for those who suffer by it; and of the dread and terror of punishment.''

There is no "terror of punishment" for the psychopath, except perhaps an understandable aversion to the death penalty. Reprimand is a waste of time, and penitentiaries never teach them penitence. Incarcerated psychopaths reinforce each other's lack of remorse, virtually assuring that any expression of heartfelt shame and regret is more show than sincerity, more performance than penitence.

Fear of punishment is not the primary reason "normal" people don't commit horrid acts such as those perpetrated by Robert Lee Yates Jr. "Most important perhaps is the capacity for thinking about, and being moved by, the feelings, rights, and well-being of others," stated Dr. Hare. "There is also an appreciation of the need for harmony and social cooperation, and the ideas of right and wrong instilled in us since childhood.''

There was no lack of proper upbringing in the

life of Robert Lee Yates Jr. He was raised by loving, nurturing parents with a strong moral code. There is no place for external blame in the equation. No fault in parenting or upbringing made him a killer. True, he was molested as a child, but not all victims of molestation become serial killers.

Burl Barer
May 10, 2002

Update for the 2012 Edition

I am sure you will be relieved to know that Robert Lee Yates, Jr. has been convicted on two counts of aggravated first-degree murder by a jury in Tacoma, Pierce County, Washington, and that the selfsame jury found insufficient cause to grant leniency for the murders of Connie LaFontaine Ellis and Melinda Mercer. Consequently, on Thursday, October 3, 2002, we twelve summarized more than eight weeks' testimony and witnessing into a singular sentence: death, wrote Juror #7, William Warren, on October 4, 2002, in his letter to, and published online by, the Internet Crime Archive. *I cannot commend my fellow jurists highly enough: there was no infighting or bickering, no power plays or bullying, but a cohesive and intelligent and sensitive group of people doing a tough job and taking care of each other in the process. We became a family in our time together, a bond we hope to maintain now that our job is done.*

Robert Lee Yates Jr. made a statement of apology in Tacoma, similar to the one he had made in Spokane. "I've prepared this statement so that I might leave nothing unsaid that needs to be said to all my victims' families, my family, and the people of the communities I terrorized," Yates said. "The world is a frightening place, and I've made it more so for so many.

"I'm so very, very sorry I took those loved, wonderful, important people from you. I've devastated your hopes and dreams and left you with only photographs and memories."

The serial killer admitted that he was previously in denial about the depth of his depravity. "I couldn't see the enormous devastation I had caused," he said. "I had to confess to God before I could see the enormity of my evil. Nothing I can say today will justify and excuse my wrongs. There's absolutely no excuse. I'm sorry beyond what words can express."

Prosecutor Barbara Corey-Boulet found his remarks offensive and disingenuous. "Yates is a self-centered, manipulative man obsessed with his own ego and what he could get away with," she said in court. "He never once accepted responsibility for what he did. He didn't say, 'I did this.' What did he really say? He said 'sin' entered him and 'sin' made him do it. What the defendant is telling you is that the Devil made him do it."

The victims' families were equally unimpressed. "The apology here meant absolutely nothing," said Kathy Lloyd, the sister of victim Shawn McClenahan. Lloyd's view was shared by others who were touched by the killer. "He was talking a great deal about how his life belongs to Jesus, but I'm not buying into that. It's too late," Lloyd asserted.

The convicted killer's father, Robert Yates Sr., was prepared for the jury's decision. "I didn't hold out much hope with them coming back this fast," he said. "After that, I just knew it was going to be death. But I think he's prepared."

Yates's then–eighteen-year-old daughter, Michelle Yates, took some solace from her father's remarks. "I'm happy that he at least said he was sorry. . . . I think that in time I could forgive him."

That was in 2002, more than a decade ago, and today no one hears much about Robert Lee Yates Jr. The appeals made on his behalf by some of Washington's finest attorneys did not result in overturning his conviction in Pierce County, nor was he given a new sentencing phase. His sentence of death by lethal injection did have one very clever argument presented against it: He must first serve the 408-year sentence handed down by the Spokane Court. After all, Spokane convicted him first, and sentenced him first. When he is done serving the Spokane sentence of 408 years, then he can be executed.

As of this writing, the Spokane Serial Killer sits on death row in the author's hometown of Walla Walla, Washington, the town where he killed his first victims. He doesn't grant interviews, although he occasionally receives requests from television stations, including KREM-TV in Spokane, Washington. *KREM 2 News* anchor Jane McCarthy wrote to him on death row in Walla Walla, and Yates declined to be interviewed on camera. He did, however, write her a five-page missive on life and guilt, an expatiation of sins:

> *What good could possibly come from having me, the object of much scorn, brought before the eyes and ears of the viewing public? Haven't I caused enough pain and suffering already? I needed long moments of personal conviction where an individual becomes obligated to respond to the convicting power of God's truth. It was that crisis encounter with truth . . . while reading the Bible in jail, that brought me humbly to the foot of the cross, to find hope, grace and cleansing by the blood of Christ, my savior. I'm confident that in Christ alone we will find the grace to heal, be reconciled, and be made whole. . . . That is my hope and prayer for each person upon whose life I have brought so much grief, suffering and loss.*

Legal issues aside, sooner or later, Robert Lee Yates Jr. will die. It is inevitable. I hear people say that Yates will have to face another judge and receive another punishment—this one eternal. But as this is theoretical, I'm not going to concern myself with esoteric arguments over potential post-death punishments.

Face it, the guy is really screwed up. He killed people, and he enjoyed it. He did it often, and with preparation and enthusiasm. He killed people I personally knew; but had I not known them, it would make no difference. They are dead because Robert Lee Yates Jr. killed them, and caused their families and friends tremendous pain.

Arthur Armstead, who watched Darla Sue Scott drive away to her death in the car of Robert Lee Yates Jr., passed away before I could get him a copy of this book's first edition. There were those, even in his own family, who were not always crazy about Arthur or his lifestyle. I will put it on record that he was—to the full extent of my experience—always a good friend to me. My memories of him will long be cherished.

The law enforcement folks of the Spokane Homicide Task Force have all moved on, moved out, or retired completely. Cal Walker took a new position in Spokane Valley and ran for Spokane County sheriff; following his defeat for that position, he retired from law enforcement. "Personally, my goal was to work major crimes as a detective—to work with all those fine people. I never looked much beyond that," Walker said.

Everyone murdered by Robert Lee Yates Jr. is—quite obviously—still dead. Nothing will reverse their condition, and no future edition of this book will contain the glorious news of their renewed health and happiness, and their reunification with those from whom they were previously estranged. Could all this have been averted? Some of it yes, some of it no.

Serial killers are well known for killing prostitutes, especially those women whose lifestyle involves recreational drug use, or actual drug addiction. In my original manuscript for *Body Count,* there was a section that was deleted, which both my editor and I agree should be made available to you in this second edition.

In the early 1900s, the majority of America's drug addicts were respectable white women, primarily in the southern United States, and there was no link between addiction and crime in America because drugs were not illegal.

In 1914, The United States passed the Harrison Tax Act which instituted a one dollar a year tax on companies and individuals authorized to prescribe narcotic medications. There is no mention of addicts or addiction in this revenue generating legislation. It is simply a tax to be collected by the United States Treasury Department. Registered physicians were required only to keep records of drugs dispensed or prescribed in the course of their professional practice.

After passage of the law, the phrase "in the course of their professional practice," was interpreted by law-enforcement officers to mean that a doctor could not prescribe opiates to an addict to maintain his addiction. Since addiction was not a disease, the argument went, an addict was not a patient, and opiates dispensed to or prescribed for him by a physician were therefore not being supplied "in the course of his professional practice." A law apparently intended to ensure the orderly marketing of narcotics was converted into a law prohibiting the supplying of narcotics to addicts, even on a physician's prescription.

In 1924, Dr. Charles O. Linder, completing a lifetime of honorable practice in Spokane, Washington, was persuaded by an undercover patient from the Treasury Department to write a prescription for four tablets of cocaine and morphine. Several U.S. Treasury agents thereupon descended on his office and broke in on him in the midst of a consultation. He was indicted, convicted, and sentenced for having supplied narcotics to a patient to relieve her withdrawal symptoms. Dr. Linder lost his intermediate appeal to the circuit court. However, he persisted all the way to the United States Supreme Court. The U.S. Supreme Court's unanimous decision came on April 13, 1925, in which his conviction was reversed and he was completely vindicated. The Supreme Court confirmed that the Harrison Act was a tax act, had nothing to do with medical issues, declared that addicts were "diseased and proper subjects for treatment," and that it was not illegal for a physician acting in good faith—and according to fair medical standards—to prescribe moderate amounts of narcotics for purposes of alleviating withdrawal symptoms.

The Court also expressed its view that drug addiction is a disease and that relieving the "conditions incident to the addiction" may be medically appropriate. The Court, being a judicial body rather than medical, acknowledged that it was neither qualified nor empowered to intervene in matters of medicine. The U.S. Supreme Court, by its own admission, was incapable of defining "reasonable treatment," leaving that decision to the medical community. Doctors, however, were fearful of the Treasury Department, and felt it was much safer to simply ignore treatment requests from addicted or dependant patients. When doctors stopped meeting their patients' needs, the needs did not go away. Organized crime filled the void, and in the process, raised prices. Instead of receiving their medication from a doctor, addicts were (and still are) compelled to purchase them at inflated prices, and of unknown quality, from illegal sources. Making access to these drugs illegal increased harm rather than reducing it.

Had the Linder Decision been widely promulgated, and if doctors had not become fearful of interference in their practices by the Treasury Department, it is possible that the entire drug subculture to which the majority of Yates' victims belonged would not even exist.

In the United States, it is not illegal to have the disease of addiction, nor is it illegal to be dependent upon, or addicted to, controlled substances, either legal or illegal. It is, however, illegal to have, sell, or distribute controlled substances without proper licensing by the government, and paying appropriate taxes. If you were to apply for a license and request a tax I.D. number to sell many of these substances, your application would be denied. Obviously, this is a problematic approach.

The person suffering from the medical condition of addiction must also endure the pain of social stigma due to prevailing misunderstandings. They are wrongly viewed as immoral and/or weak-willed, when they are, in truth, suffering from a primarily genetic medical condition remarkably similar to heart disease, diabetes, or asthma.

Recent international research by medical organizations asserts that the negative impact of social stigma is far more damaging to the individual and society than is the disease itself.

It is the stigmatized and marginalized women whom serial killers such as Robert Lee Yates Jr. select as their victims.

It is my fervent prayer that this country abandons its destructive and inhumane antidrug and antiprostitution policies of punitive action and replaces them with the harm-reduction methodologies that have proven, worldwide, to save lives, and increase the health and safety of the individuals and society.

As long as there are those who are marginalized, there will be easy prey for the likes of Robert Lee Yates Jr. The more cohesive and accepting a community, the less victimization takes place.

Burl Barer
March 2012

Turn the page for a gripping excerpt from
Burl Barer's acclaimed true-crime thriller . . .

FATAL BEAUTY

Now available from Pinnacle!

Prologue

The story of James "Jimmy" Joste and Rhonda Glover has all the ingredients of a Shakespearean tragedy: the rich prince, the beautiful ingénue, true love, hot sex, backstabbing, intrigue, conspiracy, intoxicants and the contemporary equivalent of witches and ghosts.

For fifteen turbulent years, Glover and Joste had all the trappings of marriage—except the certificate. He purchased her a $350,000 engagement ring and numerous extravagant residences; he fathered her son. The storybook romance of the wealthy Prince Charming and the all-American princess is heavily footnoted with episodes of irrational violence, illegal drugs, delusional mental states and frequent visits to their residences by law enforcement.

Any story that combines vast wealth, exotic locales and beautiful women, with mind-altering drugs, Devil worshipers, demons and a Glock 9mm handgun, is, as the saying goes, "all good fun until someone gets hurt."

We're talking death here. Rhonda shot Jimmy at least ten times. "I emptied the gun into him," she told police. "I just kept shooting until he fell, but I honestly didn't think I mortally wounded him. I wasn't that good a shot."

She didn't have to be a good shot. This was close range, rapidfire. One expert insisted that six of the shots were fired into Joste after he was on the ground, including two well below the waistband of his shorts.

To Rhonda Glover, the entire issue is the right of a woman to protect herself in her own home. "I am," she proudly asserted, "the self-defense poster child.

"On July 21, 2004, just five days before my birthday, I was brutally attacked, choked, and my life threatened by my ex-boyfriend, in my home in Austin, Texas," said Glover. In her version of events, she was separated from her longtime millionaire boyfriend, Jimmy Joste, because she feared his violent and abusive nature.

"I lived in fear of Jimmy Joste," insisted Rhonda Glover, and her personal recollection of their fifteen-year relationship could very well be something along these lines:

"When I met him, he was warm, kind, clever and crazy about me. We moved in together, but it wasn't long before his drunken rage and violent outbursts had me shaking in terror. I couldn't live with him, and he said he couldn't live without me. He wouldn't let me go. He stalked me, he scared me, he bought me and he forced himself on me. I bore him a son and placated him by allowing him to do what he wanted—to play the part of the generous lover. He could buy me gifts and houses, but he couldn't claim my heart or my soul: No one except me knows what Jimmy Joste was like behind closed doors. He had one face to his friends, but it was a mask. The dollars he flashed blinded people, including me, to his dark side. He was sick, perverted, evil and dangerous. He wasn't alone in his duplicity and deceit. I can give you names—important names of important people who use their wealth and prestige to obscure their true nature."

Rhonda claimed that she broke free from Joste, as best she could, living in a different city, and avoiding him at all costs. "I was terrified that I would be a missing person," said Glover. "I would be one of those skeletons in a remote area where hikers go, or that I would be a mother searching for her child on an AMBER Alert. Life was very weird for me. Jimmy had lost his mind. He had a secret life, and after he got comfortable doing drugs in my house, he decided to let me in on his alternative lifestyle. I am not crazy. I was with a crazy man. He was out of his mind. He threatened me, called me a bitch, said he was going to kill me, and then grabbed me by the throat. He was choking me. I shot him because I thought he was going to kill me. It was self-defense. I feared for my life."

The story of a battered beauty who, in final desperation, ends the cycle of violence sounds like a made-for-television movie. "It is more a made-up excuse for murder," insisted a Travis County assistant district attorney (ADA). "She was waiting for him in the upstairs bedroom wearing a lovely flowerprint sundress with no pockets. In her hand was a Glock nine-millimeter handgun. This was cold, calculated murder."

1

You never forget your first car, first kiss or first corpse. That new car smell only lasts so long, and the olfactory sensation instigated by your best girl's perfume, or lover's cologne, lingers as treasured nostalgia. The stench of death clings to you like a parasite, fouling your mind and haunting your memories. No homicide detective forgets that first dead body.

When you're a homicide detective in Texas, snuffed lives litter your career's landscape like so many scattered leaves. Each victim's dignity must be preserved, and each crime scene must be kept pure. When you discover a corpse, investigate, don't contaminate.

The bullet-riddled body of Texas millionaire/oil entrepreneur James "Jimmy" Joste was discovered July 25, 2004, in the upscale Austin Mission Oaks residence technically owned by his estranged girlfriend, Rhonda Lee Glover. This event triggered a multistate investigation requiring involvement by the Bureau of Alcohol, Tobacco, Firearms and Explosives (ATF), the United States Secret Service, the Kansas State Police and the homicide division of the Austin Police Department (APD).

Prior to arresting the person responsible for Joste's death, Austin homicide detectives Keith Walker and Richard Faithful uncovered allegations of conspiracy, financial fraud, manipulation of oil markets, kidnapping, child murder, drug dealing, satanic rituals and perverse sexual behavior by respected members of Texas's social elite. The investigation began with a phone call from Janice Van Every on Sunday, July 25, 2004.

"I came up to Austin to visit my son, Paul Owen," explained Van Every. "At approximately nine-thirty P.M., Saturday night, July twenty-fourth, we went to the residence of my niece [Rhonda Glover] at Mission Oaks. I observed that the garage door was open, and a car parked inside. No lights were on, and we decided not to go in. We came back the next morning. The garage was still open, and a navy blue Volkswagen was still parked inside. I could see that the utility door was open. I tried knocking on the door and ringing the doorbell several times, with no luck. I also tried calling on the phone, but received no answer. I tried the front door, and it was unlocked. I opened it a crack, and then closed it. I yelled for whoever was inside to answer, but no one came. We became concerned and called police."

The first respondents on the scene were Officers Martinez and Paez. Knocking on the front door, they repeatedly made loud announcements of their presence, but no one responded. "We entered the house," said Officer Richard Paez, "and immedi-

ately noticed the foul smell of something rotting.
There were also large insects throughout the house—
a possible indication that there was a dead body inside the home." As the two Austin police officers
moved up the stairs, the offensive odor increased
in intensity.

"Almost as we reached the top of the stairwell,"
said Paez, "I saw what appeared to be a deceased
person lying on the hallway floor. We decided not
to go farther, walked out the way we came in, and
then called our supervisor, and advised dispatch to
summon all necessary units to the crime scene."

Homicide detectives Keith Walker, Eric De Los
Santos and Richard Faithful were soon on their
way to the Mission Oaks residence, along with
Austin's crime scene analysis team. "I'd been with
the Austin Police Department about eleven years
when that call came in," recalled Keith Walker,
"and I'd been a detective for about five and a half
years. Homicide detectives investigate any unnat-
ural death or any death that is not known to be
natural. That includes accidental, overdoses, homicides, anything of that nature that doesn't involve
traffic."

It was Walker's turn to take the role of lead
detective under Austin's rotation system. "Once
you are assigned to a case," explained Walker, "you
then start again at the bottom and work your way
up. Detective De Los Santos was there to assist me.
Detective Faithful was number two, my backup
detective, so to speak, and we also use other members to take statements and assist in the investigation, as needed."

When Walker arrived, the crime scene specialists had not yet entered the house: "That's because we didn't know at that time who owned the house, and we didn't know for sure the identity of the victim. Once it was determined that the death was suspicious, the house was left alone, pending entry into the house in a legal manner. In this case a search warrant was required. We needed to know who owned the house, whose name was on the utility bills and who was paying the property taxes. Our Detective Fortune got right on that, Eric De Los Santos was already canvassing the neighborhood, and Ms. Van Every told Detective Faithful that the victim in the house was most likely Mr. James Joste, father of her niece's nine-year-old son."

"Okay, here's the story," Faithful told his fellow detectives. "She says that her niece, Rhonda Glover, and Joste had split up, and that Glover had their son. There was supposed to be some sort of custody problem over their son, and neither of them was supposed to have custody of the boy. The aunt came looking for Glover because no one had heard or seen her for several months. She says that she was concerned for the boy and Glover, and she hoped that maybe Glover and the boy came back to Joste, or at least talked to him, and that he might know where they were. That's why she came to the house."

The only thing detectives knew for sure was that there was a dead body, not yet identified, in the upstairs hall. The fact that the individuals who called the police were looking for Rhonda Glover and a nine-year-old child weighed heavily on Walker's mind.

"We didn't know what had happened in that

house," affirmed Walker. "We didn't know if there were other crimes involved as well. We had two major concerns. One was that Ms. Glover might be a suspect, and that her son could be in danger from her. The other concern was just as disturbing. It was equally possible that Glover and her son had been abducted, and both of them were in danger for their lives. We issued a broadcast nationwide to be on the lookout for them based on what little information we had at the time."

By the time everyone dispatched to the scene arrived, and Faithful had elicited basic information from Janice Van Every, Detective De Los Santos had spoken to most of the neighbors, including Andy and Judy Granger.

"Andy Granger began to tell me how he only saw an older white male at the unit," recalled De Los Santos, "but Judy Granger interrupted. She said that they would give us information, but did not want to be called into court. I tried to explain to her that if the information they provided was considered significant by the district attorney, then there was a possibility they could be called in. Judy stated that if that were the case, they have nothing to say. I left it at that and continued canvassing."

At 11:43 A.M., De Los Santos spoke with April Lord, Shannon Hopkins and Allison Atchley. "The three women could only recall that an older white male lived in the unit. They recalled that he seemed nice, waving, and he had a black motorcycle."

"The last time I saw the guy who lives there," Paul Mathews told De Los Santos, "was on Tuesday. I saw him come in through the gate, and backing the VW into the garage. I didn't pay a lot of attention because I was simply getting my mail."

Neighbor Nellie Byrne walked the neighborhood frequently, but did not notice anything out of the ordinary. She did recall seeing Joste's garage door open on Thursday. Kathleen Dunegan also recalled seeing the garage door open on either Monday or Tuesday.

"I had never seen him leave it open before," she said. "In fact, I walked over and knocked on the door to check on him. I didn't get any answer, so I left."

Jack Young told De Los Santos that he knew an older man lived in that unit, but didn't know him personally. "I think he may have had a girlfriend," said Young, "but that was some months ago."

"I know my neighbors slightly," said Patricia Reichle. "I haven't seen Rhonda Glover in about a year, or her son. Mr. Joste told me that Rhonda was living in their house in Houston. He's had different people house-sitting from time to time," Reichle explained, "but I think the last time anyone house-sat was several months ago. As for the garage door, I think I noticed it open since about Wednesday, the twenty-first."

Sara Buss also spoke freely. "I haven't seen anyone around the house other than the man who lives there," she said. "The overhead garage door has been open for several days. I don't recall if he left the garage door open all the time, but I definitely remembered that it has been open several days, and that there was that car backed into the garage. I haven't seen anyone at the house for a few days."

Detective Faithful was standing in front of the residence when Wanda Stevens, a member of the home owners' board for the community, pulled up to him. She kindly offered assistance. "Stevens informed me that the access codes to get into the gate are personalized, but that they have no way of tracking them," said Faithful. "Stevens also informed me that there are no cameras in the community to monitor entry and exit."

Forty-five minutes after his final interview with Jimmy Joste's neighbors, De Los Santos left the scene and drove to the station to draft a search warrant. Detective Fortune completed the required research, passing it on to De Los Santos.

"According to Travis County Appraisal District information," Fortune told him, "the home on Mission Oaks is owned by Rhonda Glover. City of Austin utility records also show an active account in Glover's name for that same residence. The Texas Department of Public Safety has records confirming that Rhonda Glover is a white female born July 26, 1966, and she has a Texas driver's license."

In addition to the information acquired by Fortune, De Los Santos also checked Austin Police Department records for any previous police response to the address on Mission Oaks Boulevard.

"Austin PD was very familiar with Rhonda Glover," confirmed De Los Santos. "I found plenty of activity for both Rhonda Glover and James Joste."

"Activity" is a polite way of saying that there were numerous calls to 911, all placed by Rhonda

Glover, and all contained the notation of *EDP,* the abbreviation for emotionally disturbed person.

A review of the records pulled by De Los Santos provides a chilling glimpse into the terrified mind of Rhonda Glover, a woman so beset with fear and panic that she called 911 to report a burglary in progress almost every other day. When Officers Funderburgh and Fiske arrived at the Mission Oaks home on March 3, 2003, they found Rhonda Glover still on the phone, updating 911 on the demons in her walls and the disembodied life-forms threatening her.

"This was the third time in the space of a week or two that Ms. Glover called 911 to report a burglary in progress," confirmed Officer Fiske. "Rhonda was sure that there was someone in her house. Even while I talked with Rhonda, she kept looking around the house for the intruder."

There never was an intruder. "This wasn't the first time that week that police had been called to her house," revealed Fiske, and there were no intruders the other nights either. Unlike the other responding officers, Fiske wasn't responding to the burglary. "I am a mental-health officer, so one of the officers on the scene called me. I am really just a regular police officer who has had training in mental illness and the procedures that police use when dealing with the mentally ill."

The officers on the scene had searched Glover's residence up and down and didn't find any intruders inside. "I talked to her for some time, but she didn't believe that there was not a person or persons in the house, and she kept repeatedly asking

me, 'Did you hear that?' and stuff like that. It was
difficult to talk to her because she was so paranoid. I remember one time while I was talking to
her, she got up and went into the kitchen and was
searching the kitchen and just left me sitting in
the other room. She was acting in a very bizarre
fashion.

"She never calmed down the entire time I was
with her," said Fiske. "She was fearful, distraught
and paranoid.

"My main job," said Fiske, "is to assist with mentally ill people that become involved with law
enforcement. One of my responsibilities is if I get
called to a scene, or am at a scene, and there is a
mentally ill person actively dangerous to either
themselves or others, I have the authority to have
them committed to the hospital to be evaluated."
Her job description was seemingly custom crafted
for her encounter with Rhonda Glover.

The threshold by which dangerousness is measured is quite high, and they have to be so out of
touch with reality that it is feared that if this person is left alone, they may hurt themselves or others. "The institutions I take them to," explained
Fiske, "public or private, have some very high standards of what they will and will not accept for immediately dangerous. That is a determination that
they make independent of my own concern. I have
had several rejected by the hospitals.

"Rhonda Glover told me that she was seeing Dr.
Jones at MMHR," said Fiske. "Well, I determined
that she wasn't an immediate danger to herself or
others, but since she was under so much stress and

fearful, and she told me that she was bipolar, I
asked her if she would like to go to Psychiatric
Emergency Services to talk to somebody. She
agreed, and she followed me to Psychiatric Emergency Services.

"What I do," explained Fiske, "is when it is on a
volunteer basis like that, when she wants to speak
with somebody, she wants the help, I will go in,
and I will help them fill out the forms. It just gives
[the staff] a small synopsis of why we are even
there, and what that does a lot of times is it will ex-
pedite them talking to her as opposed to having
her wait in a line that is generally very long." Once
there, Fiske did not stay with Rhonda Glover. "I
don't stay there," she said, "because it could be
hours before they see her."

As De Los Santos flipped the pages of the APD
reports, a definite pattern became evident—Rhonda
Glover calls 911 in a state of panic. Officers arrive,
find nothing, and leave. Rhonda was not always
alone, discovered De Los Santos. Most often, the
one calming influence was Mr. James Joste.

At 6:25 P.M., November 15, 2003, Rhonda Glover
called 911, out of breath, asking for police. "I arrived a short time later," recalled Officer Kelly
Moore, "and noticed that there were a few items
lying in the driveway, including a disposable camera, travel map and various papers. I rang the
doorbell and a male answered the door. His name,
James Joste."

Moore interviewed Jimmy Joste, and it didn't

take long to get to the bottom line. Basically, Joste advised him that Rhonda Glover had been diagnosed with two different forms of mental illness, but he couldn't tell which condition was responsible for her current symptoms. "His wife, Rhonda, had been prescribed medication to control her condition," said Moore, "but she hadn't taken them in about a month."

Joste informed Moore that Rhonda had been able to self-medicate by consuming no fluids other than Austin tap water. Moore had good reason to doubt the power of the tap water, due to the fact that Rhonda, according to Joste, was becoming increasingly irritable and irrational. "She had thrown a fit, called various people saying Joste was holding her hostage, wouldn't let her leave the house, et cetera. Joste, however, had let her take their son in their Suburban and leave."

Rhonda called Joste twice while Officer Moore was at the Mission Oaks home. "Joste was very calm with her, and seemed to fully be aware of the subtleties of her condition, and how to handle her. The second time she called, she told him that she wanted to stay in a hotel in Austin, and he agreed quite easily to this. Joste told Rhonda to call him back, and he would book her a room at a downtown hotel. He later told me," said Officer Moore, "that he believed that she would simply come home, and that she sounded like she has returned to normal during the second conversation."

Several times during his conversation with Joste, Officer Moore asked him if Rhonda Glover was a

danger to him, herself or anyone else. "No," said
Joste. Again he was asked if he was in any danger
from Rhonda Glover. "No, absolutely not," replied
Jimmy Joste. "I am not in any danger from
Rhonda, none at all."

MORE SHOCKING TRUE CRIME
FROM PINNACLE